T0293099

'This is a hugely fascinating book offering a range of insights from seasoned and well-regarded deliberators on both their personal and professional lived-experience of the Covid pandemic. It is important in times of such overwhelming existential peril for leading thinkers in the academic and professional world to disclose their experiences by writing about and describing their own angst, dependencies, disconnectedness, physical reaction, sense of time, being and freedom – or deprivation of – extraordinary thinkers thinking about extraordinary times. The potential for this book to become an exemplar of philosophical critique, phenomenological account, and authentic reflection of living through the pandemic presents itself with this range and collection of writers.'

Prof. John Nuttall, *Assistant Dean and Head of School of Psychotherapy and Psychology, Regent's University London. Certified Management Consultant*

'With this latest book Monica Hanaway and her chapter authors offer us a further brilliant insight into the power and relevance of the existential and phenomenological lens. Since the start of the pandemic, we have all faced numerous challenges, as well as some potential unseen gifts. In response, this book sensitively and intelligently helps to ground these experiences initially in theory, then with client case studies, before looking at wider implications and lessons for society and business. As a consequence, I cannot recommend this book highly enough. It speaks to all that are ready to listen.'

Jamie Reed, *Team and Leadership Coach, Director of Human Leadership Ltd*

'Monica is uniquely placed to write this book as an internationally renowned practitioner whose work is founded on existential principles. Her expertise as both a therapist and a coach inform key issues that illuminate the range of challenges experienced by people and businesses alike. An impressive breadth of contributing authors helps us understand the existential threat of the pandemic, how people regain a sense of equilibrium, and possible opportunities for growth, purpose, and authenticity.'

Dr Mark Burgess, *Research Lead and Teaching Fellow (Social Psychology), Oxford Brookes University, Oxford*

'The pandemic has confronted humanity with several complex and unprecedented challenges. This book excellently dissects the impact to human lived experience from an existential viewpoint e.g. the physical, personal, relational and spiritual experiences and the often paradoxical meanings we attach to them. Like any existential threat, the pandemic is rich in helping reveal who we are to ourselves and this book facilitates the reader in making sense of it all.'

Nigel Smaller, *Psychotherapist and Coach*

'The pandemic turned out to be for many of us nothing less than a mirror reflecting our biggest challenges and shadows as well as greatest gifts and virtues. It is crucial now not only to look at this experience as a "crisis to overcome", but as a reason to dive into the questions it raised. Monica does that brilliantly in this book by bringing in existential paradigm to rethink what we collectively and individually have gone and are going through. An excellent array of co-authors and personal stories/cases makes this work very personal, allowing it to speak not only to our minds but our hearts.'

Svetlana Hetrick, *Clinical Psychologist, Director of the Educational Centre for Psychological Education, St Petersburg, Russia*

'Existential thinking has seen a remarkable comeback during the COVID 19 pandemic. The common thread running through is a sensitivity to human fragility that is felt to be particularly relevant. Our most important existential lesson is that our fears are inherent in the human condition. Anxiety is a wake-up call and not pathological. It is up to us to anchor ourselves, to value life in the midst of death, to nurture relationships in the midst of isolation, and to voice against shame and stigma of psychologically stressful experiences. And above all, to be there for our clients and show them that and how we can be responsible for our own resilience. Monica Hanaway's latest publication, together with her chapter authors, follows along this trail. It is with great enrichment to accompany her on this journey.'

Dr Georg Martensen, *Logotherapist, Existential Coach, Supervisor, Brunswick, Germany*

Existentialism in Pandemic Times

Building on Monica Hanaway's previous publications, this timely volume considers the benefits of bringing an existential approach to psychotherapy, coaching, supervision and leadership, particularly in times of crisis.

The book uses an existential lens to examine the impact Covid-19 has had on our mental health and ways of being, making connections between situations that challenge our mental resources and the unique ways existential ideas can address those challenges. Featuring contributions from renowned existential thinkers and practitioners, the book connects personal experiences with clinical examples and philosophic ideas to explore concepts like anxiety, relatedness and uncertainty as they relate to key existential themes, helping to inform coaches and therapists in their work with clients.

Existentialism in Pandemic Times is important reading for coaches, therapists, psychologists and business leaders, as well for scholars and researchers interested in applied philosophy.

Monica Hanaway is author of several books on coaching, leadership and conflict resolution, including *The Existential Leader, An Existential Approach to Leadership Challenges, Handbook of Existential Coaching Practice, Psychologically Informed Mediation* and *An Existential and Phenomenological Approach to Coaching Supervision*. She is committed to introducing applied existential thought into new contexts, particularly the world of business.

Existentialism in Pandemic Times

Implications for Psychotherapists, Coaches and Organisations

Edited by

Monica Hanaway

Routledge
Taylor & Francis Group

LONDON AND NEW YORK

Cover image: Duncan Mitchell & Monica Hanaway

First published 2023
by Routledge
4 Park Square, Milton Park, Abingdon, Oxon OX14 4RN

and by Routledge
605 Third Avenue, New York, NY 10158

Routledge is an imprint of the Taylor & Francis Group, an informa business

British Library Cataloguing-in-Publication Data
A catalogue record for this book is available from the British Library

Library of Congress Cataloging-in-Publication Data
Names: Hanaway, Monica, editor.
Title: Existentialism in pandemic times : implications for psychotherapists,
coaches and organisations / edited by Monica Hanaway.
Description: Milton Park, Abingdon, Oxon ; New York, NY : Routledge, 2023. |
Includes bibliographical references and index. | Summary: "Building
on Monica Hanaway's previous publications, this timely volume considers
the benefits of bringing an existential approach to psychotherapy, coaching,
supervision, and leadership, particularly in times of crisis" – Provided by publisher.
Identifiers: LCCN 2022009156 | ISBN 9781032186894 (hardback) |
ISBN 9781032186870 (paperback) | ISBN 9781003255765 (ebook)
Subjects: LCSH: Personal coaching. | Existential psychology. |
COVID-19 Pandemic, 2020—Psychological aspects.
Classification: LCC BF637.P36 E99 2023 | DDC 158/.9–dc23/eng/20220223
LC record available at https://lccn.loc.gov/2022009156

ISBN: 978-1-032-18689-4 (hbk)
ISBN: 978-1-032-18687-0 (pbk)
ISBN: 978-1-003-25576-5 (ebk)

DOI: 10.4324/9781003255765

Typeset in Times New Roman
by Newgen Publishing UK

This book is dedicated to all those who have suffered loss during the Covid-19 pandemic

Contents

Acknowledgments   xi
List of contributors   xii
Preface   xv

Introduction   1

PART I
The internal world – self-reflection: Thoughts from
individuals about their own pandemic experience
from an existential viewpoint   21

1 From fear, uncertainty, and loss to embodiment, dreams
   and awakening   25
   MONICA HANAWAY

2 'Without music, life would be a mistake': The experience
   of a musician in Covid-19 times   35
   LAURENCE COLBERT

3 The paradox of freedom in lockdown   45
   DIANA MITCHELL

4 My pandemic pregnancy: A self-reflection via the words
   of others   52
   CLEO HANAWAY-OAKLEY

5 What really matters? A phenomenological exploration of
two YouTube dialogues on living through Corona times 66
GREG MADISON AND ERNESTO SPINELLI

PART 2
The therapy world: Psychotherapy and coaching clients 79

6 Birth, death and isolation: Motherhood during a pandemic 87
CLAIRE ARNOLD-BAKER

7 Relatedness and relationships in the time of Covid-19 101
LUCI MOJA-STRASSER AND MICHAEL WORRELL

8 Existential resilience and Covid-19: What existential
coaching can offer 112
YANNICK JACOB

9 'It's been a good pandemic for me': Working with
coaching and psychotherapy clients, with a focus on
clients with a diagnosis of pure obsessive compulsive
disorder 126
MONICA HANAWAY

PART 3
The business world and other communities: Existential
issues for businesses, communities and organisations to
consider post-pandemic 137

10 East of Eden: An existential view of the pandemic 139
RENÉ MÄRTIN

11 Existential challenges for business leaders post-pandemic 148
MONICA HANAWAY

Conclusion: The existential legacy of the Covid-19
pandemic 160

Index 173

Acknowledgments

My thanks go to all the authors who have contributed chapters to this book. Their honest sharing of personal insights and their knowledge of the existential have added richness to my original idea.

I would also like to thank Lyra Hanaway-Oakley for allowing me to include her two poems, and Diana and Allan Mitchell for allowing me to use a painting by their son, Duncan Mitchell, as inspiration for the book cover.

I would also like to thank my husband and our dogs who have been by my side during lockdowns, and with whom I have enjoyed the occasional rural escape when we were allowed.

Contributors

Claire Arnold-Baker is an existential therapist and counselling psychologist specialising in working in perinatal mental health in her private practice. She is course leader for the DC Psych programme at NSPC, where she is also the academic director, lecturer, supervisor and researcher. She is the author of *The Existential Crisis of Motherhood* (2020) and has co-authored several books.

Laurence Colbert is a professional drummer, composer and writer. He is particularly interested in the phenomena of soundscapes and is currently conducting research into this for a PhD. He is an accredited mediator bringing an existential approach to resolving conflicts. He also plays in the band RIDE.

Monica Hanaway is author of several books on coaching, leadership and conflict resolution. She is committed to introducing applied existential thought into new contexts, particularly the world of business. She works privately as a psychotherapist, executive and leadership coach, consultant, mediator and trainer. She has worked in South Africa with residents of the Cape Town townships to address gender-based violence, and with paramilitaries in Belfast for the Desmond Tutu Foundation. She works internationally training mediators and coaches using an existential framework and is due to start a running a course on existential coaching in St Petersburg early 2022.

Cleo Hanaway-Oakley is lecturer in Liberal Arts and English at the University of Bristol. Her research is rooted literary studies but intersects with history, philosophy, film studies and medical humanities. She is interested in embodiment, sensory experience and modernism. Her first book, *James Joyce and the Phenomenology of Film*, was published by Oxford University Press in 2017. She is the founder of the Oxford Phenomenology Network and the Bristol Senses Cluster, is on the executive committee for the British Association for Modernist Studies, and is part of the steering group for Bristol's Centre for Health, Humanities and Science.

Yannick Jacob is a coach, positive psychologist, trainer and supervisor, and course director of the Accredited Certificate in Integrative Coaching (School of Positive Transformation), member of the teaching faculty at Animas Centre for Coaching, the International Centre for Coaching Supervision, and the School of Life. He is the author of *An Introduction to Existential Coaching* and regularly presents internationally at conferences.

René Märtin is a logotherapist/existential counsellor, supervisor, and coach, author, lecturer, and founder of the German Empowerment Institute. He works existentially with executives and associations. He has worked in the areas of strategic communications, strategy consulting and organisational development and is engaged in international training, and consulting activities (UNAIDS, FES, IMOE, NDI) in the areas of empowerment processes, participation and democracy, and community building in African, central and eastern European, and Scandinavian countries.

Diana Mitchell is a psychotherapist, mediator, trainer and supervisor. She has a private psychotherapy practice in Walton-on-Thames. She has written a number of articles and book chapters. She has worked with paramilitary groups in Belfast for the Desmond Tutu Foundation. She has presented at several conferences internationally.

Greg Madison is an existential psychotherapist and psychologist, supervisor and trainer, with a particular interest in focusing. He is the author of several books. These include works on focusing, existential therapy, existential migration, and HIV and being.

Lucia Moja-Strasser is an existential psychotherapist, supervisor, trainer and mediator, based in Paris. She is a founder member of the Society for Existential Analysis. She has contributed to many academic books and journals and is particularly known for her work on phenomenology and on silence.

Ernesto Spinelli is a counselling psychologist and psychotherapist, executive coach and supervisor. He has an international reputation as a leading contemporary trainer and theorist of existential analysis. He is the author of many influential books on existential therapy and more recently has published two books of fiction.

Michael Worrell is a consultant clinical psychologist, existential psychotherapist, CBT therapist, supervisor and trainer. He is the trust lead for evidence-based psychological therapy training in Central and Northwest London Foundation NHS Trust. He was involved in the establishment of Behavioural Couples Therapy for Depression for the National Improving Access to Psychological Therapies Programme.

Preface

I work as a psychotherapist, trainer, mediator and coach, drawing on existential philosophy to inform all my practice. Most of these professions require close contact and a deep exploration of oneself and others. As we moved into 2020, I had development plans and the possibility of several exciting projects in all these areas, and the future looked exciting. However, times were definitely 'a changing'.

By the time I started to write this book, we were again in lockdown due to Covid-19, and the numbers admitted to hospital each day were continuing to grow. Things have moved on, many adults have received at least one vaccination against Covid-19, and the easing of lockdown is underway. However, there is no certainty that things will continue to move in a positive direction, and new variants may provide fresh challenges, as we are currently experiencing with the Delta and Delta Plus variants. If we take a positive view and believe there is hope in sight due to the rollout of vaccinations and other measures, we are still experiencing conditions of life which we have never experienced before and are having to find ways of living within new parameters.

This is not the first pandemic with global implications. Perhaps one of the earliest we can recall from school history lessons is the Black Death (1346–1353), which claimed the lives of 30–60% of the European population. Epidemics of smallpox, influenza, scarlet fever, 'plague', cholera, Dengue fever, Ebola and others are found across history. But this is perhaps the first time for most of us that we are encountering a 'lived experience' of a pandemic, which carries the potentiality for taking our lives or the lives of those we know and love and, even if we survive, will inevitably change our lives not just while we are 'in it' but also in the future.

If we do regain all our previous freedoms, it will no longer be with a sense of certainty that these will continue, and our experiences during the pandemic are likely to have altered our worldview in some way. Indeed, as Vos (2021:1) points out: 'the world has not merely been put into crisis by this microscopic virus, but also by a larger enemy: ourselves'. Vos sees the virus as the first pandemic but identifies a second one: 'the psychological and political responses to the risks and uncertainties posed by COVID-19' (ibid.). It is this psychological response which may have the most lasting impact and is the focus of this book.

Initially, I intended to explore my own response to the pandemic experience through an existential lens and to consider this alongside the experiences of my psychotherapy, coaching clients, and organisational clients, whose worlds have been turned upside down. I aimed to reflect on my understanding of self, and others who were attempting to chart unknown territory. However, after talking to many friends and colleagues, particularly my colleagues René Märtin and Georg Martensen in Germany, I decided that it would provide a much richer exploration if I was to include the thoughts of others who also use an existentially orientated approach in their work.

It seems that each of us has been affected by our experiences on both personal and professional levels, and so I have divided the book into three main sections. Each chapter does not necessarily fit neatly into one section, as we cannot easily separate our responses into the professional or personal. However, I have found it helpful, in structuring my thoughts, to consider our personal world, our therapeutic world, and the wider world, when examining the impact of the pandemic.

Some readers may not be sure what is meant by existential. A simple definition is that existentialism is about 'lived experience'. In the introduction, I offer a short exploration of the way the Covid-19 pandemic has often been described as an 'existential crisis' or an 'existential threat' and lay out some of the main themes in existential thinking.

Moving to the main body of the book, in Part 1, individuals offer their self-reflection on their 'lived experience' during the pandemic, all using an existential-phenomenological framework as a baseline for their reflections and referring to some of the main existential themes such as, Anxiety, Authenticity, Emotions, Freedom and Responsibility, Meaning, Relatedness, Time and Temporality, Uncertainty, Values and Beliefs. Moustakas (1996:172) suggested that 'we may not consciously question how things happen to us in our daily life, but when a crisis or tragedy occurs, it is almost inevitable that we will be thrown off course and plagued by a sense of "Why is this happening to me?"' We can choose to put our heads in the sand and hope there will come a time when we can safely lift them again, or we can engage with the situation and seek to discover what it tells us about ourselves and our world. Although we are not through the 'crisis' or 'tragedy' which is Covid-19, it does provide us with an opportunity to consider our lived experience during these times and to gain a richer understanding of self and others. The chapter authors in this section seek to draw and share learning and meaning from their own personal journey during the pandemic.

I start this section with my own reflections of lockdown, which are followed in Chapter 2 by insights from Laurence Colbert, who writes on the existential experience of being a professional musician, husband and father during the pandemic lockdown, at a time when his industry was brought to complete standstill and he needed to spend the time shielding with his family, as his partner was designated as a 'vulnerable' person. In Chapter 3 Diana Mitchell, a psychotherapist, mediator, trainer, and supervisor offers her reflections on the existential issues raised for herself during the pandemic, mainly those concerned with uncertainty, time, freedom/responsibility, relatedness and anxiety. My own experiences over 2020 included seeing my daughter go through the pregnancy and birth of her second child, in very different circumstances from those of her first. At the time we saw national protests about the treatment of expectant mothers who were unable to have their partners with them during ultrasound scans and sometimes not even for the birth itself. In Chapter 4, Cleo Hanaway-Oakley shares the existential issues she encountered while pregnant and giving birth during a pandemic. It is interesting to see these alongside the thoughts of Claire Arnold-Baker, who in Chapter 6 presents some of her thoughts and work around motherhood in the pandemic. Finally in Part 1, in Chapter 5 Ernesto Spinelli and Greg Madison draw on some of the existentially focused conversations they shared and recorded during the pandemic period. These focused mainly on exploring the question 'what really matters?' when considered within the context of a pandemic.

Part 2 changes the focus from reflecting on our own experiences, to looking at those of our clients. It draws from work in the fields of coaching and psychotherapy, sharing some reoccurring existential themes and considering the overall existential relevance of these approaches. It includes consideration of the required changes to therapeutic boundaries, including moving sessions online. In Chapter 6, Claire Arnold-Baker, an existential psychotherapist, focuses on the concerns of those women who experienced pregnancy, miscarriage or birth during lockdown. This is followed in Chapter 7 by a jointly authored chapter by Luci Moja-Strasser and Michael Worrell, both therapists and trainers, which focuses on the existential theme of relatedness in the context of a pandemic, as they discussed in their supervision sessions. Chapter 8 moves away from psychotherapy to coaching. Yannick Jacob considers the relevance of existential coaching in fostering resilience in the light of existential threat. In Chapter 9 I consider the impact of the pandemic on some of my psychotherapy clients, with a focus on those who had previously been diagnosed with pure obsessive compulsive disorder.

In Part 3, the final part of the book, the focus moves outside of the therapeutic setting itself to the community and business world. It considers the relevance of existential coaching, and existentially informed organisational and leadership training, while seeking to identify some of the future challenges to business models post-Covid-19. Chapter 10, authored by René Märtin, logotherapist and coach, explores the existential concerns for people and communities which the pandemic has brought to the fore. It notes how we have been called upon to re-examine what is meaningful and avoid taking on the role of 'helpless victim'. Finally, in Chapter 11 I highlight some future existential concerns for organisations, considering potential existential changes undergone by staff and the organisations themselves.

The conclusion looks at what we have learnt so far and what we may identify as the possible existential impact of the pandemic. This is considered in terms of its implications for psychotherapists, coaches, organisations and individuals.

References

Moustakis, C. (1996) *Existential Psychotherapy and the Interpretation of Dreams.* Lanham, MD: Jason Aronson Inc. Publishers.

Vos, J. (2021) *The Psychology of Covid-19: Building Resilience for Future Pandemics.* London: Sage Swifts.

Introduction

'Toy Dogs Don't Die'

Toy dogs don't die.
Not like that butterfly that someone
Did step on.

Real dogs do die.
But my dog is not dead because
She is alive.

Butterflies do die.
But they are very pretty and have
Very beautiful wings.

Dinosaurs did die.
And now we have their big bones
In the museum.

People do die.
And they have bones and skeletons
Inside of them.

Words don't die.
'L' is at the start of my name and 'a' is
At the end.
    (Lyra Hanaway-Oakley, aged 4)

I start this section with a piece of 'existential' writing from a four-year-old. She had just come across a dead butterfly on the pavement. The writer is my granddaughter, whose first year at school has been disrupted by reoccurring school lockdowns. She has made new friends and then been separated from them. At the start of the pandemic, she understood that no one must come near her, and grew accustomed to see people as 'the other' and potentially dangerous, making her cautious about human touch. She learnt that she must

DOI: 10.4324/9781003255765-1

wash her hands many times a day and 'stay at home' in order to 'be safe'. She saw her paternal grandfather admitted into residential care where he has remained throughout the pandemic, most of the time without access to visits from family. She declared that she 'hates this coronavirus and wants it to go away, it is bad, it kills people, it stops me being with my friends and hugging people'. She has been tested for Covid-19 every time someone in her school recorded a positive test (which was often). She has seen two Christmases and two birthdays pass without the usual celebrations. She has seen her mum become pregnant, miscarry, and become pregnant again and she has finally welcomed the safe arrival of a new brother.

All these experiences have happened within pandemic times, which make up nearly half of her life. These experiences have formed her perception of the world in which she lives. As we see in 'Toy Dogs Don't Die' children do think about existential issues, including the meaning of death and temporality. Her sense of relatedness has changed from welcoming physical warmth and hugs, through an active attempt to keep 'two metres' apart, and, with the introduction of 'bubbles' she has more recently been able to reengage physically and joyfully with a small number of people. So far, her life has been hedged by uncertainty: … will I be able to have a birthday party next year … my dog is old, and I love her, but she will die, can I have a stick insect when she does die … will I go to school tomorrow, or will it be closed again … when can I see my best friends again? She told her mother about a dream in which she and her three friends were sitting in her bedroom playing with her toys and that it made her cry because she did not know if this would happen ever again! Although there was a sadness in all she spoke about, there was a resilience. Perhaps the level of uncertainty and change she has already encountered in her short existence will make her better equipped to deal with uncertainty in the future. I have no doubt that this generation of children will be much researched over the years to come. For her, Covid-19 could be said to have presented several small crisis points, but perhaps it carries less of a threat of loss, as she is less grounded in the past 'normal' than adults are.

Covid as an existential threat or crisis

It is easy to find references to the Covid-19 pandemic in which it is described as an 'existential crisis' or 'existential threat'. The word 'existential' seems to spring readily to people's minds in this unprecedented situation, but what do people really mean when they describe it in this way, and to what extent are existential issues evident in our experience of our changed situation and the issues brought to therapy and coaching?

When people speak of an existential threat or crisis the meaning is dependent on the writer and the publication. It could be considered that Covid-19 poses a universal threat, not just to our health but to ways of living and being which for most people have merely been accepted up until now. For many it has raised new questions about the meaning and purpose of life, what we mean by 'normal', what normal looked like before, what is has come to mean and what it may be in the future.

When we speak of a 'threat' we are implying that someone or something has power over us. This can threaten to change our lives. This is more commonly used when speaking of an event which is massive in scale, such as war, or climate change. However, we may be threatened through small or large actions, the threat of a bully to take a child's sweets, or the threat of one nation to obliterate another.

An 'existential threat' requires us to ask questions about our understanding of life and meaning and the way we have so far chosen to live our lives. Existentially, we would be required to reflect on the extent to which we have invested power in the other for them to be able to threaten us. When we are under threat from an unseen virus it is harder to see where our responsibility sits in relation to its creation. It could stem from our treatment of the world we live in, or the arrogance sometimes found in our desire to know everything and perhaps take universal risks in pursuit of knowledge. We may simply have been too preoccupied with our own daily lives to note what was going on around us.

The term 'existential threat' began to be commonly used during the 1960–1980s. It was used in relation to the threatened use of nuclear weapons during the Cold War. Since then, the phrase has been attached to many situations such as the attacks of 9/11, and terrorism of various kinds has been seen as an existential threat most commonly to the West.

van Deurzen (2021:37) suggests that using the term 'existential threat' is a way in which the government can engender increased fear around Covid-19 and thus 'increase the likelihood that citizens follow the government guidelines'. He suggested that any sense of a feared true existential threat would stimulate a less critical attitude towards government policy and action. In a previous book on existential leadership (2019) I noted that in times of crisis people tend to look for a charismatic leader. This does not necessarily mean a good or competent leader, but one with a big personality. It may not be coincidental that the pandemic started with Trump, Johnson, Bolsonaro and others in power, who would fit within the category of charismatic leader.

Giving up our freedom and responsibility are 'a defense against uncertainty and gives ... a project; "survival", through which I can find meaning. It is all part of that fundamental question "Why am I here?"' (Hanaway, 2019:26). We are more willing to give up our freedoms if we believe our very existence is under threat. Yalom proposed that we look to either personal specialness or an ultimate rescuer to save us from uncertainty and ultimately from death and that if this fails, we look outside ourselves. 'Some individuals discover their rescuer not in a supernatural being but in their earthly surroundings, either in a leader or in some higher cause' (Yalom, 1980:129).

Belief in a leader (or government) provides a perceived defence against our existential freedom.

> If there is someone 'above' me making the decisions, then I can live in denial of my own freedom to decide. It is the decision maker that carries the blame if things go wrong, and they provide the perfect mechanism for absorbing any guilt.
>
> (Hanaway, 2019:26)

We look to leaders to provide a human shield we can hide behind. In this way we invest them with 'personal specialness' and give up our freedom so that they can write and live by their own rules, which are not necessarily the same ones they inflict on us.

The German sociologist Max Weber (1968) speaks of the followers' response to such leaders as a devotion born of distress. 'Charismatic leaders can induce a sense of dissatisfaction in followers thus creating the conditions required for their ascension to power. Such leaders are very powerful and hold power they can wield for good or bad' (Hanaway, 2019:31). They tend to focus on projecting an image of grace and charm, and evidence a great deal of uncritical self-belief. They rely on their ability to 'work the room', 'play the house' and build an image of the group or company in which they themselves are central. The emphasis for them is on how to use their personality and charm (sometimes even physical attractiveness), how they communicate to followers, and their ability to gain followers' trust to persuade them to follow by using verbal and body language. Musser (1987) notes that charismatic leaders seek to instill both commitment to ideological goals, and devotion to themselves. The extent to which either of these two goals is dominant depends on the underlying motivations and needs of the leader. Interestingly, only followers expect the leader to display charisma. Their entourage does not, and they can tolerate the leader being human and flawed (Bailey, 2001). I leave it to you to consider to what extent the above is true of our current government.

When we speak of a 'crisis', this is more often focused on the outcome of a threat which has been carried out and knocked us off kilter, taken away security, and required us to consider our sense of what is 'normal' in a different way. An investor who loses money on the stock market may suffer a financial crisis, a person whose home is destroyed by an earthquake or hurricane suffers, at the very least, a housing crisis, but when we speak of existential crisis, we are speaking of a crisis effecting the spirit and creating deep anxiety. The anxiety is centred on a crisis of existence and identity and, as Kierkegaard wrote in 1844, 'whoever has learnt to be anxious in the right way has learnt the ultimate' (1844 [1980]:155):

The anxiety experienced during a pandemic feels deeper from the more usual anxiety attached to concrete concerns focusing as it does on our very survival physically and psychologically and is therefore a crisis of existence, and so fundamentally 'existential'. Existentialism considers existential anxiety as an inevitability of human existence and something we need to learn to live with. It is not a negative, and an existential crisis is considered as an awakening or part of life's journey. Such a crisis is a complex phenomenon which puts us in touch with our vulnerability, physically and psychologically. We are faced with the temporality of our existence and the truth that our whole existence is surrounded with uncertainty which cannot authentically be removed. What we have previously taken for granted is questioned and behaviours we have unquestionably engaged in are now under scrutiny as to their meaning. In an existential crisis we may be uneasy about our future, our health, our understanding of our own meaning, our freedom, values, and beliefs. However, the anxiety caused by Covid-19 has also provided us with the opportunity to move toward learning 'the ultimate'; what is truly important to us.

In the following chapters the authors are all writing with an existential-phenomenological framework in mind. Some of the authors are steeped in existential theory and they use the approach in their daily work. Others are not scholars of philosophy, therapists, or coaches and so the level of theoretical input varies in the style and the content of each chapter. They all bring their unique ways of thinking about the existential and phenomenological aspects of their pandemic experiences and so give prominence to different existential elements.

For those readers new to existential thinking, in the following section, I aim to give a brief overview of some of the main aspects of the philosophy underpinning the approach.

What is meant by 'existential'?

Existentialism is concerned with our lived experience of being in the world, and as Heidegger (1949:1) eloquently put it: 'Being is the bell that rings into our life and gradually dies away.' Existentialism focuses on the time in which the bell is ringing; the space between our birth and our death. The temporality, uncertain nature, and vulnerability of this time-space has been heightened for many by the Covid-19 pandemic.

Moustakis (1996:5) offers a lovely definition of existential philosophy: 'Existential philosophy recognises mystery, embraces the unknown and unpredictability, and asserts that regardless of past impoverishment, the potentials for health and well-being in life and in relationships are within reach.' I hope this overview shows why it is particularly relevant in pandemic times when the reality of uncertainty cannot be ignored.

Existential human givens

An existential approach values the uniqueness of individual experience, believing that, through our emotions, values and beliefs, and phenomenological experiences we create a worldview. Despite our uniqueness, we all share common aspects of what it is to be human, and I shall refer to these as universal existential 'human givens' which we experience within different dimensions of our existence. Although shared, we will each give a different level of priority and a different set of individual meaning to each of these givens.

There is no agreed list of human givens, but I have grouped the main ones in Figure 0.1. Enveloping all of them is existential anxiety and the given that we are all emotional; we feel things. We also experience our being in an embodied way which requires us to take note of our physical body, its vulnerability, and the way it relates to itself, others and its environment; the way it operates in the world.

From an existential perspective, to maintain psychological health is to develop and maintain the ability to navigate these givens and the complexities of one's own life, the world, and one's relationships with the world. To not do so opens us up to psychological anxiety and disturbance; the outcome of avoiding life's truths and of working under the shadow of other people's expectations, beliefs, and values. Just hearing the word 'anxiety' has the power to conjure up further anxiety in many people. However, although anxiety may feel uncomfortable it is an authentic response to experiences, including the

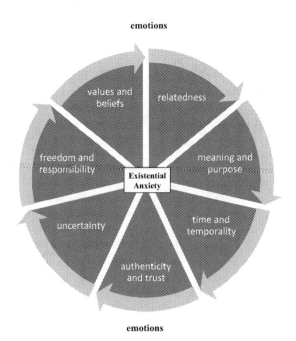

Figure 0.1 Existential human givens

holistic experience of being-in-the-world as a temporal being. It can act as a stimulus for growth enabling us to become increasingly aware of our freedom, and the consequences of accepting or rejecting that freedom. When we make a decision involving the reconstruction of our life in all or any of the existential dimensions, the accompanying anxiety can be a signal that we are ready for personal change. If we can be brave and, instead of seeking to dismiss anxiety, we learn to listen to its subtle messages, we may dare to take the steps necessary to develop and change.

Of the givens shown in Figure 0.1, there are some which may immediately spring to mind when thinking about the new circumstances and challenges presented by living in a pandemic when our sense of time, temporality and mortality may have shifted. It may be useful to give some thought to how each of these existential aspects are brought into the foreground by the current situation.

Authenticity

Existentialism values authenticity, which it considers to be essential in building and maintaining trust. When we are in a crisis, afraid and surrounded by uncertainty, we look for an authentic voice which we can trust to guide us. We long for it to give us the certainty we seek while looking for something to grab hold of in the fog of chaos.

However, Heidegger reminded us that 'Not all language is authentic. It may be imitated, copied, and worn out by repetition and overuse. Language may distort meaning. When this happens, it becomes a form of "mouthing and dispersion"' (Heidegger 1949:174). The lack of authenticity at government level has led to increased anxiety in many people. It has also laid fertile ground for the growth of conspiracy theories, the spread of which has been aided by social media. How each person decides for themselves which voice they believe is authentic will be influenced by their own worldview, but also the way in which they understand their responsibility to self and others, and their need for unrestricted freedom.

Throughout the pandemic we have listened to many voices, some of which have used their positions to speak with apparent authority. Sometimes we have been told that there is nothing to worry about; at other times we must fear for our lives. Often these voices have proved to be inauthentic and confusing, dictating what the majority should do, while applying different rules to themselves.

Outside of the public arena we have heard different things from friends and family. Some declaimed that they were having a wonderful time, enjoying the quiet, not having to commute to work, having extra time for sport and leisure, or to redecorate. Others expressed how lonely, afraid and frozen they felt. When confronted by such different responses to the same situation it can be hard to find your own authentic voice and accept that one's feeling may be paradoxical, moving quickly between the positive and negative.

In addition to having to contend with the inauthenticity of others, we need to work hard not to deceive ourselves, telling ourselves only what we want to hear. Such self-deception may provide a powerful psychological defence mechanism but prevents us from living authentically. It is not easy to remain authentic, it is a struggle for everyone; the question is not so much how to avoid inauthenticity but how to face it with openness and a willingness to engage with life rather than a tendency to retreat, withdraw or refrain from responsibility.

It is often quoted, but never referenced, that Kierkegaard said, 'There are two ways to be fooled. One is to believe what isn't true; the other is to refuse to believe what is true.' This is certainly a challenge which we have all been faced with during the pandemic.

Freedom and responsibility

An existentialist defines freedom as personal autonomy and responsibility, and it is the weight of the responsibility accompanying freedom which leads to existential anxiety. The importance of responsibility is often forgotten when people describe existentialism as a 'selfish' philosophy; a free for all in which one can do whatever one likes. Indeed, Berlin (1969:134) claims that 'conceptions of freedom directly derive from views of what constitutes a self' and to that extent the self is central, in that existential freedom focuses on your inner freedom to choose, even when your choices are externally constrained. However, although we must continually reflect and be honest with ourselves, existentialism requires us to consider ourselves as beings-in-the-world-with-others, carrying responsibility not just for self but others, and so emphasises the importance of relatedness. When we are considerate of others, we may freely choose to limit our personal freedom.

Our choices have felt constrained during the pandemic, with different levels of social freedom available to us at different times. Paradoxically, Sartre and Frankl have pointed out that it can be at times when we are most externally restrained that we may be at our most free. Sartre saw the German occupation as pushing us 'to the extremity of the human condition by forcing us to ask questions which we can ignore in peacetime' (Sartre in Gerassi 1989:12). The same has been true in the pandemic. Through the asking of questions, we take responsibility for our own answers and every action which flows from that becomes a commitment. It is this pause which occurs during our internal questioning that is

> especially important for the freedom of being, what I have called essential freedom. For it is in the pause that we experience the context out of which freedom comes. In the pause we wonder, reflect, sense awe, and conceive of eternity. The pause is when we open ourselves for the moment to the concepts of both freedom and destiny.
>
> (May 1999:164)

Frankl, a survivor of the holocaust, focused on the human capacity to remain free to find meaning in the most awful experiences. He believed that a prisoner's reactions are not solely the rest of the conditions of his life, but also of the freedom of choice he always has, even in severe suffering.

Whatever we experience in life we hold the freedom to choose to respond to that event in a particular way. When we are told we must go into lockdown, we have the freedom to comply or to ignore the injunction. We ask ourselves questions: Is this best for me? Is this best for those I love? Is this best for the majority? We then decide and commit to our action.

Frankl wrote: 'Everything can be taken from a man but one thing: the last of the human freedoms – to choose one's attitude in any given circumstances, to choose one's own way' (1985:142). We cannot be given freedom, 'freedom is something people take, and people are as free as they want to be' (Baldwin in Cooper 1967:376).

At times during the pandemic, we have felt our freedom limited. We have had different constraints placed on us depending on which area of the world we live in. We have been required to wear masks and socially distance. Camus (1947:100) described the initial reaction of people to the plague as seeming to accept being cut off from the outside world with 'more or less good grace' as they may previously have put up with 'any other temporary inconvenience that interfered with only a few of their habits'. However, he observed that later they 'abruptly became aware that they were undergoing a sort of incarceration under that blue dome of sky, already beginning to sizzle in the fires of summer'.

These were new restrictions for most people in the West who have experienced quite a high degree of day-to-day freedom. The link with freedom and responsibility is clear. If I choose to not follow the rules, am I being irresponsible, and could my actions lead to the death or suffering of others? If I choose to prioritise my individual freedom and take a decision based on my own needs and values, is this an example of authenticity? These may be difficult philosophical questions which we have been faced with, no longer just as theoretical or academic research, but as the very stuff of daily pandemic existence.

The pandemic may bring about a change in how we understand freedom and its associated responsibility. For some, freedom and responsibility may become paradoxical, e.g. the freedom to decide not to be vaccinated against Covid-19 when this action is considered to put others at risk. As a result of needing to consider such dilemmas we may be more open to questioning both our freedom and responsibility in the future and being more mindful in how we experience and use our freedom.

Meaning

One of the aspects which defines human beings is that we are a species which seeks meaning. Existentialism does not provide the certainty of a doctrine and so there is no convenient 'oven ready' meaning to adopt. We are left to find our own meaning. As Davis and Miller (1967:206), noted:

> Man is an existential being whose life is more than logic and who must discover the meaning of existence. There are no answers to the human predicament to be found in the back of a book; Philosophy is to be lived, something to be proven in action.

As meaning 'does not flow from the rational, we must live our lives based on our own unique perception of the world, and others in it, and our understanding of our lived experiences' (Hanaway 2020:8). The understanding that we create our own world and meaning draws on the work of Husserl (2009) who described us as living in 'an interpreted world' in which we come to our own conclusions about the meaning we choose to give things.

Personal meaning is a complex achievement of the human spirit and is found in the individual's confrontation with the challenges of the world and one's own being. Meaning flows from the individual's worldview and experiences. The experience of living in a pandemic challenges us to reassess what is really meaningful to us. We cannot take it for granted that what was meaningful pre-pandemic remains so.

People cannot find meaning for someone else, for us to find authentic meaning it must flow from self-reflection and inner questioning. As Frankl (1985:131) put it: 'Everyone has his own specific vocation or mission in life … Therein he cannot be replaced, nor can his life be repeated. Thus, everyone's task is as unique as is his specific opportunity to implement it.' It is through our 'tasks', or existential projects that we find and live out our meaning.

Van Deurzen (2021:113), when considering the importance of connectivity during times of crisis, noted that a crisis 'shreds us of our connective existential tissue … we literally become detached, disconnected and frequently alienated and disenfranchised'. This disconnection from the framework which gave our lives meaning makes it harder for us 'to make sense of the world and our role in it, the meaning of our life can become diminished and, in the worst-case scenario, non-existent' (ibid.). We can no longer just take on what is meaningful to others as our own meaning.

Pre-pandemic we will have defined and lived out our meaning through our daily lives which to the most part offered a degree of security. We may have invested meaning in our work, our relationships, our hopes and our projects. The pandemic immediately altered all these things, which we had probably taken for granted. We found ourselves with new ways of being, work may have been taken away or changed how it operated, we may have found ourselves separated from loved ones, or locked down with people we hardly knew. This required us to find new meaning.

It is not possible to authentically decide to take on new meaning in an instant. Heidegger (1949:206) wrote:

Waiting until some meaning is ready to disclose itself requires a clearing of time and space. It requires gradualness and unusual patience in an age which regards as real only what goes fast and can be clutched with both hands.

Lockdown provided us with just such 'a clearing of time and space' if we chose to recognise and use it.

Relatedness

Whether we like it or not we live in this world with other people. Their existence is the source of our greatest happiness and our deepest despair. We discover who we are by looking to others, choosing to ally with them or separate ourselves from them. Existential thought starts with the belief that, although humans are essentially alone in the world, they long to be connected to others and so it calls for us to acknowledge our relatedness to others, whether that is a positive and enabling experience or negative constricting one.

We seek to have meaning in one another's lives but must realise that we cannot solely depend on others for validation, and so need to acknowledge and understand that we are fundamentally alone (Yalom, 1980). Despite this aloneness, Weixel-Dixon (2017:20) writes that 'it is not possible to be totally isolated, nor is it possible to be fused with another person; we stand always in relatedness, in some form'. Bugental refers to this, using the dimensions of 'a-part-of' and 'apart-from' (1992:239). At all times we are never, and can never, be truly detached nor totally connected. This knowledge results in anxiety, as we accept that our validation must ultimately come from within, and not from others. This is a challenging responsibility to acknowledge.

The existential writer Camus (1947:207) in *The Plague* (*La Peste*) noted that 'each of us has the plague within him; no one, no one on earth, is free from it'. This perfectly described my own feelings as I observed country by country falling under the influence of Covid-19. I felt a personal sense of responsibility for potentially carrying and passing on a deadly virus. As Camus warned: 'we must keep endless watch on ourselves lest in a careless movement we breathe into someone's face and fasten the infection on him' (ibid.). This new thinking about the impact of ourselves on others, and of others on us, has been evident during the Covid-19 pandemic, during which our sense of relatedness to others may have altered, and the ways in we 'be with' others has changed. We may have discovered that we need the company of others more than we thought, or that being locked down with others felt stifling. Indeed, we may even have come to see others and ourselves as dangerous.

As we have become more aware of our own bodies (whether we have a cough, where we are standing etc.) we have also become more aware of the embodied state of others. Our natural tendencies have had to be held in check. I am quite a tactile person who greets friends with hugs and kisses, and this was something I had to become more mindful of; an action which previously signalled affection could now be perceived as dangerous and unwelcome. At one point in my career, I worked alone, often late at night, taking 'street therapy' to the homeless, drug and alcohol misusers, and sex workers. The groups I worked with were seen as volatile and potentially dangerous yet, during this time, I never felt afraid. However, in the early stages of the first lockdown I found myself crossing the road to avoid walking anywhere near any other person.

It will be interesting to see, as greater freedom is allowed, how we will physically relate to one another. Just after the ending of most restrictions my husband and I met up with my brother and sister-in-law for a rural al fresco lunch. We had not seen each other for nearly two years, and we all were 'double jabbed'. As we approached one another we stopped, uncertain of whether to greet one another as usual with a long bear hug or politely say hello. We stood there for a few seconds before my sister-in-law said, 'Well are we going to hug or not?' after which we enjoyed the intensity of a wonderful physical embrace.

Returning to Camus' *The Plague* there is an increased understanding of our connectivity. Camus (1947:151) noted: 'No longer were there individual destinies; only a collective destiny, made of plague and the emotions shared by all. Strongest of these emotions was the sense of exile and of deprivation, with all the crosscurrents of revolt and fear.' He reminded us:

> Everybody knows that pestilences have a way of recurring in the world; yet somehow, we find it hard to believe in ones that crash down on our heads from a blue sky. There have been as many plagues as wars in history; yet always plagues and wars take people equally by surprise.
>
> (1947:31)

Time and temporality

Heidegger (1962:39) states: 'Time must be brought to light – and genuinely conceived – as the horizon for all understanding of Being.' He is not focused here on ordinary, external time but an individualised experience of time 'grounded in the temporality of a *falling* person' (Moustakis, 1996:24); by this he means a person who is living in their own temporality, who is moving forward towards potentialities for growth. Indeed, in *Being and Time* Heidegger refers to time as presence, something which is allowed to exist, linger, and grow.

For months now we have been faced with daily updates on the numbers of people who have died from Covid-19. This constant reminder of the inevitability of death is not something we have lived with so starkly until recently. We are more in touch with our temporality and mortality, and so the fear of death is more conscious than previously. We may fear a hospital admission and a distressing lonely death, or we may fear a kind of self-imposed living death which some people have experienced as part of their lockdown experience unable to do the things which had previously brought meaning and joy to their lives, fearing to leave their home for any reason. For others this more conscious acceptance of life's fragility has led to an increased determination to make the most of every minute.

Most people report that their sense of time changed during lockdown. Paradoxically they have experienced time as going both fast and slow. Each day may have felt very long, but each month and year may have appeared to pass very quickly. The passing of time may have brought a sense of loss for things we had planned to happen, but which did not.

We have experienced time taking its toll on our bodies. We may look different to how we did pre-pandemic. The inaccessibility of hairdressers led to new lockdown hair; for some they returned to their original colour after many years of colouring their hair, in some cases stress saw the rapid increase of grey hair. Our body shape may have changed as our eating habits changed for the better or the worse, or we may have increased or decreased our exercise. These bodily changes remind us of time passing.

Birthdays marked out time in a new way. Parties were postponed and postponed again. People's long held plans for weddings and starting families altered. We had to confront our inability to control time. When thinking of the future now, it is with a different sense of time and certainty than previously.

However, we have experienced time during the pandemic, it is worth reminding ourselves:

> Time is the substance I am made of. Time is a river which sweeps me along, but I am the river; it is a tiger which destroys me, but I am the tiger; it is a fire which consumes me, but I am the fire.
>
> (Borges, 1964:234)

Uncertainty

Most human beings are creatures of habit and long for a generous amount of predictability and certainty. They want to know what will happen so that they can plan accordingly. They look for information, clarity, and black and white answers:

> The concept of uncertainty is one with which many of us struggle, and which perhaps lies at the heart of death anxiety; we know we will die, but we do not know how or when, and we have no certainty about what, if anything, happens to our 'being' after death.
>
> (Hanaway, 2020:198)

We cannot avoid the truth that uncertainty is a constant challenge throughout life. We start our lives in a very uncertain manner. A pregnancy will not necessarily end in a birth; if it does, we cannot accurately predict when, we cannot guarantee whether the birth will be easy or difficult or that the baby will be healthy. Our lives do not move from birth into more certain waters even if we would like to believe that they will. Although we may not like to acknowledge it, life is 'uncertain in its meaning, uncertain in its future, and uncertain because there exists no certainty beyond the finite nature of our existence and the uncertainty itself' (Hanaway, 2020:191).

Johal (2021:10) noted: 'Uncertainty is recognised as a leading cause of worry, anxiety and stress.' Not knowing what will happens makes us vulnerable and on edge. 'This edginess is exacerbated when official advice seems to be conflicting or constantly changing, as knowledge of the virus unfolds, or official bodies offer differing opinions' (ibid.). The unprecedented nature of the Covid-19 pandemic means we are faced with internal and external uncertainty.

Existential thinkers have always been interested in how humans react to uncertainty. Heidegger used the word *Geworfenheit* or 'thrownness' to describe the harsh fact that we have very little control over our own existence; we are thrown into a particular family, country and culture, and the decisions we will make have to involve a leap of faith as we can be certain of very little beyond the fact that we are born and will die. Heidegger notes that to deal with this uncertainty and the angst it causes we may choose to 'fall in with others' in a group attempt to deny reality.

Camus expressed the feelings associated with the uncertainty of our confrontation with the irrational world we inhabit as 'Absurd'. He explored these ideas in many of his novels and essays. He believed that the hopeless human desire to make sense of our condition and to establish certainty where it does not exist, was essentially absurd and impossible. He challenges us to respond appropriately and bravely, and to live in full consciousness of our state of uncertainty and absurdity. If we can do this, he suggests there are three possible consequences – revolt, freedom, and passion. By 'revolt' he means defiance, 'with the truth being experienced as not hopeless, but giving life in its essential temporality, a certain grandeur' (Hanaway, 2020:200). He believed that if we can accept the absurdity of our state, we can 'free' ourselves from habit and convention and be liberated from mindlessness convention and habit, bringing a 'passion' to live as intensely as possible. We can see during the pandemic people struggling to decide whether to revolt, use their freedom and allow their passion. The important thing is not to be frozen by the uncertainty of the situation.

Kierkegaard too emphasised that we all face a future that is uncertain and unknown and calls on us to find our own truth and meaning. He knew a lot about uncertainty, having lost his parents and five of his seven siblings before he was 30. He focused his thinking on what he termed the 'uncertain-certainty' of death and called for us to live our lives with an 'earnestness' living each day as if it were the last and also the first in a long life. He posed the challenge not to cling to false certainty, nor to give in to nihilism, but instead to live as if anything is possible. This requires us to face and accept uncertainty, and to front up to the facts rather than trying to cut deals with reality. Right now, those facts are that, for many of us, much of our lives are on hold, and our responsibilities to each other may require us to do painful things. We cannot say when this period of our lives will end or what life will look like on the other side of the pandemic.

This uncertainty can feel both seductive and terrifying. It can cause us to freeze, or it can free up our creativity, and make life full and exciting. As I have asked in previous publications, if we really knew everything that would happen before it occurred, where would that leave us? Would we enjoy the challenge if we always knew the outcome? Would we embark on creative activity if we could be sure of the end product? As Auguste de Villiers de L'Isle-Adam (2000:62) wrote: 'Uncertainty is a quality to be cherished, – if not for it, who would dare to undertake anything?' There is no antidote to uncertainty, and it is a mistake to seek it. This uncertain time opens new creative possibilities if we can break free from the desire for certainty.

Values and beliefs

Our values and beliefs influence our behaviours and, by being conscious of them and continually reflecting on them, then they form the framework of authentic living. I have indicated the main existential values with the emphasis on acknowledging our authentic uniqueness in the world while always being in relationship to others and accepting the importance of freedom, choice and responsibility. Sartre in *Being and Nothingness* (1943) says that values appear with the character of 'demands' and as such they lay claim to a' foundation' or 'justification' requiring us to challenge ourselves as to why we think or act in the way we do. By remaining true to our values and beliefs we behave authentically.

Often, our values and beliefs may have been handed down to us through our families, cultures or religions. We may rarely question them and assume the values of others rather than formulate our own through internal questioning. It is common for people never to question their values and to be able to list them quite easily. Yet, for values to be meaningful they must be reviewed and interrogated. A too rigid adherence to a long-held value may be problematic for an individual: 'If an individual places "loyalty" high on their list of values they may feel the need to unquestioningly follow behaviours of their gang, peer group or institution even when they experience the behaviours as destructive or wrong' (Hanaway, 2020:391).

During the pandemic people needed to ask themselves what is most important to them and to reflect on their values and beliefs. This caused difficult dilemmas for some, often in relation to their beliefs and values about individual freedom and collective responsibility.

By giving more time to considering to what extent we trust others, ranging from those making and presenting government policies, to those closest to us, and the level of their adherence to Covid-19 rules and restrictions, we are called upon to face and question our values, our degree of authenticity, and to what extent the new situation may challenge our values and beliefs.

These existential givens are evident in all aspects of our being-in-the-world. To explore our own, or other people's, 'lived givens' it may be helpful to look at them in relation to the contexts (dimensions) in which they are demonstrated. I think we can all recognise that, while remaining authentic, we do not always feel or act the same in all contexts.

Existential dimensions

Each existential theme is experienced in a context of what may be referred to as an existential dimension. These dimensions make a person's worldview, that is their 'Being-in-the world'. This can be explored through the dimensions in which they exist and move.

Existential thinkers have used a framework of four different existential dimensions to explore a person's worldview, which affects their choice of behaviour, and their decision making. These four, separate but interconnecting, existential dimensions are concerned with the person's way of being in the social, environmental, psychological and spiritual aspects of their existence.

Binswanger (1930) spoke of a relatedness between the environment (*Umwelt*; 'around world'); the world of social being and its signals (*Mitwelt*; 'with world'); the personal or psychological world (*Eigenwelt*; 'own world'); and the world of actions (*Aliticwelt*; 'doing world'). The use of *Aliticwelt* has somewhat fallen out of use. In 1984 van Deurzen-Smith added the *Uberwelt*, or the spiritual dimension.

Umwelt

Umwelt literally means the world around; the natural world of objects that surround us, including the environment and the biological world. We are 'thrown' into the world, without a choice of whether, how, or when to be born or to which parents, or the nature (gender, health etc.) of the body we inhabit.

Personal and global events and circumstances can radically alter our relationship to our *Umwelt* causing a sea of confusion and doubt. The pandemic has affected how safe we see our environment. For many of us the world shrank to the inside of our own home, and our relationship with our own bodies changed with a deeper understanding of their vulnerability and capacity for change. Van Deurzen (2021:101) wrote: 'The more we feel we can enjoy our body, the more confident we are in our sense of mastery and do not feel burdened by the threats of death, illness ... or other forms of bodily diminishment.' She notes that the Covid-19 pandemic resulted in many of us becoming 'aware of how dependent we are on there being a state of harmony, not just in our own bodies but in the physical world' (ibid.).

We have become more aware of our bodies and the bodies of others. We have experienced fear and shame at every cough, and the change in the structure of our lives has given more time to reengage with our embodied self. This may have resulted in a greater awareness of our own ageing, causing anxiety as we note every physical change or actively try to ward off the ageing process.

Mitwelt

Mitwelt is concerned with the social world, our interaction with one's fellow human beings, and the world of interrelationships generally. This means that we may be in danger of becoming caught up in each other's ways of being and risk our authentic self. It can be tempting and too easy to take on another's standards, preferences, and desires or to separate ourselves out from those we feel are different to us. Heidegger (1962:220) describes this as a 'fallenness into the world', through which we can become absorbed with others leading to temptation, tranquilisation, alienation and self-entanglements – the nullity of inauthentic everydayness, averageness, and leveling down. (ibid.: 223). There is a danger that in falling, or being absorbed in others, one becomes superficial and inauthentic, an imitation of who one really is. In falling, we live in social worlds in which we have lost ourselves in everyday routines and relationships. Heidegger (1962:422) exclaims:

> In everydayness Dasein can undergo suffering, sink away in the dullness of it, and evade it by seeking new ways in which its affairs may be dispersed. In the moment of vision, indeed, and often just for the moment; existence can even gain the mastery over the 'everyday'; but it can never extinguish it.

The pandemic has forced many of us out of a non-reflected way of being with others. It may have enhanced the experience of otherness, of me and them, or us and them. 'Them' may be the ones I am lockdowned with, the ones who share my views on the virus, on whether to follow the rules and become vaccinated, whereas another 'them' may be the 'others' who are seen to represent danger, who can infect us or make us challenge our views and values.

Through the very physical disconnectedness of lockdown and social distancing we have been made more aware of the separation between self and others. Some people may have experienced this positively, while for others the loss of physical connectedness may have been difficult to bear.

Eigenwelt

In this third mode of being-in-the-world, the *Eigenwelt* is concerned with the relationship to self. This presupposes a level of self-awareness sand self-relatedness. It involves grasping what something means in its connection to oneself and in its potentialities for self-expression and development: 'The Eigenwelt is the source of creative unfolding, self-searching, and inventive discovery ... in its inauthentic state it is dominated by the expectations, standards, and values of others' (Moustakis, 1996:24).

Our sense of who we are may have been challenged by the imposed restrictions of the pandemic. We may previously have defined ourselves by professional success only to lose our jobs, or we may have considered ourselves to be 'earth mothers' only to find that being with our children 24/7 was more demanding than we had anticipated. Without the onlookers who usually surround us we are released from the question 'what will others think?' Instead, we are afforded the moral freedom to choose our own way-of-being-in the-world, a freedom which was always there but which at times may have been ignored.

The acknowledgement of our freedom brings the requirement to acknowledge both its positive and negative aspects. Carter (2008) explains the distinction as being 'negative liberty is the absence of obstacles, barriers or constraints ... Positive liberty is the possibility of acting ... in such a way as to take control of one's life'. The pandemic has not deprived us of our internal freedom and our ability to choose, but as van Deurzen (2021:101) wrote: 'When we have our freedom taken away from us in some way (as for example in the lockdowns to control the spread of the Covid-19 pandemic), we will need to find a new inner balance.' The pandemic has set us new challenges within the *Eigenwelt* requiring us to take a fresh look at ourselves and our values, and to consider what our authentic self may be post pandemic.

Uberwelt

The *Uberwelt* is concerned with our spiritual dimension, values and beliefs, and those ideas that influence how we understand the world. It is the dimension of meaning and moral responsibility. It helps us to prioritise aspects of our being using our values to set our behaviours.

For most of the time we may fail to sit back and consider what makes life meaningful, or what we believe in, or how to confront some apparent paradoxes in our thinking. The pandemic gave us the time to stop and think and it challenged us to make some value judgements, which may have been far from easy. I may value my freedom but do I do so at the risk of putting others in danger by refusing the limitations placed on me by Covid-19 rules. Will I refuse to wear a mask or be vaccinated because these limit my freedom or will I freely choose to prioritise the potential health benefits for self and others if I follow the rules? In making our decisions we are forced to do so without any certainty that what we are told is correct leaving us to use our own values as a framework for action. As van Deurzen (2021:102) wrote: 'In the Covid-19 pandemic many people began to worry about the lack of ethics and truth in the world and began to realise that these things matter more than we sometimes think.' We are having a very harsh lesson in living with uncertainty.

These existential givens and dimensions are referred to by chapter authors throughout this book. This brief overview is included for those new to existential thinking to place what the authors have written within the broad spectrum of existential and phenomenological thought.

References

Bailey, J. (2001) Leadership Lessons from Mount Rushmore: An Interview with James MacGregor Burns. *Leadership Quarterly*, 12.91, 113–128 http://dx.doi.org/10.1016/S1048-9843(01)00066-2.

Berlin, I. (1969) 'Two Concepts of Liberty', in I. Berlin (ed.), *Four Essays on Liberty*. Oxford: Oxford University Press.

Binswanger, L. (1930) Traum und Existenz. *Neue Schweizer Rundschau (Zürich)*, IX, 673–685, 766–779.

Borges, J.L. (1964) *Labyrinthes*. Ed. D.A. Yates and J.E. Irby. New York: New Directions Books.

Bugental, J.F.T. (1992) *The Art of the Psychotherapist: How to Develop Skills which take* Psychotherapy *beyond Science*. New York: NY Norton.

Camus, A. (1947) *La Peste* [*The Plague*]. Paris: Gallimard.

Carter, I. (2008) *Positive and Negative Liberty. Stanford Encyclopedia of Philosophy*. http://plato.stanford.edu/entries/liberty-positive-negative/ (accessed 23 May 2020).

Cooper, B. (1967) *12 Prose Writers*. New York: Holt, Rinehart & Winston.

Davis, E. and Miller, D. (1967) *The Philosophic Process in Physical Education*. Philadelphia: Lea & Febiger.

Deurzen, E. van (2021) *Rising from Existential Crisis*. Monmouth: PCCS Books Ltd.

Deurzen-Smith, E. van (1984) 'Existential Therapy', in W. Dryden (ed.), *Individual Therapy in Britain*. London: Harper & Row.

Frankl, V.E. (1985) *Man's Search for Meaning*. New York: Washington Square Press.

Gerassi, J. (1989) *Jean-Paul Sartre: Hated Conscience of his Century*. Chicago: University of Chicago Press.

Hanaway, M. (2019) *The Existential Leader: An Authentic Leader for Our Uncertain Times*. Abingdon: Routledge.

Hanaway, M. (2020) *An Existential Approach to Leadership Challenges*. Abingdon: Routledge.

Heidegger, M. (1949) *Existence and Being*. Trans W. Brock. South Bend, IN: Regney/Gateway.

Heidegger, M. (1962) *Being and Time*. Trans J. Macquarrie and E. Robinson. New York: Harper Row.

Husserl, E. (2009) *The Basic Problems of Phenomenology: From the Lectures, Winter Semester 1910–1911, New Edition*. Trans I. Farin and J.G. Hart. New York City: Springer.

Johal, S. (2021) *Steady: A Guide to Better Mental Health Trough and Beyond the Coronavirus Pandemic*. London: Equanimity Ltd.

Kant, I. (1781 [1966]) *Critique of Pure Reason*. Trans M. Muller. New York: Doubleday.

Kierkegaard, S. (1844 [1980]) *The Concept of Anxiety*. Princeton, NJ: Princeton University Press.

May, R. (1999) *Freedom and Destiny*. New York: W.W. Norton.

Moustakis, C. (1996) *Existential Psychotherapy and the Interpretation of Dreams*. Lanham, MD: Jason Aronson Inc. Publishers.

Musser, S.J. (1987) *Positive and Negative Charismatic Leaders*. Grantham, PA: Messiah College.

Sartre, J.-P. (1943 [1972]) *Being and Nothingness: An Essay on Phenomenological Ontology*. London: Methuen & Co.

Villiers de L'Isle-Adam, A. (2000) *Tomorrow's Eve*. Champaign, IL: University of Illinois Press.

Weber, M. (1968) *On Charisma and Institution Building*. Chicago: University of Chicago Press.

Weixel-Dixon, K. (2017) *Interpersonal Conflict: An Existential and Psychotherapeutic Model*. London: Routledge.

Yalom, I. (1980) *Existential Psychotherapy*. New York: Basic Books.

Part I

The internal world – self-reflection

Thoughts from individuals about their own pandemic experience from an existential viewpoint

It may seem a little self-indulgent to give quite a lot of space to personal thoughts and reflections on individuals' pandemic experiences. However, as Jung pointed out, 'Your visions will become clear only when you can look into your own heart. Who looks outside, dreams; who looks inside, awakes' (Sreechinth, 2018:19).

Learning from subjective experience is increasingly valued as a way of better understanding the world, and essential to effective future planning. The Galileo Commission, made up of a diverse group of scientists, together with others from different disciplines, argued that

> the current scientific paradigm with its focus explicitly on the physical, that which can be measured, is no longer fit for purpose. If science, they recommend, is to reflect both the objective, outer, and subjective, inner, sensed aspects of reality, then it needs to embrace our felt experiences.
>
> (Beasley, 2021)

This calls for importance to be given to people's personal narratives:

> Feelings expressed during interviews, ideas gleaned through story-telling and perceptions highlighted through analysis of personal journals; all provide essential clues as to what is going on in the hearts and minds of those under study. Some might call this the inner dimension to being human.
>
> (Beasley, 2021)

Existentialism is focused on the 'lived experience'. Kant (1781:2) reminded us that 'all our knowledge begins with experience there can be no doubt'. We are going through a time which, for most of us is unique; we need to take the opportunity to reflect on our new experiences and see what we can learn

DOI: 10.4324/9781003255765-2

from them. So, to start an existential reflection on the pandemic with personal 'lived experiences' seems appropriate.

Whatever our professional background, it is important we find time for self-reflection (Williams et al. 2008). The phrase 'know thyself', often attributed to Socrates, is a motto inscribed on the frontispiece of the Temple of Delphi. This assertion indicates that a person must stand and live according to their true nature. This in turn carries with it the understanding that one must accept that we do not remain static and so, to be our true authentic selves, we must continually question who we are, what we believe in and what values flow from that belief. If I can know myself on any one day, I can understand my limitations and my potentialities, I can openly acknowledge my vulnerability and fears, and celebrate my strengths and achievements. I can learn not just from the past but from my present, noting my feelings in all my experiences.

If I can honestly examine all these aspects of my externally and internally lived experience then, as Socrates believed, I might come to know myself, which he saw as the beginning of wisdom. In Plato's *Philebus* dialogue, he states that people make themselves appear ridiculous when they are trying to claim or gain knowledge of obscure things before they even know themselves. He stresses that the unexamined life is not worth living.

In the case of therapists and coaches it would be arrogant and dangerous to believe that we can 'know' and understand others if we give no time to knowing ourselves. Indeed, the level of self-awareness in a therapist has been identified as a critical component of successful and ethical psychotherapy (Strong & Schmidt 1970; Edwards & Bess, 1998; Jennings & Skovholt, 1999; Mattison, 2000). These studies use the term 'self-awareness' to refer to 'self-knowledge' or 'self-insight' particularly in relation to knowing one's own issues, biases, strengths and weaknesses.

During the pandemic I often read or heard the statement 'we are all in the same boat now'. Indeed, this is the title of the first chapter of Zizek's (2020) book on the pandemic. Although we are living through some of the same challenging circumstances, we will each experience them differently. Perhaps it could be true to say that we are all adrift on the same sea of uncertainty, but the truth is there are lots of different types of boats floating on it, ranging from luxury yachts to mere bits of wood off a sinking ship providing something for those with nothing better, to cling on to while awaiting rescue.

Each person has their own history, views, thoughts, emotions, plans and hopes which provide the lens through which we view and make sense of our daily experiences. However, even though we are so different, we experience similar patterns of self-analysis, which make up who we are today.

If we can be self-aware, we can see ourselves authentically, without blinkers. This is not easy as it requires us to find a kindness and empathy towards ourselves, without ignoring any of our vulnerabilities, or areas of which we may justifiably be self-critical. If we can find such openness, we can find learning in our experiences. Dr Kabat-Zinn (2005:96) wrote:

Dwelling in stillness and looking inward for some part of each day, we touch what is most real and reliable in ourselves and most easily overlooked and undeveloped. When we can be centred in ourselves, even for brief periods of time in the face of the pull of the outer world, not having to look elsewhere for something to fill us up or make us happy, we can be at home wherever we find ourselves, at peace with things as they are, moment by moment.

Lockdown gave us the time and opportunity to look inwards.

For this section of the book, I invited the authors to give their reflections on their pandemic experience. In line with the existential approach, they were asked to retain their authentic voice rather than to adopt a 'house style' which limited their freedom of expression. As the reader will see there are commonalities and differences in their self-reflected experiences. I offered no structure for the authors to follow, nor gave them access to what their fellow writers produced. I gave them free rein to use existential-phenomenological thought as a framework for their reflections in whatever way they wished.

References

Beasley, K. (2021) Beyond Disciplines: Evolving Research Methodology for the Post-Pandemic 'New Normal'. *Academia Letters*, Article 2301 https://doi.org/10.20935/AL2301.

Edwards, J.K. and Bess, J.M. (1998) Developing Effectiveness in the Therapeutic Use of Self. *Clinical Social Work Journal*, 26(1), 89–105.

Jennings, L. and Skovholt, T.M. (1999) The Cognitive, Emotional and Relational Characteristics of Master Therapists. *Journal of Counseling Psychology*, 46, 3–11.

Kabat-Zinn, J. (2005) *Wherever You Go, There You Are: Mindfulness Meditation in Everyday Life.* New York: Hachette Books.

Kant, I. (1781) *The Critique of Pure Reason.* Konigsberg: Friedrich Nicolovius.

Mattison, M. (2000) Ethical Decision-Making: The Person in the Process. *Social Work*, 45(3): 201–212.

Sreechinth, C. (2018) *Musings of Carl Jun* Slough: CreateSpace Independent Publishing Platform.

Strong, S.R. and Schmidt, L.D. (1970) Trustworthiness and Influence in Counselling. *Journal of Counseling Psychologist*, 17, 197–204.

Williams, E.N., Hayes, J.A. and Fauth, J. (2008) 'Therapist Self-Awareness: Interdisciplinary Connections and Future Directions', in S.D. Brown and R.W. Lent (eds), *Handbook of Counseling Psychology.* Hoboken, New Jersey John Wiley (pp. 303–319).

Zizek, S. (2020) *Pandemic: Covid-19 Shakes The World.* New York: Polity Press.

Chapter 1

From fear, uncertainty, and loss to embodiment, dreams and awakening

Monica Hanaway

Although Rainer Maria Rilke, the German poet, writing in 1910, in *The Notes of Malte Laurids Brigge* (2009) was concerned with war, I felt a resonance in her writing with some of my own feelings in relation to the start of the Covid-19 pandemic:

> There is a creature that is completely harmless for your eyes: you scarcely notice it and forget it immediately. But as soon as, invisibly, it somehow gets into your ear, it develops there and, as it were, finally comes out of its cocoon; and there have been cases in which it penetrated to the brain and there spread devastation, somehow like the pneumococci of the dog which enter through the node.
>
> (Kaufmann, 1963:116)

For Rilke, this creature represents 'fear of war', but it could equally apply to Covid-19. You have a vague feeling something is going on, somewhere in the world. You notice some small, unusual news items appearing in the media, you scarcely notice their gravity and tend to forget about it immediately, believing it to be harmless to you. However, as it keeps appearing over and over again, you find it gets into your head, and provides a soundtrack to your thoughts. Eventually the moment comes when you can no longer deny its severity and it whirls around your brain.

I had heard that there was concern about a new virus taking hold around Wuhan, China. How awful I thought, but my immediate reaction was to remember Ebola and the terror that generated in the UK for a relatively short time. I recalled photos of aid workers and medics kitted out in full PPE and how strange and detached it looked, with people's individuality literally masked, seemingly robbing them of their humanity. I remembered the Ebola threat becoming more real to me when cases were confirmed within the UK, and we heard of the Scottish nurse Pauline Cafferkey contracting and beating the virus twice, before going on to give birth to twin boys. For some reason

DOI: 10.4324/9781003255765-3

these events were shocking but remained in my peripheral vision 'scarcely noticed'.

My first visceral awareness of the Covid-19 pandemic came through watching the news and seeing film of terrified, screaming people in China being forcefully dragged from their homes and thrown into the backs of windowless vans. The surfacing of the videos (www.nbcnews.com/news/world/video-appears-show-people-china-forcibly-taken-quarantine-over-coronavirus-n1133096) came after a Chinese government official visited Wuhan in February 2020. Sun Chunlan, vice premier of the state council, referred to a 'wartime condition' and warned that 'no person or household should be left out' of the system of checks, observation and quarantine considered necessary to contain the virus. These images terrified me, not primarily because of the severity of the virus, but because its cause and future trajectory was uncertain. I have never believed myself to have much difficulty with uncertainty, as generally I see it as an invitation to engage in creativity. Certainty does not offer me security, it constrains me. Rebecca Solnit (2014) reminds us:

> Creation is always in the dark because you can only do the work of making by not knowing what you are doing, by walking into the darkness, not staying in the light. Ideas emerge from the edges and shadows arrive in the light, and although that is where they may be seen by others, that is not where they are born.

I did not, and on a personal level still do not, have any need to know with certainty where the virus started, whether it was the result of the sale of pangolins, the state of markets selling animals for food, or an escape from a lab. I feel I should want that certainty, but it would not change anything; it is now present across the world. Paradoxically the idea that it came from pangolins may have helped focus the world's attention on their endangered plight and improved conditions in some food markets where live animals are sold. Of course, if it came from a leak, and the lab holds the answer to its treatment, that raises political and moral questions: but I must confess these were not what preoccupied me.

In the videos, I was faced with people reduced to nameless and faceless groups, robbed of their individuality and their freedom. This conflicts with the existential way of seeing the world and its emphasis on the uniqueness of the individual within a set of existential givens, and the individual's freedom and responsibility to respond to their worldview. The Wuhan government officially divided the population into 'four types of people'; those confirmed to have Covid-19; those suspected to have the virus; people with fevers who could not be ruled out of having the virus; and those who had been in close contact with people with confirmed cases. Being confined to groups and labelled may have been, and continue to be, essential for our physical survival, yet it felt to be in opposition to the existential commitment to the belief in the individual as a unique responsible being. Of course, even with a label, we have a choice of how we live with it, to what extent we accept or reject it, how we define its meaning and choose to live in relation to our own definition or a more global one, or indeed whether we choose to quietly reject it or overtly fight against it.

I felt an existential dread. Where were these people being taken? What would happen to them? Would they die Did their friends and family know where they were? Would they be cared for? Would anyone ever hear from them again? Eventually I allowed the thought to penetrate my brain: could this happen here? Could I, and those I love, become just a number, or be experienced as a threat to others, instead of being experienced in the complex richness of our humanity. Was it possible I would lose contact with those I loved? Even worse, could I lose them permanently through my death or theirs? My own awareness for the need for relatedness and human contact was brought to the forefront of my mind.

Twinned with this was a desire to keep safe and, more importantly, to keep my family safe. This was intensified with the first two confirmed cases of Covid-19 in the UK at the end of January 2020. I found myself experiencing an existential anxiety the depth of which I had not experienced before. I feared for my partner whose health required the daily use of immune-suppressant medicine. As time moved on and my elder daughter discovered she was pregnant, I worried for her and her unborn baby. I missed my younger daughter and worried when she and her partner, both self-employed and initially not considered eligible for furlough or self-employed support, were without work or income. I slept badly and experienced intense dreams. I faced the eternal existential dilemma of squaring the circle between freedom and responsibility. My choice was to embrace my freedom to be responsible and accept new limitations on my daily existence.

As the initial shock and encounter with uncertainty faded a little, I became more occupied with issues of relatedness and loss (*Mitwelt*). A family member died of the virus and older members of the family in residential care were not allowed visitors. I felt my sense of power over my daily existence diminishing (*Eigenwelt*). I was faced with several decisions which highlighted existential concerns.

Some decisions were very hard and linked to the existential importance of relatedness and the *Mitwelt*/social dimension. I love meeting new people; now, I was expected to experience other people as dangerous, with the potential to make me ill, or even kill me. Zizek (2020:1), when considering the requirement not to touch people, draws our attention to the resurrected Christ's requirement that he could no longer be touched but 'He will be there not as a person to touch, but as a bond of solidarity between people' – so, 'do not touch me, touch and deal with other people in the spirit of love'. This was quite a challenge. Zizek (2020:3) is hopeful that social distancing will 'strengthen the intensity of our link with others' as, he believes 'it is only now when I have to avoid many of those who are close to me, that I fully experience their presence, their importance' (ibid.). We may recognise this shift in importance if we have lost someone close to us as their importance and the intense pain of their loss is only experienced fully after their death.

For most of my professional (and personal) life I have always desired to understand others and their ways of being-in-the-world. I am essentially a nosy person. Now my experiences with those outside my bubble would be limited to experiences separated by a screen. For the foreseeable future, I would be confined with one person, fortunately my partner, who I love, plus our two dogs (one of whom we lost during the pandemic). Was I finally going to agree with the quote from Sartre, that 'hell is other people'?

We must firstly remind ourselves where that quote comes from. It is found towards the end of his play *No Exit* (*Huis Clos*, in French), written in 1943. The play depicts the arrival of three characters – Garcin, Estelle and Inez – in hell (a drawing room). The characters struggle to understand what sin has led them to this fate, and what their punishment may be, but they come to understand there is no torturer and no eternal flames. It is just the three of them, trapped together. Just sharing their space with the other characters in the room was the punishment: 'You remember all we were told about the torture-chambers, the fire and brimstone, the "burning marl." … no need for red-hot pokers. HELL IS OTHER PEOPLE!'

Fortunately, the proximity of another for 24 hours a day, every day, was not a punishment. I felt grateful that I was not living alone. My appreciation of my partner grew and, although we are busy on our separate projects, we came together to touch base, have a drink or food, and share our thoughts. This quite simple, and in many ways accepting, way of being has grown as the Covid-19 situation has developed.

However, I was confronted through the lives of my clients with many hellish situations caused by lockdown. Many of my psychotherapy clients live alone and so their days do not contain the option to easily connect 'in the flesh' with another person. My coaching work is focused on work with business executives and leaders and for them the challenge is often the opposite; they are expected to work from home and, instead of the sanctity of their office, they are working surrounded by their families, often with children requiring home schooling and a partner who shares the same work pressures as they do. My supervisees have all been faced with the challenges of working virtually and with increased workloads and pressure at a time when also dealing with the personal impact of Covid-19.

Lockdown presented clients not just with challenges in the *Umwelt*, accustoming themselves with new or changed environments. The lives of several clients were made harder through increased pressure from situations which already existed. These included the woman who was locked down with an abusive husband, another trying to manage the withdrawal symptoms of a son unable to access his heroin supply, a woman who had struggled for many years with fertility problems whose treatment was just about to start and which was 'put on hold', families confined and at war with each other, and clients 'trapped' in multi-occupancy shared houses with people they hardly knew.

The sense of difference, including the inequality, which was highlighted in terms of domestic comfort, financial security, access to others, quality of home teaching, access to support, access to outside space etc., highlighted how easy it is for people to be divided into opposing groups. Experiencing fellow beings as 'Other'. This followed on from the Brexit experience where people were divided into Brexiteers or Remainers (Remoaners) – a division which I encountered when a client voted differently from his identical twin in the referendum and reported they had not spoken to one another since. Covid-19 has further divided us: we are 'vulnerable' or less so; we are vaccine adopters ('one jabbed or two') or anti-vaxxers and conspiracy theorists; we are those who believe the government and believe they are doing a good job, or who have no respect for them and consider them to have acted irresponsibly, illegally and inauthentically. One future challenge will lie in trying to tear down those walls of separation again so we can welcome difference and not be frightened by it.

My own lockdown journey, which I described as starting in fear and uncertainty, moved to an acceptance of the situation. Taking responsibility for how I chose to give meaning to my experiences. Like others I began to see opportunities in the time it gave me. Although my psychotherapy work did not lessen, my leadership and coaching work continued but without the travelling; but my training work stopped completely. Like many others, I decorated my rooms (it seems so long ago now that they are ready for a further coat of paint). This gave a sense of agency and control over my environment (*Umwelt*). I responded to the knowledge that the virus was less transmittable outside by buying new garden furniture and watching as my partner filled the garden with glorious new plants.

Time and temporality were experienced in a very concrete manner. Seasons came and went. I missed my annual trips to Italy. I missed the smell of the place, the quality of the light, the sound of its poetic language. I missed the sea, the heat, and the sunshine. I missed the architecture and the art. I asked myself whether I would ever go there again. The answer still eludes me. However, when the sun began to shine brightly and beautifully in summer 2020, I acknowledged my loss of Italy and the meaning it holds for me and sought to address some of that loss by taking a glass of Italian wine into the garden and indulging myself in old downloads of episodes of *Montalbano*, a detective series set in Sicily, where I could see places I had visited, I could listen to the language and try yet again, not very successfully, to learn Italian. I read Gianrico Carofiglio, Maurizio De Giovanni, Marco Vichi and others, reading of fictional death instead of tormenting myself with reading the daily

Covid-19 statistics. I discovered that I could allow myself to drift away, feel the heat on my skin, smell the flowers in my garden, and be grateful to be alive and lucky enough to have that space in which to revisit my memories, always conscious that others were trapped inside flats and houses with no outdoor space. I acknowledged to myself how rarely pre-pandemic I allowed myself to drop everything I needed to do and head into the garden. I noted to myself that I needed to take greater care in ensuring that I did not ignore the personal external environment.

Within the more personal realm of my body, things were less glorious. I had engrossed myself in activity, I was busy, but it was a motionless busyness – sitting down, staring at a computer screen for Zoom meetings with clients, writing, and designing several online courses (despite my dislike of working online). I experienced the time passing and I experienced myself becoming older. Time slipped quickly away and yet could also feel endless.

It is not surprising that for many of us we became more focused on our embodied self during the pandemic. Many of us do not hold a consciousness of our body throughout the day. Leder (1990), in his exploration of the body with regards to subjectivity, reminds us that although the human experience is always embodied it is 'seldom a thematic object of my experience'. Despite this, Merleau Ponty (2002) speaks of the 'self-giveness' of the body so that, even when non-reflective, I am aware of my body.

During the pandemic we became hyper-aware of coughs, breathlessness, temperature shifts, shivering, hotness, headaches. This does not just apply to awareness of our own bodies but an increased awareness of those we try to distance, in order that they do not spread the virus to us, and those we long to hold, but who were forbidden to us. There is a danger that we see others and ourselves as a set of symptoms which are either present or absent. The image of the virus passing through the air from one person to another puts us in concrete consciousness of the interconnectedness of bodies.

It is not just the relationship between our bodies and those of others that has come under the spotlight. Daily, we have been confronted with images of ourselves on screen. As Merleau-Ponty (2002), points out to see oneself through the eyes of others, may evoke a 'dys-appearing body' or we may experience ourselves as alien (Zeiler, 2010). Leder (1990) described how the body, at times of dys-appearance, is often experienced as separate from one-self. In Zoom meetings, we experience our body as both sitting on our chair looking at our screen, and as existing in the corner of the screen, while a third person watches us on their screen. Merleau-Ponty speaks of two views of 'me and the body: my body for me and my body for others, and how these two systems can exist together' (Merleau-Ponty, 2002:122). When we are closely connected to the gaze of others it may evoke shame: 'in so far as I have a body, I may be reduced to the status of an object beneath the gaze of another person, and no longer count as a person for him' (Merleau-Ponty, 2002:193).

Indeed, I may experience my own image in the tiny box in the corner of the screen as an object and as an affront to my self-image.

As I talk to someone through the screen, I am reminded of the words of Wittgenstein (Klagge & Norman, 2003:393): 'What you say, you say in a body; you can say nothing outside of this body'. And yet most of the time I am ignoring my own. Do I fear that paying it attention will draw me down into the contemplation of its vulnerability, particularly at a time when a deadly virus is tracking our steps? Is the existential anxiety such contemplation might create too great and so distract me from my busy task? As many friends committed themselves to Pilates, yoga, running, wild swimming etc., my existing disability became worse, and my mobility decreased. I put on weight and disliked my body. I missed what my body had done with ease in earlier life, and I became fearful for its limited future ability. It was difficult to access doctors and those who succeeded spoke of nightmare visits to hospital, confronted by staff in full PPE, not able to be visited by loved ones and surrounded by fear and pain. Our bodies took on an air of vulnerability, people were afraid to cough even behind a mask and we became super aware of small changes in our health. Clients brought dreams of suffocation and annihilation. Our relationship to our bodies was changing, for some positively, for others less so.

My own body felt constantly tired, and yet I was doing less physical activity than ever before. Of course, I needed to remind myself, I had taken on more clients and spent my days in Zoom meetings which I hated, a format which for some reason drains me. It helped me to discover that researchers from Stanford University working for Professor Jeremy Bailenson, (2020) had identified causes for 'Zoom fatigue'. The first cause was the excessive amounts of close-eye contact. When a person's face is that close to ours in real life, our brains interpret us as being in an intense situation which will lead to intimacy or conflict. Thus, when on Zoom, we tend to remain in a hyper-aroused state. Secondly, seeing oneself on video chats is tiring and distracting. If, in the real world, somebody followed you around with a mirror constantly, so that you were always seeing your own image when you were talking to people, such scrutiny would feel overwhelming. Being under constant examination by others, but also by oneself, makes us more critical of ourselves. As already mentioned in relation to myself, Baileson reminds us that video chats dramatically reduce our usual mobility, and the cognitive load is much higher. In effect, humans have taken one of the most natural things in the world, an in-person conversation, and transformed it into something that involves a lot of thought which is not centred on relatedness. Indeed, one can become concerned with making sure that your head is framed within the centre of the screen. We may feel the need for exaggerated gestures to ensure we are understood, or we may try to remain still so that our natural gestures are not distracting. We are not authentically and truly connected to the person we are in dialogue with, and the cognitive overload can be tiring. I have found a way of being with my online experiences but always feel dissatisfied with them.

My acceptance of my own 'new normal' saw me move from intermittent, disturbed sleep to experiencing long, deep sleep which held a quality I do not believe I had experienced before. My dreams were not nightmarish but deeper and more vivid than previously remembered. Science has considered long dream content and emotions as connected to wellbeing while we are awake. It is posited that through bizarre dreams laden with symbolism dreamers may be enabled to overcome intense memories or everyday psychological stressors. Nightmares can be interpreted as warning signs of anxieties that we might not otherwise perceive in our waking lives.

Some dream experts suggested that the withdrawal from our usual range of daily stimuli during the pandemic left dreamers with a dearth of inspiration forcing us to draw more heavily on our past. Patrick McNamara, an associate professor of neurology at Boston University School of Medicine and considered to be an expert in dreams, in an article for the National Geographic by Rebecca Renner (2020) was quoted as saying: 'We normally use REM sleep and dreams to handle intense emotions, particularly negative emotions … Obviously, this pandemic is producing a lot of stress and anxiety.'

Lyon Neuroscience Research Centre is currently researching dreams during the pandemic and report that the Covid-19 pandemic has caused a 35% increase in dream recall among participants, with respondents reporting 15% more negative dreams than usual. Research by Associazione Italiana di Medicina del Sonno (the Italian Association of Sleep Medicine), which is analysing the dreams of Italians who were confined during the pandemic, reports many subjects experiencing nightmares and parasomnias in line with symptoms of post-traumatic stress disorder. Revonsuo (2000) in his study of nightmares during the pandemic reported a threefold increase in participants reporting nightmares once or more times each week, with two-thirds describing their nightmares as containing pandemic content.

When looking for an existential understanding of dreams we can turn to Medard Boss (1903–1990), a Swiss psychiatrist who published two books on the subject: *The Analysis of Dreams*, and *I Dreamt Last Night*. In these, he challenged the traditional views of Freud and Jung, believing that the dreamer should arrive at their own personal meaning, without the therapist imposing analysis, making interpretations, or offering a predetermined meaning of symbols within the dream. For Boss, there is no such thing as a hidden repository within the brain called the unconscious and therefore no difference between waking and sleeping worlds. Both are interrelated and connected by the individual's lived experience. The dream offers a window of opportunity for the dreamer to illuminate and clarify their relationship with their waking and lived world and shows its potential and limitations if the dreamer is willing to explore this in detail. He believed that dreams were not just a visual phenomenon, but contained moods and feelings, something which Boss (1958) called 'attunement'. If, the dreamer stays with their exploration of their dream the multiple meaning would come to light.

Despite the nature of my own dreams settling and beginning to experience deeper sleep than I did pre-pandemic, the tiredness did not abate. I tried to start incorporating some exercise into my daily schedule, but felt too exhausted, and I never established a routine. Could it be that I had Covid-19 without any other symptoms … was that cough I had back in February Covid-19 and was I now suffering from long Covid? I felt very out of touch with my own body and my struggles to reintegrate and become positively embodied remain a challenge. My relationship with my body is now more authentic. I accept its age; I accept its limitations and I attempt to care for and love it. Recently, I have been helped by discovering a book by Emily Rapp Black *Frida Kahlo and My left Leg* (2021), in which the author speaks of her feeling of connectedness with Frida Kahlo as they had both suffered the amputation of a leg. At least I still have my left leg; indeed I have both, even though one can be the source of much tiredness, frustration and pain. Perhaps the pandemic experience of 'losing my legs', as they are outside the screen shot in online sessions, will go some way to helping me reclaim them, in all their authentic human vulnerability and stop me falling into bodily 'bad faith' by appearing to everyone as though I am never in pain. The pandemic and its focus on the body and its vulnerability may, if I let it, free me from feeling I need to deny my authentic bodily experience. However, I do not want to be a person who now becomes focused on the physical but as Rapp Black (2021:81) wrote:

> There is a body I long to have, the life I think I long to have, and then the body I have been given to receive, the body that I embody, the life that I live, that is mine, both strange and beloved. I embody the shadow sides of the same bright self.

The pandemic has been a timely reminder to develop a more balanced existential realm and give more space for the personal *Umwelt*. After all, I am so lucky that I am alive and well, with a wonderful body that has given me pleasure, taken me to amazing places and, most importantly, has given birth to two wonderful, bright, young creative women.

Seeking a meaningful narrative to frame my pandemic experience I looked to the Greek myth of Persephone. Like Persephone, we may have to learn to live in half years. Periods in which we are 'lock downed', while the virus swirls, and other times when the risk declines and we regain our freedom, the flowers are out, the sun shines and the birds sing. This may allow us to acknowledge and love our bodies, use our freedom more fruitfully, make better choices for ourselves, others, and the world we inhabit.

References

Bailenson, J.K. (2020) Nonverbal Overload: A Theoretical Argument for the Causes of Zoom Fatigue. *Journal of Technology, Mind and Behavior*, 2.1. DOI: 10.1037/tmb0000030.

BBC News (2020) Two Coronavirus Cases Confirmed in UK. *BBC News*, 31 January. Retrieved 2 February 2020.

Boss, M. (1958) *The Analysis of Dreams*. New York: Philosophical Library.

Kaufmann, W. (1963) *Existentialism from Dostoevsky to Sartre*. Cleveland, OH: The World Publishing Company.

Klagge, J.C. and Normann, A. (eds) (2003) *Ludwig Wittgenstein: Public and Private Occasions*. Maryland: Rowman & Littlefield Publishers.

Leder, D. (1990) *The Absent Body*. Chicago and London: The University of Chicago Press.

Merleau-Ponty, M. (2002) *Phenomenology of Perception*. London: Routledge.

Rappp Black, E. (2021) *Frida Kahlo and My Left Leg*. Kendal: Notting Hill Editions.

Renner, R. (2020) The Pandemic Is Giving People Vivid, Unusual Dreams. Here's Why. *National Geographic*. www.nationalgeographic.co.uk/science-and-technology/2020/04/pandemic-giving-people-vivid-unusual-dreams-heres-why.

Revonsuo, A. (2000) The Reinterpretation of Dreams: An Evolutionary Hypothesis of the Function of Dreaming. *Behavioural Brain Science*, 23, 877–1121. doi: 10.1017/S0140525X00004015.

Rilke, R.M. (2009) *The Notes of Malte Laurids Brigge*. London: Penguin.

Sartre, J.-P. (1943) *No Exit; A Play in One Act*. London: Samuel French.

Solnit, R. (2014) *The Faraway Nearby*. London: Granta.

Zeiler, K (2010) A Phenomenological Analysis of Bodily Self-Awareness in the Experience of Pain and Pleasure: On Dys-Appearance and Eu-Appearance. *Medicine Health Care and Philosophy*, 13.4, 333–342. dx.doi.org/10.1007/s11019-010-9237-4.

Zizek, S. (2020) *Pandemic: Covid-19 Shakes the World*. New York: Polity Press.

Chapter 2

'Without music, life would be a mistake'

The experience of a musician in Covid-19 times

Laurence Colbert

Introduction

As a band, 2019 saw us releasing a new album and undertaking a busy touring schedule around the world: a tour that at one point, ironically, included a visit to China in early November. According to the *South China Morning Post* (2020) the first Covid-19 case was recorded in Wuhan in November; fortunately for us, we were over 800km away playing a concert in Shanghai. However, a chain of events had started while we were in the middle of an active touring phase, and in February 2020 we were playing in France and Italy just as the first cases were reported in Europe. In some cases, literally hours before we arrived in the cities of Bordeaux and Milan, reports of Covid-19 appeared in the press. Regardless of this, we were able to play our final show on 13 February 2020 in Paris with no actual cases in our touring party. We then returned home to the UK for a short break from touring.

In planning the next phase of live work, it became apparent that the virus was spreading in Europe. We had to bear in mind there might be cancellations of some up-and-coming festivals. Although at this point there did not seem to be much of a sense that this would happen, an ominous feeling was beginning to materialise. On the train to one meeting, I remember reading the BBC news on my phone and saw that Italy was in 'lockdown'. The word 'lockdown' was new – it did not sound good. Yet, none of us had had any experience of such a thing happening. What really sharpened my mind were the photos in that article showing the completely deserted Palazzo in Milan, where only a few weeks ago I had stood taking my own photos surrounded by tourists, locals, buskers, students and artists. This, with the images of chaotic hospital scenes in Italy, made the situation relevant but, given news reports in the UK, it still felt distant. It was not until case numbers started rising in the UK in March that the growing speculation shattered into some stark planes of a new reality that would soon become 'normality'.

DOI: 10.4324/9781003255765-4

Lockdown begins: initial reactions, new terms, new fears

As the reality of the situation sank in, I felt disempowered by the thought of a lockdown in the UK. As a musician, my most direct mode of performance and interaction had been taken away: that of live music. It is one of the only ways bands can earn money in today's post-MP3 and streaming society. The concept of making music in a shared space with other people became quickly outdated. This loss of freedom to perform and the accompanying anxiety covered many existential themes, as they raised new questions about how I define myself and how I might understand the uncertainty I and the whole music industry faced in the future. In place of a future, a void began to open up.

It also soon became clear that if my wife, who has an auto-immune disease affecting her respiratory system, had any contact with the virus she risked death. This created an anxiety which could quite easily come into play with any interaction we may have with the outside world. This presented a paradox when 'outside': a place that once represented a casual freedom, space, sociability, relatedness and choice, could (for her) instead contain the potential of silent and hidden death.

Authenticity and emotions

Some of the emotions I felt at this time were universal, while others were specifically linked to my status as a musician. Certainly my sense of authenticity as a musician took some wild turns over the course of 2020. There was the need to undertake a lot of adaptation to the changing situations and opportunities as they presented themselves or were removed.

To start with, there was a sense of *being-in-self*. The return home from European touring in February 2020 was that of the triumphant travelling musician. I felt fully authentic as an active and engaged performer back from over nine months of constant touring: creating music in the moment with a heaving, breathing, perspiring crowd in front of me. As my meaning circle changed, life seemed to move from crowds, characters, touring companions and a musical commonality to revolve around a screen or monitor of some kind, as all relations took place via emails, text chats or Zoom. Looking back, in terms of daily activity and social/work relations, we may as well have been travelling in space. So, the identity of the daring performer living in the moment faded away and, instead, the sense of a stay-at-home father stuck on an outpost with his family emerged. Was this perhaps an inauthentic *being-in-itself* or the emergence of a new authentic *being-in-a-pandemic-self*? Although life carried on, there was an air of being 'off course' in 2020. Rather reminiscent of the 1960s' TV series *Lost In Space* (itself based on *The Swiss Family Robinson*) there was a sense of everyday survival and cooperation in unexpected times, often centred on a family unit.

Freedom and responsibility

Despite the earlier fears, for me lockdown was a revelation creatively. The overall situation, bad as it was, gave me a chance to experience a creative epiphany as a musician. The opportunity to have uninterrupted time to work meant that me and a lot of other artists found ourselves, in Sartre's words, 'condemned to be free'. Sartre writes: 'Man is condemned to be free; because once thrown into the world, he is responsible for everything he does. It is up to you to give [life] a meaning' (1948:34). This was our lot as musicians, but also for the population as a whole. Given this 'given' and the message of 'Stay at Home' – and, therefore, no concerts, tour busses or studio collaborations – it was up to us to find some meaning to each day.

As the unorganised time stretched out for hours, weeks, months, I had no certainty about what would happen professionally or personally. Instead, I created my own form of certainty, what Julia Cameron (1992) calls, 'showing up at the page' daily to write – or, more often than not – to engage with the on-screen digital 'page' of music making. A new and welcome responsibility materialised, and I went from noodling about on equipment I had never quite had the time to play with, to making finished songs or tracks … and then collections of them. I collaborated with other people remotely online, and I committed to several projects and efforts. These gave a sense of certainty, responsibility and purpose, even if the opposite was true. If there were no work briefs, then creating one's own brought a form of certainty, even if you were making steps into stones held in place by your own faith.

Working as freely as possible with my own resources, and to a certain extent their limitations, the motivation to be a creative musician felt authentic as a daily role. To me it was the business of the day. The urge to create, and the execution of this, were both uncomplicated and natural: in some ways this was an easy liberation, if unfamiliar at first. It was refreshing to be able to follow artistic urges, to structure my own time. It was empowering to be able to experiment, to make mistakes, to attempt new approaches in a safe space. All my life I have felt a desire to create, and being able to feed this desire on the same day felt like an uncovering of my true self, a dusting off of an area of my potential.

Creativity may happen in an instant, but the days, weeks and months of unstructured time gave more opportunity for those moments to happen naturally and organically.

Streaming as a new way of performing live: authenticity, audience, and relation

Eventually, like many other musicians wanting to reach out, I began to see how I could interact with the outside world through the process of live streaming. By chance this grew from my experience as part of the *Drumathon*, which took place the end of May 2020. This event was set up by Errol Kennedy and

Beverly Sage to raise funds for NHS workers and associated charities, and I and 20 other drummers took it in turns to perform to backing tracks for 12 hours at a stint. The performances were live streamed from our houses or studios, as part of a drumming relay that lasted ten days. People watched us play and donated to the causes on the same website. The *Drumathon* presented me with the opportunity to engage in a different form of relatedness, while at the same time being authentically myself. In this situation I could continue to perform live as I had been doing pre-pandemic, while supporting the people who really were acting to save lives. Perhaps in this there was a sense of both *being-in-itself* and *being-for-others*. Certainly, it came as a huge relief to do something useful.

The concept of audience, however, was now radically different. Rather than the 'clearing' suggested by Heidegger (1962), Merleau-Ponty (2002:227) put forward an idea of consciousness as being more like a 'fold'. For Merleau-Ponty, we are all connected by the same fabric, but we create our own small fold of consciousness out of it. Merleau-Ponty describes 'the fold or hollow of Being [sic] having by principle an outside, the architectonics of the configurations'. Such a model also applies our 'universal separateness' in lockdown and to the dislocated sense of an audience. People enjoyed live streams as an event, but they consumed them individually in their own private spaces and on their own personal devices, with the connecting fabric was the internet. In a wider sense, intellectually we knew that the pandemic was global, but it all transpired and took effect separately and remotely, with each of us in our 'folds' of consciousness and experience. Streaming live from one's own home was like reaching out to thousands of flickering lights in a void, paradoxically 'connected' by the empty darkness surrounding them.

The whole band got together to do a live-streamed gig from a London music venue in June 2020. It was the first time I had been out of the house in three months, and it was a big step. Not surprisingly, the world appeared different. This was the first time that I experienced at first hand other people wearing masks, avoiding each other via social distancing, using anti-bacterial gels, and dealing with interactions and transactions in a non-contact way. The freedom I felt throughout was laced with anxiety, but as the day wore on a new understanding grew that the risks I might be taking were my own 'choices', and therefore I felt a sense of control over my own destiny as the day drew to a close. With a two-week quarantine awaiting me on my return, at least for 48 hours I did not have to think about protecting the life of my wife.

It felt good to experience the instant reciprocity of a real instrument again, rather than through electronics and interfaces in my home studio. Although I had played for 12 hours during the *Drumathon,* and for many hours leading up to it at home on an electronic drum kit, there is a disconnect with this that is hard to explain. Part of it revolves around our ability to 'hear' with our bodies – you feel robbed of the visceral quality of the volume of playing the drums, something I had taken for granted.

Examining the model of streaming live online would be very interesting from an existential point of view because there is no audience. We performed to a deserted room. Only the two planes of sound and vision (via a predetermined selection of microphones and cameras etc.) are relayed to a viewer. It felt very strange to be all-out performing live to an imagined audience in an empty room. There is no immediate response or pay-off to your efforts, although later I discovered that this could come in a patchwork of comments via social media instead.

My experience went like this. Firstly, you have the excitement and preparation of a real live concert. You are in a venue with all the familiar faces of the crew. There is the process of the soundcheck, and then the countdown to the performance and the rising adrenaline as you get ready – but now with social distancing and the awkwardness of colleagues trying to avoid being near each other. Eventually, we start to play, make our familiar sound, and collectively create the instrumental 'noise' of a concert. It sounded so powerful after all the quiet time at home. There is usually a big moment of synchronisation and diffusion of energy with the gathered crowd. This can create an almost transcendental experience of relatedness and connection with a crowd, and a sense of mutual healing. However, in this particular rendering something was missing; at the end of each song there was only silence and dying reflections of an empty room. The void brought anxiety; this emptiness, this silence was unnerving – did something go wrong? Did somebody make a mistake? It caught us all off guard. Then, of course, there is no-one there, no crowd, at least not in the same physical dimension. The emptiness and the silence are thrown right back at you. Usually, the audience validates the performance, the performers, and vice versa. In this situation, having opened yourself up, you feel somewhat lost, exposed and pinned down – there is no validation and no healing.

We were on stage as a band, yet the gig seemed to be happening almost exclusively in our heads. An uncanny feeling. There is an awareness of vulnerability. The singer faces forward to where the audience would have been; we are all in a bubble of interaction with our instrument or equipment, but we are not sharing the space with the collective consciousness of the audience. Almost like clinging on to your contact with your instrument to make anything make sense. Then you open yourself up and you give out energy, passion, only to find a yawning silence, and a dimly lit absence leering back at you; a nothing.

To make matters worse, we found out halfway through that the live stream had gone wrong, we had lost the 'connection' with the internet, and we *were* just playing to ourselves in an empty room. We really were performing in a void. So, we went back and started the whole gig again … only for the same thing to happen once again. Then another lost connection, yet another message to stop playing, stop the gig. We were now going for our third attempt at 'a moment in time'.

After a while, you are questioning your existence. Am I really here? Who am I? What am I doing? Am I really playing to an empty room, with the premise of connecting with our fans, only to find out they can't hear us? Are we just caught in limbo, firing blanks into space? Who are we as a band and what does all this mean? The very questioning of our identity and actuality for a time happened in what felt like an encounter with an existential, and online-digital void. Eventually, we got used to the process and a new pattern materialised: start a song in silence, finish a song in silence, move on to the next one. It was great to be playing, but it was also like filling out a form. There might be time for a brief word or two with each other when normally this would not be possible because of the crowd noise. I felt for the singer, who had to be master of ceremonies to an unoccupied room, like a comedian practising his lines, with no reaction or feedback either way.

Despite difficulties such as these, live streaming became a new way of interacting with audiences in the pandemic, and it became the way many musical artists would choose to share their work and connect with those interested in it.

Time and temporarily

Time was felt as a series of several simultaneous cycles running at different rates. The 'everyday' spun inexorably, and mostly took care of itself, with the feeding, cleaning, education, and entertainment of four children from ages 5 to 17, alongside any work or creative duties I had and any 'time together'. In a larger and seemingly slower cycle I felt myself growing older, along with the occasional sense of seasonal time passing. However, the nature of that sense of growing older was suffused with mixed emotions. Perhaps it was a bittersweet nostalgia? I was spending more time with my children, at home, enjoying the moments and loving them and our time together but it was also bittersweet as there was the obvious reason why we were all together, and I felt their growing up, in relation to my growing older.

Relatedness

The dialogue in the media had become familiarly peppered with the mixture of new words and odd phrases. There was of course 'lockdown', but then 'self-isolation' and 'social distancing' came into parlance, and eventually 'shielding'. This new vocabulary gradually shifted the identity of the population from the perspective of being fellow human beings and individuals to more that of categories, numbers, cases and statistics. We were left to ponder how many of the 250 people that died on a particular day had 'underlying health problems' or were 'over 60', as if that was some way of writing them off?

The entire country also became divided along lines of what you might call employment status, and the pandemic proved capable of changing my relatedness to self and others. I found that my relatedness to self (myself-concept) as a professional musician, whose music had the potential to cause emotional responses in others and even, occasionally, change lives, was perceived differently by others, most importantly the government. As furlough systems kicked in, I was no longer a creative musician but a 'freelancer' who did not fit so neatly into any of their categories. According to Arts Council England, the arts and culture industry contributes more than £10 billion a year to the UK economy yet, despite being a contributor to this industry through import and export for over 30 years, the 'Fatima ad' (Independent, 2020) suggested I might do better looking for a new job instead of looking for the next gig or project. As Charlotte Bence, from the trade union Equity, said: 'Fatima doesn't need to retrain – what Fatima needs is adequate state support as a freelance artist ... Freelance workers deserve better than patronising adverts telling them to go and work elsewhere.' So, did I need to totally reassess my self-concept and future identity? My identity and the meaning of music in my life seemed devalued.

Despite being divided up into categories of age, health ranking, weight category and work status, there were also 'bubbles'; and in addition to having to renegotiate my relatedness to self, I noted how strangely we experienced the challenges of relatedness in the pandemic. Within my household I could lose my connectedness with others and their experiences of the pandemic. The harsher implications of the pandemic tended to become real only in communication with people outside of our bubble (a metaphorical rather than clinical bubble). Within the wider family bubble, we continued to relate to each other without continual reference to the pandemic and to make efforts to 'cope' cheerily. I noticed the more worrying situation through my relationship to other professionals. Email communications about work forced me to engage with and relate to the news and to other's experiences of the situation. Their stories came through loud and clear, and beyond the cheery 'we are coping' chats of family and friends there were stark indications of the current reality and future implications, with people losing jobs, struggling for work, home educating, working at home in unsatisfactory conditions, or having working hours reduced, there were companies being dissolved overnight, employees dealing with restructures or attempting to deal with distant sick or elderly relatives that they could not comfort. Beyond our shielding bubble, people were dying, friends were catching the virus, people giving up jobs. The whole world order seemed to be restructuring and not for the better. Despite reading news on my iPhone mornings and evenings in bed, it would be more often through one-on-one exchanges that the truth came to me. The news came in small squares on my phone in the mornings, and it was a constant repetition of the facts: pandemic; NHS struggling; more people dying; stay at home. Being unable to pop round to see someone, take them out for a drink, hug or put your arm around them posed the question what had been lost in our relatedness to other human beings?

The final battle (but still the eternal war) for freedom

'Freedom may prove to be *the* great puzzle for the early 21st century' suggested Bakewell in 2016, and we may well say that she has been proven right. So many people; so many interpretations of freedom. We have seen that, although initially it felt like a prison sentence, lockdown became a freedom in itself, but it was a strange kind of freedom as many terrible battles and protests raged at home and overseas related to, and fighting for, liberty. Beyond the immediate Covid-19 restrictions that held our lives in check: in Hong Kong there were the Anti-Extradition Law Amendment Bill Movement protests and riots, there was the complex and controversial situation of the US presidential elections; there were Extinction Rebellion protests against the destruction of our environment by industry; and, as if this was not bad enough, within the cloud of a deadly virus, we watched horrified as the news showed the footage of George Floyd being asphyxiated by a police officer on camera. So many questions concerned with freedom: freedom to live; freedom to breathe; freedom to walk the streets safely; freedom to be treated equally, how can these *not* be given? The resulting protests that came after the murder of George Floyd – Black Lives Matter – took place across the US; and then in the UK in London, Bristol, Newcastle, Manchester, Liverpool, and shook the foundations and the institutions of Oxford University and their Rhodes scholar legacy. Freedom in this sense became very problematic, with the Capitol riots and the far right citing their actions and motives as 'freedom of speech'. How then do we all navigate these freedoms even within our own workplace, family, relationship? With freedom comes so much responsibility, if we are all to enjoy it.

Conclusion

Musicians adapt because they are always having to adapt to radical and changing situations. We are used to improvising. We experience the void and its uncertainty all the time, as a necessary part of the creative process. Therefore, when the pandemic hit and physical contact with the other was removed, most of us simply went 'inside' ourselves to discover and uncover inspiration. Despite the limitations of shielding and staying at home, with the migration of everything online collaboration became possible with people all around the world: 'performing live' could take place in your own house to a potentially global audience. There were new ways of connecting with other artists, and to the 'atomised' audiences of the lockdown.

The void exists for all musicians before the moment of creation. Terrifying though it is, it becomes part of our lives. Kierkegaard's 'leap of faith' (1985) is essential: how else can you make something that was not there before? There is no blueprint for our career path and our lives; our entire living is based on a leap of faith.

A choice in the past might be epic/historic; for example, I remember when I decided I was going to be a musician/actor/painter/dancer/poet. But also the leap into the dark happens every day for creatives – even when going out on stage, performing live, making a new album or painting. These are leaps of faith, as quite simply making new art or material requires it.

How musicians relate to audiences and to the political system was a challenge highlighted by the pandemic. Musicians exist at the moving point of a pendulum that swings between exaltation and ridicule. We are often treated as if we are outside of society, which gives us a unique perspective *on* society. The musician can exist in the same framing as 'Shaman'. As Attali (1977:11) writes:

> Musician, priest, and officiant were in fact a single function among ancient peoples. Poet laureate of power, herald of freedom – the musician is at the same time within society, which protects, purchases, and finances him, and outside it, when he threatens it with his visions.

The history of music and art is interwoven with the history of civilisation itself and how societies develop and ultimately express themselves beyond 'better farming', 'better commerce', or 'better killing of armies'. A history of art will contain many of the existential themes faced by us all at some point, whether this history might relate to an artist struggling for recognition, or whole nations and the changing *Zeitgeist* in their relatedness to technology, war, peace, conflict, morals. Despite this powerful connection between art and society, it was noticeable in the pandemic how far outside the system the creative industries were pushed.

The pandemic gave many of us the artistic dream: time to create. But it also brought into focus the fragile nature of working in creative industries. The paradox of being both exalted and rejected in society was never felt more intensely.

References

Attali, J. (1977) *Noise: The Political Economy of Music*. Manchester: Manchester University Press.

Bakewell, S. (2016) *At The Existentialist Cafe: Freedom, Being, and Apricot Cocktails*. New York: Random House.

Cameron, J. (1992) *The Artist's Way: A Course in Discovering and Recovering Your Creative Self*. London: Pan MacMillan.

Heidegger, M. (1962) *Being and Time*. Middlesex: The Camelot Press.

Independent (2020) Government Advert Encouraging Ballet Dancer to Retrain in IT is 'Crass', Admits Minister. *Independent* independent.co.uk/news/uk/politics/coronavirus-government-advert-ballet-dancer-retrain-it-cyber-oliver-dowden-b987403.html.

Kierkegaard, S. (1985) *Fear and Trembling: Dialectical Lyric.* Ed. Johannes de Stilentio. London: Penguin Classics.

Merleau-Ponty, M. (2002) *The Phenomenology of Perception*, 2nd edn. London: Routledge.

Sartre, J.-P. (1948) *Existentialism and Humanism.* London: Methuen.

South China Morning Post (2020) First CV19 case in China: *South China Morning Post.*

Chapter 3

The paradox of freedom in lockdown

Diana Mitchell

The first lockdown took place in Britain on 16 March 2020. Suddenly all my commitments that involved travel had to be cancelled indefinitely. This left me with my small private therapy practice clients. Zoom became my 'good enough' way to be with my clients and to continue with my Pilates classes, which required me to move furniture out of my office and therapy room to create space for my exercise mat and my Pilates paraphernalia.

My room changed from being my therapy room and office to my office/ Pilates/Zoom space. This new setup reminded me a bit of a stage set where the audience on the other side of the screen only saw the front façade. My clients only saw and, as I write this, still see me from the shoulders up with what is, to me, a presentable and rather orderly section of my room behind me.

My inner and outer world and sense of time started to shift and change. It was a bit like floating in a boundaryless world that made me feel free and carefree, and yet my husband and I were confined to the boundaries of our house and garden with no idea when the situation would change. This was a new experience; finding myself in a situation that I had never experienced before where there seemed to be no commitments outside our house. The pressure that came with preparing workshops and courses was suddenly gone and so was the responsibility and stress that came with delivering and facilitating courses that sometimes required travelling abroad. The following quote touches on some of what I experienced at the beginning of the first lockdown: 'Between stimulus and response, there is a space. In that space is our power to choose our response. In our response lies our growth and our freedom' (quoted by Steven Covey, source unknown).

Between stimulus and response, there is a space

I have a tendency to be too quick off the mark; too quick to respond without stretching the space and giving myself more time to breathe before I respond. As a therapist, I do try to leave a space and be silent to let the moment be, without me interrupting my client's invisible, emerging thoughts. I know

DOI: 10.4324/9781003255765-5

that I still interrupt and fill the space when I could have remained silent. As a multi-tasker and as a person who tends to instantly respond to emails, it is very rare for me to savour the moment and wait and allow something to unfold – to be in the moment.

Then along came the pandemic and everything changed. The Covid-19 lockdown gave me stillness. I did not have to make anything happen; I could just be in this unfamiliar, yet familiar, space. The rest of 2020 was cancelled almost before it had begun in earnest. 2020 had become my surprise gap year.

My friends on Facebook started getting busy and creating projects, the newspapers were full of advice; telling us to learn new skills, read books about faraway lands, join groups on Zoom, meditate, do yoga, watch opera, concerts, theatre, exhibitions, and ballet on YouTube. But I did not want to leap into action, which was my familiar way of being. I did have a very vague plan to paint my study/client room at some point, but I had no idea when or if that would happen.

In that space is our power to choose our response

Lockdown had become a giant guilt-free procrastination chamber. I could now give my attention to practical tasks; the tasks that I might have turned to when I was procrastinating, but without feeling guilty that I should be doing something more important.

To begin with I felt like a ten-year-old who did not have to go to school; I could do whatever I wanted. No homework to do, no deadlines ... nothing.

Here I was, doodling from one day to another. I sat at my computer and read the news online and watched medical experts being interviewed between bouts of playing in Facebook where I was also being bombarded with advice on how to survive lockdown. I indulged in the joys of ordering 'stuff' online for the first time. The doorbell never stopped ringing!

I did not want to disturb this new clear safe place. This feeling of contentment continued into the night – waking up around 4 am did not bother me from a practical point of view – after all, I had no serious commitments waiting for me once the night was over – and yet there seemed to be a faraway feeling of anxiety lurking in the dark, just out of reach. I can now see that my newfound comfort during the day also camouflaged my unease at living through something so new, unfamiliar and uncertain. My anxiety seemed to emerge at night, waking me up at odd times. Contact with clients continued online, almost as if nothing had happened and my weekly Pilates classes evolved into daily classes via Zoom.

It was strange and rather puzzling that I did not regret or miss the cancelled courses I loved doing and the trips to foreign lands, or even my regular outings to the ballet. Meanwhile my friends seemed to miss going out to restaurants, museums, concerts, the theatre, opera and the ballet.

I loved what I did and what I do, but I discovered that I also loved not doing what I normally love to do.

The experience was surreal – it felt a bit like reclaiming an imaginary basic me, a me that felt unrestricted, unjudged and free. Lockdown became predictable and familiar. I felt safe and secure, knowing that the world 'out there' was unsafe and full of the unknown. I was in control and responsible for my wellbeing. I kidded myself that I had banished uncertainty in my safe little bubble. Erich Fromm said something similar when he wrote about security and insecurity; how tempting it is to hold on to what we have, we fear the unknown when we step into new territory: 'Every new step contains the danger of failure, and that is one of the reasons people are so afraid of freedom' (1978:108). There was no fear of failure during lockdown, but it was always a real possibility every time I stepped out into the world.

In our response lies our growth and our freedom

I read about a man who sailed across the ocean during the pandemic from Portugal to Argentina to be with his father who was almost 90. His account highlighted how freedom can swing from the practical – being stuck in a restricted situation, and the psychological and emotional way we can exercise our freedom. The son felt he was in a quarantine of sorts, imprisoned by an unrelenting stream of foreboding thoughts about what the future held. Here he was, as free as a bird in the middle of the ocean but his thoughts created a sort of lockdown. He recalled: 'I was locked up in my own freedom.'

Freedom is never total and there are always limits and boundaries, some come with a particular situation and others are self-made, others are within relationships and so on. Boundaries between people vary but they are always there. Freedom can also be experienced when accepting 'a new reality' with new boundaries. A change in attitude can set us free while the physical situation remains the same. The term 'thinking outside the box' is a good example of creative psychological freedom in action. I think this happened to me in that first lockdown, I discovered new possibilities within the boundaries of our house. My thinking floated outside my usual box.

Martin Adams quotes Simone de Beauvoir in his book on human development (2018:144) where she writes about the paradox faced by the young person who steps out into the world:

> But whatever the joy of this liberation may be, it is not without great confusion. The adolescent finds himself cast into a world which is no longer ready-made, which has to be made: he is abandoned, unjustified, the prey of a freedom that is no longer chained up by anything. What will he do in the face of this new situation?
>
> (de Beauvoir, 1947)

My life during lockdown was 'ready-made' and so wonderfully controllable. My experience of staying at home, a home I had lived in for almost 50 years, was familiar, but the context and the situation had changed. Suddenly my home became my world and that was what made me feel so free. Knowing that at some point the wheels of life 'out there' would start turning and beckoning made me grateful to be given this opportunity to take stock without the distractions that came with being sucked back into a life full of multi-tasking, challenges, commitments and responsibilities.

Meaningful moments

Before the arrival of Covid-19 my way of being in life was mainly in the present and future while I carried my past less consciously; during lockdown my focus seemed to be in the present and past, while the future also remained just out of sight. Something new happened and I started thinking about my 'past lives' in a different way. I noticed patterns that repeated themselves in my life and how these patterns continued to still be actively present. I became aware of the me that remained constant despite constant changes within me and my life (Mitchell, 2021). I was caught between being unchanged and changed.

Merleau-Ponty writes about this paradox in relation to liberty where he refers to true liberty that comes about when we go beyond our original situation, while we also continue to be the same:

> Two things are certain about freedom: that we are never determined and yet that we never change, since, looking back on what we were, we can always find hints of what we have become. It is up to us to understand both these things simultaneously, as well as the way freedom dawns in us without breaking our bonds with the world.
>
> (1964:21)

My relationship with death, my death, was not loud, but it was expressed in my attitude and way of being. I became acutely aware that in four years' time I would be 80, if I am still here, so I decided to make the most of being fit and energetic now. Strike while the iron was hot and get our house in order while I could still climb up and down ladders! My idea was to repaint every ceiling and wall in our old and neglected house. There were no pressures and no interruptions.

I attacked my DIY painting project in the same way I would have attacked my oven or fridge when I am in full procrastinating mode, but with a slight shift in how I experienced this task. I did not rush, I took my time, and I got a buzz out of doing the finishing touches with a tiny brush. I experienced this hands-on practical job as highly creative. I caught myself smiling at times as my brush smoothly covered each wall in a different shade of blue and green.

Over the years I have come to embrace my procrastination activities as part of my process in a positive way. But my lockdown experience magnified and clarified this phenomenon. I rediscovered how practical I am and how my procrastination projects were very satisfying in themselves, but hurried and short-lived. Lockdown became my never-ending guilt-free procrastination project. I was filling that space with the most meaningful unrushed, enjoyable and satisfying experiences.

Ernesto Spinelli writes about how important meaning is, while implying that our meaningfulness is at times tied up with our identity, that can become stuck like a broken record:

> If I conclude that my meaning – my identity, let us say – is defined by certain fixed characteristics, attitudes, patterns of thought, and so forth, then when I am experientially confronted with evidence to the contrary, or which expands the 'meaning' of myself, I must either accept the evidence and reshape or extend my meaning of myself, or reject, or disown, the evidence in order to maintain my fixed meaning.
>
> (1994:295)

Not doing what I have done for years had given me the chance to stop, take stock, and tune into who I was from moment to moment, and then to tune out to how I wanted to be in my life. In other words, lockdown highlighted the importance of having a good emotional and psychological clear-out and honouring what really mattered to me.

Despite my constantly changing needs – it was so easy to hold onto the familiar without pausing to check if my pattern had become outdated and out of sync with my changing needs.

Is that what had happened to me? Had I become an unquestioning creature of habits?

Taking stock is something that some people do regularly or that can happen in therapy and mediation if the therapist or mediator knows how to leave a space for the client to listen to, see, and question themselves. I realised that pausing and taking stock had been thin on the ground in my life.

This is when what really matters can come to the surface – sometimes as a revelation.

Greg Madison and Ernesto Spinelli (Chapter 5) highlight how what really matters is one of their greatest gains and 'take aways' from lockdown.

Emerging from lockdown

We all respond differently to the situation we find ourselves in, while knowing deep down that our lives will come to an end at some point. This ultimate deadline can act like a kick up the backside. Knowing that I will die can act as a motivator. I have found how to cope and make sense of this fact in different ways throughout my life. Sometimes my awareness seemed to be clear, while at other times it fades into the background as some of my projects and tasks evolve into habits – habits that gave my life structure, purpose and meaning, but habits that also by default can restrict other options and possibilities.

My very first 'stepping-out' experience happened during lockdown when on Thursday 28 March at 8 pm millions of people in Britain stepped outside their front doors and clapped for the NHS. To suddenly see groups of clapping people emerging from their houses was very moving and powerful. We did not just clap but we waved and gestured to each other in such a warm-hearted way, despite not knowing each others' names. Up until that moment the houses seemed still and empty, the streets were empty and quiet without the sound of cars and people. At five minutes past eight, we all retreated into our houses and the stillness resumed.

Emerging from that first lockdown was like slowly coming out of hibernation, and yet I had not been asleep. There was something unreal and dream-like about the situation; I was swapping a soft, safe, familiar world of my own creation for the harsher more grown-up world that was populated with potentially dangerous people who might infect me with Covid-19. I did not want to wake up from this semi-dream world, but I did become fully awake; it was like trying to remember and hold on to a dream that I did not want to lose.

I had resolved to be selective and focus on what really mattered to me in terms of relationships and work. I am not a lover of Zoom, but I decided to continue seeing clients via Zoom rather than face to face like some of my therapist friends. I loved my messy private room, and I did not want to tidy it up for anyone – like a teenager not wanting anyone to mess with a much-loved bedroom. I did not want to socialise if I did not really want to, and I decided not to use PowerPoint for any of my presentations!

But what I experienced stepping out of lockdown muddied these waters; my confident predictions about what mattered started to change as my needs shifted. It had slipped my mind how influential the context was. The lockdown situation had created a new setting that was full of possibilities for me in a particular way and at a certain time in my life. I could see that I was trying to hold onto something that was already behind me; a way of being me in a situation that had come and gone.

Stepping out of lockdown started with tentative cautious steps; these steps morphed into more confident strides. My Oyster and rail card got renewed, face-to-face courses resumed, flights and ballet tickets got booked.

My simple life was beginning to fill up once again and I was enjoying this more demanding and yet familiar way of being that I had put on hold and that I had assumed did not matter that much anymore. I was getting back to do what I loved doing, but with the knowledge that I can also replace doing what I love doing, if I must, with a different way of being me; that is also satisfying.

Uncertainty had now become part of my life in a heightened way. It was one thing to talk about uncertainty, quite another to now know in a very concrete way that nothing is certain apart from my death at an uncertain moment. When I had booked a flight or ballet tickets in the past, I had assumed that these would not be cancelled. These certainties have now become at best tentative certainties surrounded by uncertainty in every direction.

The certainties I experienced during lockdown have now become watered down and less certain. Everything seems reversed now. My safe, predictable lockdown bubble has burst; now that the world is opening once again, I enjoy being involved, challenged and part of that world again. Gone are my predictions or having fixed ideas about what really matters.

Lockdown has shown me how my response to a new experience, in a new context, can reveal aspects of me that I might not be aware of. But that is not the end of it; once the context changes, I adjust and tap into different aspects of myself, my needs change and what really matters changes as well, and yet I remain the same. Hans W. Cohn's poem *Sleep* (1999:55) comes close to how I felt waking up from lockdown and finding another familiar version of myself.

Sleep: retreat
through dark passages
until suddenly
from the mirror of dreaming
you run into yourself
and wake colliding.

References

Adams, M. (2018) *An Existential Approach to Human Development*. London: Palgrave.

Beauvoir, S. de (1947 [2015]) *The Ethics of Ambiguity*. Trans. B. Frechtman. New York: Citadel.

Cohn, H.W. (1999) *With All Five Senses – Sleep*. Trans. F.G. Cohn. Newcastle upon Tyne: Menard Press.

Fromm, E. (1978) *To Have or To Be*. London: Jonathan Cape Ltd.

Merleau-Ponty, M. (1964) *Sense and Non-Sense*. Trans. L. Dreyfus and P. Dreyfus Allen). Illinois: Northwestern University Press.

Mitchell, D. (2021) My Being in Time: How My Past Lives Reveal Who I Still Am. *Society of Existential Analysis Journal*, 32.1.

Spinelli, E. (1994) *Demystifying Therapy*. London: Constable and Company Ltd.

Chapter 4

My pandemic pregnancy

A self-reflection via the words of others

Cleo Hanaway-Oakley

On Monday 23 March 2020, prompted by the spiralling spread and severity of a novel coronavirus named 'Covid-19', Prime Minister Boris Johnson announced the first UK lockdown. The nation was urged to 'stay at home, protect our NHS and save lives' (Johnson, 2020). On Tuesday 24 March 2020, my husband and I had a tearful conversation. For over a year, we had been trying, unsuccessfully, for a second baby. Given the apparent gravity of the situation the world now found itself in, we decided it was wise to put our baby-making plans on hold; we felt it was foolish to bring a baby into a virus-ridden realm, and unhelpful to add extra burden to the already overstretched NHS. On Sunday 29 March 2020, I discovered I was pregnant.

Via engagement with existential-phenomenological ideas and concepts, this chapter reflects upon being pregnant, and giving birth, during the Covid-19 pandemic. I focus on my own personal experience, but certain phrases and images from the minds of others weave their way through. As Maurice Merleau-Ponty states, '[i]nside and outside are inseparable'; the 'world is wholly inside and I am wholly outside of myself' (1994:474). As a lecturer in Liberal Arts and English, my ('inside') thoughts are always inescapably inflected with snippets of ('outside') literature. While this essay presents a first-person viewpoint, its perspective is always already interwoven with hand-me-down words.

My thoughts, in this piece, are bookended by Beckett. Samuel Barclay Beckett (1906–1989) is an existential-phenomenological writer *par excellence* (Maude and Feldman, 2011). He is intrigued by human consciousness, perception, interaction and mortality. Near the beginning of the first UK lockdown, I Tweeted a poll asking my (largely geeky and literature-loving) followers to vote on which Beckett work best reflected the world we were currently living in. Was it *Endgame* (1957), with its confined characters and apocalyptic backdrop; *Waiting for Godot* (1953), with its ever-delayed wait for certainty; *Film* (1965), with its fear of perceivedness and perceiving (prefiguring our Zoom-obsessed existence); or, in a similar vein, *Not I* (1972), with its disembodied talking mouth? *Endgame* topped the poll, but it was agreed that each work of

DOI: 10.4324/9781003255765-6

fiction vividly – yet unintentionally – conveyed different aspects of pandemic life and, in doing so, helped us to express some of the shared thoughts and fears we were experiencing.

For me, it was *Waiting for Godot* (1953) that most accurately reflected my feelings. In the play Beckett writes: 'They give birth astride of a grave' (Beckett, 1953). This quotation encapsulates several of the emotions and concerns I explore below. At first glance, the line may appear morbid, grotesque and pessimistic. The juxtaposition of 'birth' and 'grave' conjures up a rather gruesome and disturbing image, an image that – during pandemic times – provides a fairly accurate depiction of reality. In 2020, with hospital beds in short supply (due to the influx of Covid-positive patients), many births took place, not in graveyards, but in close proximity to gravely ill people. So, Beckett's words paint a vivid picture of some of the practical issues faced by birthing people during the coronavirus outbreak.

Interpreted through an existential lens, the quotation can be seen to convey sentiments akin to Jean-Paul Sartre's assertion that '[o]ne is still what one is going to cease to be and already what one is going to become'; '[o]ne lives one's death, one dies one's life' (Sartre & Frechtman, 1963:19). Both Beckett and Sartre invoke the spectre of death (the only certainty in our future) to force us to reflect on the life we are currently living (the uncertainty of the present moment). In Beckett's play, the quotation under discussion is spoken by Pozzo, a character who is only too aware of, and furiously disgruntled by, the onward march of time. In Act 2, just before exiting the stage, Pozzo asserts:

> Have you not done tormenting me with your accursed time! It's abominable! When! When! One day, is that not enough for you, … one day we were born, one day we shall die, the same day, the same second, is that not enough for you? (*Calmer.*) They give birth astride of a grave, the light gleams an instant, then it's night once more. (*He jerks the rope.*) On!

The quotation is, therefore, less about death and more about life – about the time we have on Earth and what we can do with it. For me, as a pregnant person, rather than prompting entirely new fears and feelings, the coronavirus outbreak served to intensify the recognition of my own mortality and the revitalising nature of procreation that is often felt when one discovers they are gestating a new life. Thus, my musings in this chapter – upon uncertainty and anxiety, a changing sense of self, and warped temporality – are as much about my general experience of being-in-the-world (in *non*-pandemic times), as they are about the specific conditions which prompted them: pregnancy and the Covid-19 outbreak. Like a *Gestalt* image (I am thinking, here, of Edgar John Rubin's famous vase-faces figure; 1915), the pandemic brought to the foreground thoughts and feelings which were, for me, already in the background.

Pregnant with uncertainty

When I stated, above, that 'I discovered I was pregnant', I meant that – after realising that my period was late – I urinated on a strip of compressed fibres covered in reactive antibodies and, after a three-minute wait, saw two inky pink lines appear. From this event, knowing how pregnancy tests work, I was able to infer that I was pregnant. But what does it mean to *be pregnant*? According to existential-phenomenological thinking, the answer will vary from person to person. As Merleau-Ponty explains, rather than providing an objective explanation, phenomenology 'offers an account of space, time and the world as we "live" them' (1994:viii). Pregnancy, like any other bodily occurrence, is always a 'lived' experience, undergone and understood in a unique way by a specific human being (or animal). What it means for *me* to *be pregnant* will be different to what it means for *you* to *be pregnant*. The two pink lines we perceive on our positive pregnancy tests will look virtually identical, but they will prompt distinct resonances and bring to mind – often drastically – different images.

For me, on 29 March 2020, the appearance of two lines on a pregnancy test indicated little more than raised human chorionic gonadotropin (HCG) levels. Having suffered three first trimester miscarriages, I was well aware that two pink lines do not equal a healthy baby; they merely show the presence of particular hormones. As I knew from bitter experience, HCG can be detected by a home test for several weeks after a 'blighted' embryo or foetus has stopped developing. Thus, rather than offering a sense of certainty with regards to my bodily state, my positive pregnancy test provoked intense feelings of *un*certainty. The inky lines ushered me into a liminal place, between not-baby and baby. And it appears that I am not alone in my feelings of anxious ambiguity regarding pregnancy tests. In her 2018 study, 'Provisionally Pregnant: Uncertainty and Interpretive Work in Accounts of Home Pregnancy Testing', Emily Ross concludes that 'the pregnancy test was not able to definitively indicate a pregnancy, but could instead exacerbate the uncertainties of early gestation' (Ross, 2018:101).

To acknowledge uncertainty is, of course, to begin to think existentially. As Simone de Beauvoir asserts, '[f]rom the very beginning, existentialism defined itself as a philosophy of ambiguity' (de Beauvoir, 1986:9). I like ambiguity. My job, which I enjoy immensely, involves teaching and writing about notoriously complex modernist texts – texts, such as James Joyce's *Ulysses* and *Finnegans Wake* (1922 and 1939), and Virginia Woolf's *To the Lighthouse* and *The Waves* (1927 and 1931) – which revel in the indefinite and indeterminate. These texts beautifully express 'this varying, this unknown and uncircumscribed spirit', this messy and 'incessant shower of innumerable atoms' which we call life (Woolf & Bradshaw, 2008:9). Uncertainty in my own body and feelings is, however, something I find much harder to cope with. So, I was eager to get an early ultrasound scan in the hope of achieving greater certainty with regards to the state and status of my (potential) pregnancy. Due to my history of pregnancy loss, I was under the care of the recurrent miscarriage clinic. I was, therefore, permitted a 'viability scan', at six to eight weeks' gestation, on the NHS. But would this scan still be possible during the pandemic, when hospitals were becoming overwhelmed with Covid-19 cases and were delaying, or even cancelling, non-Covid-related treatments and tests?

Pandemic appendages

Despite our conversation about not bringing a baby into a virus-ridden world, in the first few hours after the positive pregnancy test, the pandemic was not at the forefront of my partner's or my own mind. We were focusing on what those two pink lines might lead to: another miscarriage; a healthy baby; an unhealthy baby? But it was hard to keep thoughts of the pandemic at bay when we were being bombarded – via television, social media, emails and texts – by news of Covid-related statistics, policies, and concerns. Our questions regarding the positive pregnancy test soon took on pandemic appendages (Covid-prompted fears which cleaved themselves onto our pre-existent worries): another miscarriage? – and what miscarriage treatments would be available during the pandemic?; a healthy or unhealthy baby – and how well could health be monitored, *in utero*, with reduced NHS resources? Our thoughts quickly became inflected with the Covid-19 infection, leading to multiple – and multiplying – layers of uncertainty. Rather than the regular anxiety experienced by expectant parents, we endured pandemic levels of angst – a multi-tiered wedding cake of worry, if you will, as opposed to a double-layered sponge cake of unease. I value Søren Kierkegaard's assertion that we must 'learn to be anxious in order that [we] may not perish either by never having been in anxiety or by succumbing in anxiety' (Kierkegaard, 1980:155). But the multiple layers of apprehension, caused by proliferating pandemic appendages (on top of the worries already associated with being pregnant after miscarriage), caused excessive levels of anxiety.

As much as I would have liked to learn to 'live with' my uncertainty (and resulting anxiety), I was thankful to discover that, despite the worsening pandemic, my local hospital was still offering viability scans for eligible patients. At seven weeks' gestation, I was able to view a grainy black and white image of my internal organs. On the screen, I perceived a white tadpole-shaped splodge which, according to the sonographer, was a healthy embryo forming inside my womb. By this stage I was already experiencing mild nausea (a classic bodily sign of pregnancy), but this was not enough to convince me that I was pregnant. For me, it was only at this point, after the scan, that I was able to experience the emotions that some people feel immediately upon perceiving the two pink lines – the normal feelings of anxiety associated with the knowledge that you are growing a (potential) human being inside of your own body. I was still scared of miscarriage. But I was also scared of *not* miscarrying – I was scared of the prospect of growing, birthing, and raising another human being. My worries moved from 'am I pregnant?' to 'I *am* (currently) pregnant, so what happens next?'.

After the scan, it was even more difficult to focus on my work and on caring for my four-year-old daughter. Whenever I was lecturing (virtually, from my garden shed office), my pregnancy – and its pandemic appendages – was in the back, if not the front, of my mind. Watching my daughter play 'nursery' with her teddies, during lockdown, was upsetting for several reasons. As an only child, she had nobody to play with at home; my pregnancy could change that for her, could give her a sibling. But the possibility of caring for two young children at home, without the assistance of grandparents or day-care, was an uncomfortable prospect. I am not a natural stay-at-home mum. I do not define myself, nor gain satisfaction from, the sole role of 'mother'; I enjoy time alone with myself as much as I enjoy time with my family. I also had more immediate worries over the practicalities of being pregnant during lockdown. Some worries were seemingly small, such as concern over the availability of a particular brand of tortilla chips (one of a tiny selection of foods I could stomach during my first trimester), and others were larger. One question was impossible to ignore: What would happen to my baby and me if I caught Covid-19?

The existential threat of catching the coronavirus was difficult enough without pregnancy being added into the mix. As well as worrying about myself and my existent family, I was concerned about a minuscule being, deep within my body, who I was yet to meet. In the early days of the first lockdown (which paralleled the early days of my pregnancy), there was little known about the effects of the virus on pregnant people, foetuses, and new-born babies. I knew that the influenza virus was dangerous for pregnant people and their babies, and I had vague – disturbing – memories of the media coverage surrounding the Zika virus, and the birth defects it caused. On 15 April 2020 (16 days after my positive pregnancy test), news broke of the tragic death of Mary Agyeiwaa Agyapong, a 28-year-old pregnant nurse who died from Covid-19. Mary's baby was saved, unscathed yet motherless (BBC, 2020a). I felt angry for the way Mary had been treated (she should have been taken off hospital-floor duties), and sad for the family she left behind. But I was also worried about myself, as a pregnant person. Could the coronavirus harm me or my baby more severely than the general population?

My working conditions make catching viruses incredibly easy. In 'normal' times, I am a commuter; my journey to work involves two bus and two train rides each way. I am used to being squeezed right up against the sweaty bodies of fellow commuters and am regularly coughed and sneezed on. In these conditions, my chance of contracting Covid-19 was high. But my workplace does not readily make allowances for commuters; if we choose to live miles away from work, that is our choice, and we must cope with the consequences.

When the first lockdown was announced it was unclear whether my profession (university lecturer) was 'key work' or not; it was up to individual universities to decide whether in-person teaching should continue. I was terrified at the prospect of having to cram myself into busy train carriages, then mix with sociable multinational students in windowless teaching rooms. As a relatively healthy, relatively young, white woman, there was growing evidence to suggest that I was not at great risk from the coronavirus. But my risk as a pregnant person was less clear; early studies were beginning to indicate that I may be vulnerable (Royal College of Obstetricians and Gynaecologists, 2020). Thankfully, my work worries were soon allayed, as I was able to work from home. The quick pivot to 'emergency online teaching' was not easy, but it was preferable to commuting in and out of various virus hotbeds.

While I was not required to attend my workplace in person, my pregnancy meant that I would have to visit hospitals and other medical venues. Or would my appointments be virtual? Would I still have the same access to my midwife, to scans, and to other maternity services? Would I still be able to give birth in a hospital? Would I have to wear a mask during labour? Who would be allowed to look after my daughter while I was birthing my baby? Would my husband be able to join me for medical appointments and the birth? These were some of the questions that haunted my mind throughout my pandemic pregnancy.

Invisible intimidations

From the start of the pandemic, the coronavirus was described as an 'invisible killer' (Johnson, 2020). Covid-19 was an unseen, omnipresent threat, out there in the world. The invisibility of the virus was a key part of its terror; we were hiding from something which was, itself, hidden. The invisibility of my pregnancy was also anxiety-producing. My growing baby was an unseen, omnipresent hope inside my body. From March 2020 onwards, fear regarding unseen phenomena cut across my parallel experiences of pandemic and pregnancy. Sight has long been privileged in the hierarchy of the senses; like many of us, I have been conditioned to accept visual images as reliable testimony. Seeing, we are taught, is believing. I am aware that my faith in vision goes against Merleau-Ponty's existential-phenomenological philosophy of perception. Perceiving, for Merleau-Ponty, is not solely sight-based; 'touch opens on to a setting at least analogous to that of visual data' (Merleau-Ponty, 1994:223). Our tactile (and other non-visual sensations), says Merleau-Ponty, are just as valid and significant as sight. The presence of Covid-19 in our body is signalled not through visual means (there is no rash, for example), but through the loss of taste/smell, the feeling of being hot, and an audible cough. Before the invention of ultrasound or HGC pregnancy tests, one of the first clear signs of pregnancy was the feeling of baby movement, known as 'quickening'.

Although I would love to have more faith in my non-visual bodily
sensations, I drew great comfort from my seven-week scan; *seeing* my bundle
of growing cells on the screen was very reassuring. The desire to *see* one's
unborn baby is strong. This maternal longing for connection is beautifully
captured by Sylvia Plath in her 1960 poem, 'You're', in which she describes
her baby – *in utero* – as 'Vague as fog and looked for like mail'. Mothers
want to communicate with our children. We want to be pen pals. We want to
view clear, regular fogless images of our hidden, developing babies. We want
to Facetime with our foetuses. The omnipresence of visual communication
technologies, during the pandemic, made it even harder to accept the impos-
sibility of regular meet-ups with my growing babe. If I can Skype with my
friends all over the world at the touch of a button, why can I not videocall the
baby inside me?

Seeing the developing foetus is just as important for the father, and for
others involved in the pregnancy. Due to social distancing rules (prompted
by the escalating spread of Covid-19), my husband was not allowed to attend
my viability scan, nor my 12-week or 20-week scan. He drove me to the
appointments then waited in the hospital car park or drove around the block
with our daughter in the back seat. I had no one to hold my hand, no one
to gasp or cry with. I was worried that my husband's absence at scans would
make it harder for him to bond with our growing baby. As I discovered when
I wrote another piece about pregnancy and the pandemic (Hanaway-Oakley,
2020), scans are, indeed, significant for a father's attachment to their unborn
baby (Draper, 2002). One expectant father said that the 12-week scan was 'the
first time that it really crystallised into anything', while another loved 'seeing
the little legs waving about' – 'it was real close' a 'real good show' and it did
'make the reality of it so much more obvious' (Draper, 2002). I was given free
printouts of my own ultrasound images, so I was able to show my husband
photos of the scans. But it was not the same as him being there. My husband –
the father of my child – was unable to share the experience with me, unable to
view the real-time baby ballet taking place inside my uterus.

While scans enabled me to see – and connect with – the baby hidden within
me, electron microscopes allowed virologists to view – and comprehend – the
covert coronavirus. We, the threatened public, were desperate to visualise the
virus, in order to better understand our assailant – to know, or have the *feeling*
of knowing, what we were dealing with. Like a Wild West cowboy town
pasted with 'Wanted' posters, the world's media outlets – in print and online –
were soon awash with caricatured versions of images seen via technologically-
extended eyes. We quickly became familiar with the grotesquely enlarged,
belligerent alliums which came to signify our viral attacker. And we were also
bombarded with images of ourselves. The multitude of Zoom and Teams
meetings meant that I spent an inordinate amount of time staring at my own
face. But that is all I was: a garbling mouth like the disembodied protagonist
of Beckett's *Not I* (1972).

No one could see what lay outside of the carefully crafted camera shot: the mess; the piles of books; the growing baby bump. In many ways, the widespread use of face-focused interactions was a boon for me and my baby-laden belly; my pregnancy was hidden from view, cropped out of the picture. When I was pregnant with my first child, I hated strangers – or even friends and family – touching my bump without asking or looking at my bump, rather than my face, when speaking to me. I tended to wear baggy tops and dresses, rather than figure-fitting maternity wear, so as not to draw attention to the fact that I was growing a human. As Sinead Gleeson puts it in her perceptive personal essay collection, *Constellations*, the 'pregnant body is not solely its owner's domain'; '[i]n gestating another person you become public property' (Gleeson, 2019:99). Pregnant people are always on display: we are the *seen*, rather than the *seer*; objects to be perceived, rather than perceiving subjects in our own right. But, during the pandemic, it was different. Our modes of perception changed. When my only interaction with the world and others occurred via a rectangular screen focused on my face, I was – for all intents and purposes – not a pregnant person. I was, at least, not a *visibly* pregnant person. My pregnancy was closeted, only to be broadcast to those I chose to disclose it to.

While having a hidden baby bump was, for the most part, a liberating experience, the act of having to constantly 'come out' about my pregnancy was rather tiring. I had to expend energy deciding if and when it was necessary, relevant, or appropriate to disclose the fact that I was gestating a person. In non-pandemic times, I am often visible – at the lectern, in meetings, on the train, mooching round the shops. My bump would have silently declared my condition for all to see, without me having to utter a word. And, even for a somewhat shy non-exhibitionist, there is a certain pleasure in seeing oneself being seen. As Iris Young notes in her essay, 'Pregnant Subjectivity and the Limits of Existential Phenomenology' (1985), the 'pregnant woman's relationship to her body can be an innocent narcissism' and 'whereas our society often devalues and trivializes women, regards women as weak and dainty, the pregnant woman can gain a certain sense of self-respect' (Young, 1985:32). In being locked down inside my home, I had lost my societal mirror; I had lost my perceiving others. This loss was both freeing and troubling. I did not miss the unsolicited comments on the size or shape of my bump, but a part of me missed the warm smiles and nods of recognition from fellow mums and mums-to-be. I vividly recall the mix of nostalgia, sadness and relief I felt on seeing the 'Baby On Board' badge still pinned to the maternity coat I wore while pregnant with my first child. I would have no need for the badge this time around, as it was unlikely I would be leaving the house, except for medical appointments. There would be no need for anyone to offer me a seat on the bus or carry my bags onto the train. Most significantly, there would be no one to recognise me, no one to cement my identity *as an expectant mother*.

There is a sense in which we all need the other in order to help us comprehend our self. As Merleau-Ponty explains, '[m]y life must have a significance which I do not constitute'; 'I must, therefore, in the most radical reflection, apprehend around my absolute individuality a kind of halo of generality or a kind of atmosphere of "sociality"' (Merleau-Ponty, 1994:448). This is not to say that we have no agency in our own sense of identity – we do. But we are bound by the limits of the world we are 'thrown' into (Heidegger, 2010:131). In Merleau-Ponty's words, 'I must apprehend myself from the outset as centred in a way outside myself' (Merleau-Ponty, 1994:448). During the pandemic, my sense of self in my role as university lecturer was somewhat strengthened by being unhindered by visible pregnancy (my students could not be distracted by something they were unaware of), but my sense of self as a pregnant person was diminished. I felt split in two in a manner I was not wholly comfortable with. I had to make an active choice to present the pregnant part of myself when, in fact, 'lecturer' and 'person-gestating-a-human' were both important parts of my identity and, in non-pandemic times (when I engage with others in a more natural, embodied fashion), these seemingly disparate parts would have existed together in an easy and intuitive manner.

About time

VLADIMIR: We've nothing more to do here.
ESTRAGON: Nor anywhere else.
VLADIMIR: Ah Gogo, don't go on like that. Tomorrow everything will be better.
ESTRAGON: How do you make that out?
VLADIMIR: Did you not hear what the child said?
ESTRAGON: No.
VLADIMIR: He said that Godot was sure to come tomorrow. (*Pause.*) What do
    you say to that?
ESTRAGON: Then all we have to do is to wait on here.

These lines are excerpted from Beckett's *Waiting for Godot* (1953). They offer a useful route into, and a helpful illumination of, the wearisome experience of both pregnancy and pandemic time (Beckett, 1953: Act 1). In pregnancy, 'all we have to do is to wait'; there is no rushing things, and very little anyone can do – aside from induction or c-section – to speed up the process. As Young explains, for 'the pregnancy subject', 'pregnancy has a temporality of movement, growth, and change'; '[t]ime stretches out, moments and days take on a depth because she experiences more changes in herself, her body' (Young, 1985:32–33). I love this notion of days being deep rather than long. Each tiny movement felt, each maternal worry, each medical appointment, makes time feel more spatial than sequential; rather than an onward march, time is a growing mound (much like the one in which Winnie finds herself buried, in Beckett's *Happy Days*, 1961), requiring an archaeologist rather than a historian to make sense of it. Towards the end of pregnancy, bodily change is visible – and palpable – in the form of an expanding bump, meaning that space, rather than time, is dominant. I find it amazing and rather mystical that, according to midwives' charts, your symphysis-fundal height measurement (in centimetres) should roughly correspond to the number of weeks pregnant you are. In other words, if you are 28 weeks' pregnant your bump should measure around 28 centimetres. In this magical measurement, time and space fuse together; the fusion is embodied in the pregnant person and, eventually, in the new baby.

Many of us felt compelled to mark pandemic time in a similar fashion; we *made* things that took up *space* rather than *doing* things that used up *time*. Like Vladimir and Estragon, we were forced to 'wait on here'. Our 'here' – wherever we were locked-down – became our only sphere of possibility. There was 'nothing more to *do*' but, perhaps, there was something to *create*, something that – in the act of creation – would allow time to move forward without us realising it. During the pandemic, the answer to 'how many?' (banana loaves baked, pictures painted, vegetables grown) was easier to give than the answer to 'how long?' (until lockdown ends, until I can hug my friend, until my daughter can return to school). In her excellent essay, 'Something to Do' (2020), written during lockdown, Zadie Smith reflects upon this new – pandemic-induced – way of experiencing time; the way that *do* became *make*. As an artist (a creative writer), Smith is used to thinking of time as a space within which to create outputs. 'Out of an expanse of time', she writes, 'you carve a little area' (Smith, 2020:20). But 'even if you believe in the potential efficacy of art – as I do – few artists would dare count on its timeliness'; it is 'a delusional painter who finishes a canvas at two o'clock' (Smith, 2020:20–21).

Gestating a baby is, of course, less of an active pursuit than creating an artwork. The pregnant person is largely passive, until labour starts; they have 'nothing more to do here', '[n]or anywhere else' until the first contractions begin. This is not to say that nothing changes, for the pregnant person, during the *circa* 40 weeks of pregnancy. Change happens gradually, over the course of several months. Pregnancy is tripartite; it is split up into three lots of three months – of three times 13 weeks – called 'trimesters'. And time is experienced differently in each trimester. For me, the first trimester is the longest, despite it having the shortest duration (one is already around 'four weeks' pregnant' at the time of their first missed period, so the first trimester is, in fact, only nine weeks long). So, how can nine weeks be longer than 13? In order to comprehend this seemingly nonsensical statement we must 'conceive the subject and time as communicating from within' (Merleau-Ponty, 1994:410). We must understand and recognise the difference between lived time (time as we experience it) and clock time (time that is externally imposed upon us). My history of miscarriage means that, whenever I discover I am pregnant, I immediately start wondering how long my pregnancy will last (Hanaway-Oakley, 2019). Pregnancy, in my mind, does not equal a baby; it is a bodily state which can last anything from a couple of days to nine months. So, at the beginning of a pregnancy, I am always thinking in hours rather than in weeks or months; time moves at a snail's pace and every day feels like a week. This slow, slithering movement of time picks up pace, somewhat, once I am safely into the second trimester and can see my baby bump growing. Friends kept telling me that second and subsequent pregnancies go by in a flash. This was not the case with my pandemic pregnancy. Lockdown was slow-moving, too; there were fewer diversions to keep my mind off my bodily state. I was grateful for my in-person midwife appointments (which started at 21 weeks), as they gave me an excuse to get properly dressed and leave the house.

The third trimester of pregnancy is notoriously hard-going, physically and mentally; you are heavy, achy, and very much ready to meet your baby. It is also an anxiety-inducing time as there is uncertainty as to precisely when, how, and in what condition your baby will arrive. Like Vladimir and Estragon, you know you are waiting for 'Godot', but you do not know who Godot is, what Godot looks like, or the exact time at which Godot will make an appearance. Well-meaning friends tell you that your baby is 'sure to come tomorrow' (Beckett, 1953). But it does not help; nothing helps. In the final weeks of my pandemic pregnancy, I was utterly miserable. I was huge and my already troublesome hips literally buckled under the weight of my belly. The fact that I was physically unable to walk more than a few feet was both a blessing and a curse. Due to lockdown, hardly anywhere – shops, cafes, pubs, theatres – was open, so I escaped the feeling of missing out on fun get-togethers, as none were happening. But my lack of mobility meant that the stultifying nature of confinement, no doubt experienced by many people during lockdown, was intensified. I lost the small, simple pleasures that had been getting me through. I was unable to saunter round the park, unable to admire the autumn leaves or push my daughter on the swing.

The end is in sight

At 38 weeks, I was diagnosed with intrahepatic cholestasis of pregnancy, a liver condition which – if severe – has the potential to cause complications during labour, including an increased risk of stillbirth. This diagnosis exacerbated my already high anxiety levels. I felt even less certain, and significantly more concerned, about what condition my newborn would arrive in. I was even more eager to meet my baby. I just wanted to know what I would be dealing with – an induction, a c-section, a natural water birth? I was all too aware that, whatever type of birth I ended up having, I was likely to be alone for most of it. Due to Covid-19 risk, partners were not allowed to hang around. Every day, during my third trimester, I Googled 'can partners be present for the duration of labour?'. I hoped that the answer would be a clear 'yes'. But the answer kept (subtly) changing, and was always conditional: 'yes, but only during active labour'; 'yes, but they must self-isolate for two weeks prior to the birth'; 'yes, but they must be tested for Covid on arrival at the hospital'; 'yes, but they must keep two metres distance and wear a mask'. My due date was 2 December (the day on which the second UK lockdown was scheduled to end); it was to be a day of change, a day of cautious hope mixed with lingering fear. If the birth occurred after lockdown was over, my parents and my mother-in-law could assist with childcare and meet the new baby soon after the birth. However, with rules changing so rapidly, a part of me longed for the relative certainty and clarity of lockdown.

My due date came and went, and I was scheduled for an induction. Although I was nervous about the procedure, I felt a huge sense of relief in knowing that an end was in sight. I would not be pregnant indefinitely. I would meet my 'Godot'. A few hours after my conversation with my consultant, regarding my planned induction, I went into labour naturally. My mother-in-law came over, as arranged, to look after my daughter, and my husband drove me to the hospital. When I arrived, I was already in 'active labour' so, as per the current guidelines, my husband was able to stay with me (masked and alcohol-wiped) until I gave birth. In between contractions, I was Covid-tested via a swab thrust down my throat and up my nose. In the grand scheme of things, this quite invasive procedure felt rather trivial. The birth went smoothly, and, after a few hours, my baby and I were moved to the recovery ward. At this point, my husband was asked to leave. Alone with my newborn, I gazed out of the window and saw flashes of bright yellow, red and green in the distance: fireworks. When a nurse popped by to ask what I would like for dinner, I enquired about the fireworks; had she seen them, did she know what they were for? Apparently, people were celebrating the fact that, earlier that day, the first UK Covid vaccine had been administered; 'the end of the pandemic is in sight', exclaimed the nurse excitedly (BBC News, 2020b).

But what does 'the end' of a pandemic look like? Birth signals the end of pregnancy, but it brings the beginning of a new phase – life with a newborn. Vaccination signals the end of stringent lockdown and social distancing measures, but does it really herald the end of the pandemic? For me, the end of pregnancy brought about a whole new range of anxiety-inducing events and issues: my baby had problems breastfeeding (necessitating a tongue-tie operation) and was diagnosed with hip dysplasia (requiring a brace and regular hospital visits). Neither of these issues were easy to deal with alongside the birth of a new, more infectious Covid-19 variant. As I write this essay, in September 2021, my baby is developing well and the vaccination roll out is continuing apace. As of last month, I am doubly vaccinated. Mask-wearing is now optional, but Covid-19 cases continue to rise. My daughter is due to start back at school tomorrow and my baby is due to start nursery next month. Will they catch Covid-19 as soon as they mingle with their unvaccinated peers (in the UK, vaccination for under 12s is not currently available)? Will there be another national lockdown? No one knows. 'Tomorrow everything will be better'; 'all we have to do is to wait on here' (Beckett, 1953: Act 1).

References

BBC News (2020a) Coronavirus: Pregnant Nurse Dies But Baby 'Well' After Delivery. *BBC News*, 15 April www.bbc.co.uk/news/uk-england-beds-bucks-herts-52301870 [accessed September 2021].

BBC News (2020b) Covid-19 Vaccine: First Person Receives Pfizer Jab in UK. *BBC News*, 8 December www.bbc.co.uk/news/uk-55227325 [accessed September 2021].

Beckett, S. (1953) *Waiting for Godot*. New York: Grove Press.

Beckett, S. (2010 [1961]) *Happy Days*. London: Faber and Faber.

de Beauvoir, S. (1986) *Ethics of Ambiguity*. Trans. B. Fechtman. New York: Citadel Press.

Draper, J. (2002) 'It was a real good show': the Ultrasound Scan, Fathers and the Power of Visual Knowledge. *Sociology of Health & Illness*, 24.6, 771–795.

Gleeson, S. (2019) *Constellations: Reflections from Life*. London: Picador.

Hanaway-Oakley, C. (2019) Devastated, Numb and A Shattered Sense of Self – The Lasting Impact of Pregnancy Loss. *British Vogue*, 14 October. www.vogue.co.uk/arts-and-lifestyle/article/-cleo-hanaway-oakley-miscarriage-pregnancy-loss [accessed September 2021].

Hanaway-Oakley, C. (2020) I want to Zoom with the Baby in My Womb: Pregnancy During the Pandemic. *The Polyphony*, 13 August https://thepolyphony.org/2020/08/13/i-want-to-zoom-with-the-baby-in-my-womb-pregnancy-during-the-pandemic/ [accessed September 2021].

Heidegger M., (2010) *Being and Time: A Revised Edition of the Stambaugh Translation*. Trans. Joan Stambaugh. Ed. Dennis J. Schmidt. New York: State University of New York Press.

Johnson, B. (2020) Prime Minister's Statement on Coronavirus (Covid-19): 23 March 2020 www.gov.uk/government/speeches/pm-address-to-the-nation-on-coronavirus-23-march-2020 [accessed September 2021].

Kierkegaard S. (1980) *Concept of Anxiety: A Simple Psychological Orienting Deliberation on the Dogmatic Issue of Hereditary Sin*. Ed. Reidar Thomte. New Jersey: Princeton University Press.

Maude, U. and Feldman, M. (2011) *Beckett and Phenomenology*. London: Bloomsbury.

Merleau-Ponty, M. (1994) *Phenomenology of Perception*. London: Routledge & Kegan Paul.

Plath, S. (1960) *Collected Poems*. New York: Harper Collins.

Ross, E. (2018) Provisionally Pregnant: Uncertainty and Interpretive Work in Accounts of Home Pregnancy Testing. *Health: An Interdisciplinary Journal for the Social Study of Health, illness and Medicine*, 22.1, 87–105.

Royal College of Obstetricians and Gynaecologists (2020) Coronavirus (Covid-19) Infection in Pregnancy. *Royal College of Midwives* www.rcm.org.uk/media/3892/2020-04-17-coronavirus-covid-19-infection-in-pregnancy.pdf [accessed September 2021].

Rubin, E. (1915) *Synsoplevede Figurer: Studier i psykologisk analyse* [*Perceived Figures: Studies in Psychological Analysis*]. Gyldendal, Nordisk: Forlag.

Sartre, J.-P. and Frechtman, Bernard (trans.) (1963) Saint Genet: Actor and Martyr. *The Tulane Drama Review*, 7.3, 18–36.

Smith, Z. (2020) *Intimations*. London: Penguin.

Woolf, V. and Bradshaw, D. (eds) (2008) Modern Fiction. *Selected Essays*. Oxford: Oxford University Press, 6–12.

Young, I.M. (1985) 'Pregnant Subjectivity and the Limits of Existential Phenomenology', in Don Ihde and Hugh J. Silverman (eds), *Descriptions*. New York: State University of New York Press, 25–34.

Chapter 5

What really matters?

A phenomenological exploration of two YouTube dialogues on living through Corona times

Greg Madison and Ernesto Spinelli

Introduction

On 23 March 2020, in response to the growing threat of Covid-19, world leaders including UK Prime Minister Boris Johnson told their countries that people must stay at home and avoid all unnecessary social contacts, including contact with family members, friends and romantic partners living elsewhere. Severe travel restrictions were imposed and a great many businesses – including restaurants and bars, cinemas, theatres, galleries and museums, clothing stores and gyms – which were deemed to be non-essential were forced to shut for an indefinite period of time. In spite of this unprecedented restriction on so many forms of everyday social interaction, the overwhelming majority of citizens in the UK accepted this period of 'lockdown' as a necessary means with which to protect themselves against an unknown, worldwide, and life-threatening virus.

Through online and telephone discussions with their friends, clients and supervisees, the two authors quickly became aware that exploring these dramatic events from the perspective of various key ideas and themes within existential phenomenology might well help to clarify a number of the multiple, often contradictory, reactions that both they and others were experiencing. As existential psychologists living in the UK, we decided to engage in an online dialogue about our experiences of living in, and working therapeutically through, 'corona times'. The discussion, which was entirely unscripted and spontaneous, explored some of the deeper significance of lockdown on daily life events, relevant existential themes that seemed to be emerging, the possible long-term effects on society, as well as some initial ideas about practising as a therapist in the current context and beyond.

That first dialogue took place a mere two weeks after UK lockdown had begun and was subsequently uploaded onto YouTube on 6 April 2020 where it can still be viewed (Madison & Spinelli, 2020).

Just over a year later, following the realisation that many of our feelings and experiences had changed considerably, we decided to engage in a second dialogue, which was primarily focused on the longer-term psychological

DOI: 10.4324/9781003255765-7

and existential impact of this strange period in human history. Once again, the dialogue was uploaded onto YouTube on 30 April 2021 (Madison & Spinelli, 2021).

This chapter explores and elaborates upon several of the key existential themes and concerns discussed in the two dialogues.

The first dialogue

It is already a difficult task to re-enter the complex feeling-state in which we found ourselves during that early period. Quiet descended over the cities. The streets were mostly deserted, apart from the occasional citizen out for their allotted daily exercise. Many of us rediscovered the space of our homes, maybe home cooking, gardening for those of us lucky to have outdoor space, while outside the emptiness was punctuated by the mosquito buzz of delivery scooters and the occasional haunting sound of ambulance sirens. For those of us living in London, it was the sudden silence that felt most eerie – not least, the silence created by hardly any airplanes flying above us. The possibility of a vaccine seemed remote and, at best, likely to be unavailable until some years in the future. As such, we imagined ourselves as having to live with the life-threatening presence of Covid-19 for the foreseeable future, perhaps even the remainder of our lives. Unexpectedly, we found ourselves inhabiting an alien world.

Like many others, one response to this set of circumstances was that of anger and fear.

> There are various times when it just suddenly hits me in a way that I feel really I don't want to accept it and I don't like it and I get angry about it and I also get quite scared about it … particularly when I direct it back on myself and I say: 'Well I'm in that group of people that keeps being highlighted as being in danger for age or for medical reasons … and I just go: This is unfair! This isn't right! I don't want this!'

Almost simultaneously, however, a very different experience came into focus:

> I catch myself saying that and I think: 'What are you talking about?' In a strange way [living with Covid-19] opens me up to looking at things differently, more intensely … [like] listening to the bird song, or really noticing people and the silence … I notice these things much more powerfully than I did prior to two weeks ago.

In addressing these contrasting experiences, we became aware of how our views shifted back and forth between deprivation and opportunity, neither being the only truth, both being truthful.

We realised that how we responded always remained a choice. We could be curious and interested, even exhilarated by moments in this strange world and then, equally, at other times, we were consumed by grief, grieving for lost assumptions or even the unthinkable: that the world we used to take for granted might never return. We saw that we had been suddenly thrown into a strange, new world experience that had ripped open many of those cocooning assumptions that had previously maintained us. It reminded us of Heidegger's idea of the uncanny:

> where we're in a familiar world that is not familiar exactly. Where we're in something that was supposed to remain adequately hidden so that we could feel at home [but which] has been exposed such that we live in this uneasy openness to both what should have remained hidden and the home that was meant to obscure it.

In many ways, we had been struck with a hint of anxious recognition that the quotidian life we had been living was fundamentally a tranquillised reality. And yet, we also remained aware of our inability – or unwillingness – to bring about the process that might either fully confront us or fully conceal it all again.

We concluded that what had broken down to some extent had been the ordinary, everyday defences we relied upon to enable us to escape from the chaos of reality. Could it be that our sense of grief was a consequence of having to let go of these ordinary defences? So many of the habitual things we formerly did were inaccessible to us and even those that remained, such as shopping for food, had to be done in such unfamiliar ways that they were no longer part of that habitual stance. In *Burnt Norton*, one of T.S. Eliot's *Four Quartets* (Eliot, 2001), the author reminds us that human beings cannot withstand too much reality. It seemed to us as if our access to reality had changed such that it was more unfettered and, as a result, very unnerving. This unnerving quality could be experienced as both wondrous and terrifying. In either case, there was a palpable response to what had previously been hidden and was now being unconcealed.

In an immediate, practical sense we could see how much we had protected ourselves – and had been protected by, forces of order such as the media and government – from the reality of Covid-19 by focusing on what was happening from an abstract position. We had focused on data and graphs when the reality was that human beings were actually suffering and dying. Our focus had constructed a sort of illusion which protected us from confronting what was there. This desire to maintain the illusion was experienced at a more personal level as well:

> Actually, I quite like being locked in, you know? I don't know if I ever want to get out again because this feels really safe. I know where I am. Who I am. What to do and what not to do.

Nonetheless, even this cocooning experience had brought about an unexpected awareness:

> I hate to admit this but, actually, with the onset of the virus I have never felt so much in touch with myself as I do now. And I've realised that so much of my life was spent in terms of things like planning for the future or looking at things in a certain way or having a kind of diary or calendar that said this is what I'm doing today and tomorrow and the next day and so forth. And because of the threat of the virus, I've put all those things away. They don't make any sense to me anymore. I'm living a much more chaotic life in the sense that I'm open to whatever opens itself in front of me and I feel great and I feel awful for feeling great because it's a greatness that's come as a result of this awful situation.

Our dialogue touched on numerous topics – too many to discuss adequately in this chapter – but of these, one that especially stood out as being of particular relevance to an existential focus was that of *relatedness*.

In a nutshell: existential relatedness argues that every living being is, at one and the same time, both one-of-a-kind and an outcome manifestation of being as a whole. Often, when first considering this idea, it is viewed from a solely positive standpoint, a sort of 'Aww ... We're all in this together' feeling. But there is a far less 'cosy' quality to relatedness as well. In accepting the idea of relatedness, we must also accept that we can never fully know, much less control, the impact of every other living being's presence upon our way of thinking, feeling, and acting in the world. Relatedness creates an underlying, and inevitable, openness in every facet of our lives. And while that openness can feel liberating at times, it must also, inevitably, deny us the ability to ever truly know ourselves.

The rate of worldwide transmission of Covid-19 brought the issue of relatedness more and more to the foreground. However, what was being primarily foregrounded was that 'dark' aspect of relatedness. We were in this awful situation because we could not cut ourselves off in any complete sense from the rest of the world. At an everyday level, we found ourselves experiencing this more terrifying aspect of relatedness 'when walking down the street and looking at people and in a sense not seeing them as people anymore [but, rather] as agents of death'. In bringing the focus of the dialogue onto our relations with others – and with ourselves – we wondered what might be the longer-term consequences of this strange period of time once it evolved into something else. Once again, the contrasting themes of 'opening up' and 'shutting down' emerged as having equal possibility and import. From an 'opening up' perspective, we imagined that

> some number of people will not allow themselves to pretend that the world has just gone back to the way it was. [As a consequence] there

could be quite a flowering of creativity [in the Arts and Sciences] resulting in new ways of understanding the kinds of relations that we have and the ways we express them.

Similarly, one immediate shift, which was already becoming apparent, was in the ways we chose to work and the structure of the workplace.

In the opposite, 'closing down' direction, our anticipation was that there would be both a top-down and bottom-up move to try to normalise things through which we would convince ourselves that we could go back to how things had been prior to Covid-19 and that this was a desirable step to take. Once again, the desire to evade or, indeed, erase the experience of reality with which we had all been confronted was likely to be a powerful temptation.

The final part of our dialogue explored these various themes from the standpoint of their impact upon both the practice and structure of therapy. This aspect of the discussion will be addressed in a later section of this chapter.

The second dialogue

The first thing we both noticed when beginning our second dialogue was our reluctance or at least ambivalence about having a second conversation at all. We did not know if we had much to say. A bland mist had descended upon us such that we could not even face listening to the previous discussion from a year earlier. It felt like going backwards and being reminded that, as lockdown began, we had shared some excitement and optimism about the changes that might result, as well as fear about the unknown. But now that optimism had faded and it felt like we would expose ourselves to self-recriminations for what we had been unable to actualise, what had already dulled and closed over. A year earlier we had hoped that the pandemic might pass quickly and that it would leave behind fresh exciting possibilities for how we live together.

The shock and excitement and potential for fundamental social change seemed to have dispersed at some point during the physical isolation and social distancing of months of lockdown. Was this one of the effects of the lockdown and the lack of contact it necessitated?

We noticed a strong tension to go back to something familiar and secure, weary of the strange world, yet knowing there is no going back fully. Who can just bury a year, blur it out and forget it? As the lockdown began to ease, we had to consciously remind ourselves how to live again, how to go into town for a coffee, recollect previous habits and routines, how we used to live – and how we used to live together! There was no automatic return just because there were no longer government restrictions on our lives.

[I feel] like a prisoner coming out of an 18-month prison sentence and at first wanting to just stay in the familiar cell. I know this place. I may not like it but it is familiar. And maybe it is also a betrayal not to learn something profound about ourselves and our societies through this trial of the human species.

We seemed caught between wanting to stay cocooned, wanting to return to a past 'normal', and also wanting to move beyond the past by harvesting some insight from the whole experience, while actually feeling just subdued by it, and blandly bewildered.

The pandemic had elicited the predictable models of mental health advice from the psychological profession. These included how to deal with the anxiety of uncertainty, how to ward off depression as well as instructions to maintain structure, take up a new hobby, and get exercise. We noticed though that there was much less about how to face the humiliation of our species – that as human beings we are not as special as we thought we were, we are contingent upon nature's ability to wipe us away and all the uncertainty and lack of control that accompanies that insight.

We were left wondering if we could see this human situation as a brutal opportunity, unwelcome as it is, to live in a way that retains an opening to what has, until now, been very easily covered over by the way we live. It raised the question: "To what extent can we live while acknowledging the uncertainty and not-knowing and the anxiety of our existential reality? Can we resist the 'life-lies' that make 'normal' believable? And would that be compatible with 'mental health'?" As with our first dialogue, there seemed to be a tension, between the impulse for familiarity, security, protection from the release of lockdown, generally the fear of the unknown, versus an impulse toward freedom, taking personal responsibility for behaviours and broadly libertarian mores.

This foundationally existential tension highlighted that if too much protection and containment is unfamiliar so is too much freedom. We noted that, increasingly, responses to this tension seemed to have the potential for violent expression – the *zeitgeist*, we proposed, now included this tension embodied as an increase in frustration and certainly a form of 'frustration politics'.

In line with this, we considered Rollo May's idea of the daimonic (May, 1969). We wondered whether the tension of this dynamic could give rise to a destructively-focused explosion of experience that happens when things are too controlled and too protected. Rollo May wrote about the sort of scenario that occurs when societies have no means to express openness to being and how, under such circumstances, the daimonic can burst forth in aggressive and uncontained ways. May's counter-proposal was that, in order to avoid this, societies needed to establish and encourage ways to channel the daimonic – such as through society-wide festivals and mass gatherings (exactly the rituals that had been forbidden during lockdown) so that through such group rituals a more creative, artistic, means arose for the daimonic to express itself and, thereby, shepherd in a more constructive, positive transformation in our personal and social relations. May's concept of the daimonic revealed contradictory experiences, pushing in different directions. This resonated strongly with both our understanding of key existential themes and, more pertinently, our current experiences of living through the pandemic.

We noticed the shift in relational interactions due to the implicit threat of contagion as well as the experience of moving so much human inter-action into the virtual space. We missed the in-person, physical interactions once so easily available to us with their complete sensory experience, little bodily movements that happen naturally when talking to a person, the shared environment, the sounds not filtered through a microphone, and the smells. 'Suddenly, the people who are physically near, even those I've just met, become more important as sources of interaction, than family and long-term friends who are only available through the computer screen.' In line with this, we noted how our casual, everyday interactions with shopkeepers, delivery people, dog walkers and neighbours over the fence, had tended to become noticeably more intimate. We speculated whether, in terms of process and content, these instances of physically proximate interaction offer needed *processes of connection* even if the *content* of the interactions seemed more superficial. This combined with our daily experiences of maintaining phys-ical distancing on the footpath while apologetically giving each other space because being too close is a danger to ourselves or the other.

> Again, the tension between 'don't get near me' and 'I'm sorry you can't get near me'. The loosening of restrictions forces us to collapse back into a more individual interpretation of behaviour and it's a bit like 'every person for themselves'. Individualism replacing collectivism already. Along with the deterioration of a collective response there is now more cynicism. The clapping for health workers etc., all these responses have become more politically motivated and manipulated and as the cynicism grows after the first lockdown, we notice that trying to manipulate a sense of connection and comradeship, doesn't work. It is so immediately discernible from an authentic expression of appreciation and care. And now there is a guarded-ness coming back, perhaps because we have all experienced something that has been quite personal and profound and to actually talk about it is just too intimate. It's uncomfortable .... All the while we are aware that the pan-demic has not yet reached its height in some parts of the world and there is the background fear of whether we could really face yet another lockdown. And the response may bring that strange contradiction of 'Oh god! No! Not again!' and at the same time this is now familiar, I know how to live like that. Some mix of what was so strange has become somewhat familiar and what was so taken for granted is now somewhat strange.

When we spoke about the personal impact of the lockdown, as we were coming out of it, we both felt a degree of fuzziness, and, once again, multiple contradictions in experience.

Days blended into each other. Regrets were expressed about not harnessing this time in a more productive way and yet there was also the appreciation of having stayed with the feelings provoked during this odd time and not having busied ourselves too much with the distractions of productivity and work. Both of us often felt flat but then also easily moved to tears. We both reacted emotionally to music that seemed to express something of what we were feeling. These experiences of release also elicited nostalgia for a time when such music expressed the way humans lived and how much of that way of living now seemed to be in the past.

Perhaps the most existentially pertinent question we asked ourselves was:

> Do we have the courage to embrace with some honesty what we're actually experiencing and the mystery of it? [A]re we just going to pretend that this was just some kind of fantasy and almost erase everything? Or are we actually going to meet what has happened and remain open to the challenge of it? Maybe a year ago we were pretty sure that we were going to meet it as a challenge and maybe we're now much more uncertain as to whether we will. Maybe that's where the fuzziness comes in ... Is this an opportunity for human civilisation to ask the big questions like 'what do we want to do with this species that we are?' 'How do we want to continue this species if we do?' And are we willing to do what that requires?

By the end of the second dialogue, we were left with various questions. But at the heart of these was one over-arching one: What sense did we have of what really matters? What really matters to us now?

> We have had an event forced upon us that shines a light onto how we have got caught up in things that we've told ourselves are important and really matter. But actually, it takes something like this to realise that they don't mean very much at all and that we've avoided actually exploring more deeply what is it that *does* matter to us, both individually and universally?

Hopefully, it is a question that will continue being asked.

Implications for therapy

What will be the longer-term effects of offering therapy under pandemic conditions? Will the foundation that has evolved over 125 years fundamentally change? If those fundamentals of therapy do not make sense anymore, or we discovered through necessity that they are not necessary fundamentals, can therapy continue in a recognisable form?

At the beginning of lockdown, two weeks in, there was a rush to move sessions online and a corresponding increase in anxiety for therapists who had only worked face-to-face until then. Corresponding with this was a plethora of online trainings for virtual therapy, and how to work with the anxiety and depression of clients reacting to the pandemic (not always acknowledging that therapists, too, were all reacting to the pandemic). There was considerable panic but quickly it seemed that therapists and clients (most of whom seemed to transition to online sessions with more ease than their therapists) forgot they were meeting through a screen and sessions regained the feeling of therapeutic encounter. In fact, many therapists were quite quickly expressing a desire to stay online and not return to in-office work, though by the end of the lockdown online fatigue might have softened that desire.

Like many therapists, we found the online sessions more tiring, whether because there was a different kind of focus required, or the constant white light in the eyes, or the stress of living through all the uncertainty ourselves while simultaneously listening to our clients' experiences of the same situation. Whatever the reason, in common with so many other therapists, we were usually exhausted by the end of our client week.

One of the immediate questions that this raised for us was whether the ritual of keeping to 45- or 50-minute sessions needed to be maintained? Perhaps more frequent, shorter sessions would work better in this new reality? Or, perhaps a bit more radically, through platforms like Zoom, therapists might begin to work with more than one client at a time? In general, we considered how many of the traditions that make us feel secure could be abandoned or at least less rigidly held?

Interestingly, we found that working online could still generate an energetic body feeling during the session. Just because it was on the screen did not mean the interaction had to be flattened to eye–brain processing. Did this experience raise a question about human bodies and where their boundaries really end?

We also asked ourselves if our experience was that therapy sessions had become less symptom-focused and more conversational during the pandemic. If at least part of the content is a shared uncertain and unfamiliar reality that both client and therapist are experiencing, did that expand the conversation into a more mutual dialogue? In line with this, we noticed that many clients would begin their sessions with a genuine question: 'And how are *you*? Are you and your family OK?'

In the same way, focusing upon possible changes in 'being a therapist' that we ourselves might have initiated, we explored our own role in allowing – perhaps even encouraging – a more mutual discourse. This, in turn, led to our considering how much more self-revealing we had allowed ourselves to become – be it by choice or because of the conditions imposed by virtual meetings. After all, unless we took active steps to hide our surroundings from the camera's view our clients would have visual access to rooms and furnishings that might otherwise have remained private. In turn, such access was also likely to reveal our tastes, perhaps our pets, the sounds in our neighbourhood, and so forth. Again, a general question was raised: How open can we be as therapists to the sharing of our own life experience? What sort of impact would that have on how we understand and practise therapy? And will the emergence of more openness eventually close back down if we return to in-person sessions?

Overall, it seemed to us that the dialogues we engaged in had become more broadly 'existential', in that they continually raised discussions about what it means to be human under these strange conditions and therefore shedding light on human being in general. What creative therapeutic possibilities might arise from continuing a model that includes a respectful acknowledgment of our mutual human situation rather than obstruct or avoid it or even try to escape from it?

While some of these questions and concerns were repeated during the second dialogue, what was of greater focus was the question of what was going to happen to psychotherapy if there is not a clear end to the pandemic situation and people chose not to return to their offices at all? What is it to be a therapist when therapy is primarily or exclusively online?

Thinking of this once again in terms of contradictions we could see that, on one level, a very strong sense of distancing and limitation can accompany therapy that is exclusively online. But at another level, we also experienced a different sort of intimacy – no less powerful than a possible increase in ano-nymity – which emerged through our willingness to accept that, as therapists, we were inevitably becoming more self-revealing. Acknowledging that we had found ourselves naturally saying more about our own experiences, we noted that the idea of the anonymous therapist (of which there had always been issues anyway) has become even more of a questionable assumption.

Now one year since our first dialogue, we also noticed that the intention to try to hold the frame within online sessions as if it were in-person began to relax. For example, if a delivery person rang the doorbell, previously we would be likely to ignore it and continue the session. Yet from the begin-ning of lockdown everyone appreciated the importance of home deliveries so, if the doorbell rang, the therapist was more likely to apologise and answer the door.

More generally, we concluded that in online sessions it is more likely that the therapist's life intrudes. A pet might walk past in the frame, which could well lead to a little conversation about that. As the various lockdowns continued and deliveries and other interruptions became 'normal', the question arose again: 'Hold on a second, this delivery thing has become kind of normal … Maybe I should be reasserting that frame!' But why does it make any sense to reassert that more traditional frame? Or would it be more sensible to accept a new flexible and modified framework? Or, perhaps, could we seek to hold the tensions that both generate?

> Can we consider the therapeutic frame has a flexibility to it that we hadn't considered before, or were unwilling to consider before, and maybe it's

not something that should be imposed by the therapist but something that should be relationally negotiated? Why not allow the client to see me run out of the room, and sit back down slightly embarrassed? It humanises us. Therapists have had this tendency to think that many of their human aspects have to be bracketed when they are being a therapist. I have to be a superhuman being who's able to engage with you in this particular way even while I too experience a pandemic. Maybe some of the fear around being seen by the client has dissipated during all this. And maybe some of the fear about it having a deleterious impact on the client has also dissipated. Perhaps part of the fear is that if we don't hold this rigidity then therapy will collapse into just any old conversation, a neighbourly chat ... I don't think that's true. I think it is absolutely possible to remain focused on the client's experience and the relational dynamics in a way that you don't focus on when you're having an informal chat with a friend. It doesn't become a friendship just because you let in more of your humanity.

Nonetheless, we remained acutely aware that such shifts in the overall therapeutic frame can well generate the perceived danger that if the therapist becomes too human then the degree of closeness and intimacy that might be generated for either or both participants might become overwhelming.

If I reveal myself through simple acts of answering the door, letting the client see that I get excited by the arrival of a package in the post, just ordinary little things that as therapists our tendencies may be to hold back from clients, am I allowing a familiarity that weakens or strengthens the therapeutic relationship in each case? Therapy requires a depth and an intimacy, but one that's kind of unidirectional rather than mutually directional. There comes a point in my sharing that starts to feel almost slightly queasy, like there's something else going on here, it doesn't feel right to continue this. When you're getting up and answering the door and so forth while it's a very surfacy momentary insignificant act on your part, it has something to it that changes the nature of your encounter with that person because now you're showing them a version of you that maybe would be reserved for other kinds of meetings. And it's not maybe so much that a version of self is being shown as much as the therapist is *letting it* be seen, the therapist is *not hiding it*. But of course, if therapy continues to be mostly delivered online, will the shifts in therapist disclosure and flexibility in frames be reined in as the inevitable new therapist training modules tell us how to *do* online therapy?

Finally, we also wondered about the pandemic accelerating the development of other technologies that might have significant impact on both how therapy was conceptualised and practised. One example we explored was that of virtual reality therapy (VRT). The possibility of wandering around inside a virtual office or garden with a client, both dressed as avatars of some kind, raises fascinating question as to where therapy may now be headed. The Pandora's box of therapy and technology has been opened, so what might be the positive and undesirable consequences of meeting in virtual space?

Will clients feel more anonymous, be willing to speak and act more freely? And if your client appears as an avatar, do they still need to maintain a certain physical space? Imagine a scenario where in the virtual reality that both therapist and client inhabit the client makes the request to sit on your knee. Would this be permissible? Appropriate? After all, the client would not *really* be sitting on your knee. They are sat in their house on the other side of the city ... or the world. Even so ....

All in all, we discovered that many intriguing challenges, both expected and surprising, arose for us in our attempt at reimagining therapy within recurring pandemic conditions. Being existential therapists, we found it near impossible to arrive at any fully-formed or final answers.

Summary thoughts

In this present moment, Autumn 2021, we can see that, as predicted in our first conversation, there is a strong tendency now to diminish the power of the initial experience of uncertainty and possibility and, instead, to claim that we can return to the normality that we once inhabited.

We anticipated a flowering in the arts, something which may have begun to happen since venues and meeting grounds have reopened.

And we also anticipated that there will be a significant movement to harvest something fresh from the pandemic in terms of how to organise ourselves in human communities in a way that is more egalitarian, fair, respectful and, perhaps, more human.

Perhaps so. But, for the moment, dominant psychological input has been mostly focused on how to ameliorate the negative impacts of the pandemic rather than harness its possible positive impulses.

Most significantly, now that the pandemic supposedly recedes (at least for the time being, and predominantly in Europe) we are, as anticipated, seeing a top-down move to normalise things being met with a bottom-up impulse to normalise things. Schools and universities are once again centred on classroom-based learning. Air travel – for both business and pleasure – is on the increase. Out of desire or demand, people are returning to some office work. All of these plus the removal of almost all restrictions on behaviour illustrate the strong desire to re-create the previous world with as little sign as possible of our having experienced so many of the life-changing experiences and demands of living with an ongoing pandemic.

Unfortunately, there is less evidence of any enduring changes in the social-economic structure of nations. Already in the UK for example, the financial furlough scheme is being dismantled and increases in social support payments are being rolled back, while homeless persons' accommodation is again being restricted … The previous arguments that the expense of such efforts to address economic inequality is prohibitive are again being expressed unmodified and have dampened the initial excitement that government responses to the pandemic meant old arguments could never again be quite as persuasive.

We had hoped that some fundamental possibilities that previously were seen to be too radical would now be open to public debate and discussion. But that optimism is fading.

We had hoped, during the first lockdown, that eventually if we returned to something recognisable as new life routines that they would be more inclusive ways of living that did not leave out so much of the full complexity of human being.

Even so, the positive aspects of working from home, and not just for therapists, means that a full-time return to office-based work is unlikely to ever return to its pre-pandemic levels. Larger organisations that previously resisted this degree of flexible working arrangements are seeing the benefits – not least increased productivity and worker satisfaction combined with less estate costs.

Perhaps the main long-term existential impact on humans will be experienced in how we engage with one another and the ways we give expression to our relatedness.

But, if our embodied experience is anything to go by – as we believe it is – the most truthful conclusion we can arrive at, in this moment in time, is that we really do not have any clue about the long-term implications of this strange, global experiment that the whole human species continues to go through.

At this moment, it feels like the ongoing pandemic continues to have something profound to offer us. And because what its long-term ripples may bring about for humanity as a whole is far too difficult to predict, it seems to us that the best we can do for now is to remain open and unknowing.

References

Eliot, T.S. (2001) 'Burnt Norton', in *Four Quartets*. London: Faber & Faber.
Madison, G. and Spinelli, E. (2020) In Corona Times. *YouTube*, 6 April, https://youtu.be/dYmlvrutyU0 [accessed 1 September 2021].
Madison, G. and Spinelli, E. (2021) In Corona Times 2: What Really Matters? *YouTube*, 30 April https://youtu.be/Gc7AI80COVc [accessed 1 September 2021].
May, R. (1969) *Love and Will.* New York: W.W. Norton.

Part 2

The therapy world

Psychotherapy and coaching clients

The therapy world

Price-Robertson et al. (2020) noted: 'In this time of great uncertainty, we can at least be sure of this: the Covid-19 pandemic has changed the field of psychotherapy and counselling, and it will never be quite the same again.'

Throughout the pandemic there has been increased need for mental health and psychotherapy services. This reflects the challenges presented by the pandemic itself, and the subsequent changes to people's lives. While need has increased, therapists have been presented with their own personal and professional challenges. This has included how they continue to practise within the Covid-19 restrictions.

Some practical changes have been required. It is now over a year since I have seen a psychotherapy client for a face-to-face session, having moved to a situation where I 'see' clients via Zoom, or we have telephone sessions.

These changes have been welcomed by some therapists, who intend only to offer online sessions when the restrictions are lifted. At the time of writing, it is possible to see clients face-to-face, with the recommendation that face masks are worn by both the therapist and client. I have offered this option to clients but, thankfully, they have all said the use of face masks would detract from the intimacy and connectedness of the therapy session, a position I share.

I have discussed with colleagues and supervisees how they have experienced the challenges which have been presented, and their plans for after the lifting of restrictions. One positive aspect acknowledged by all was that they could now make their services more accessible to people. Therapists could offer therapy from wherever they were on the day, opening up possibilities of travel which therapists had previously had to forgo. They no longer had to travel to their 'office' or 'clinic', saving time on the travel and, if they chose, allowing them time to see more clients, or to regain personal time. For those not trapped in long-term contracts, they could choose to give up the lease of expensive rented rooms, thus allowing the possibility of reducing fees and giving greater access to clients who were not financially well-off. Some therapists working from home and intending to only offer online sessions in the future felt they

DOI: 10.4324/9781003255765-8

no longer had to keep the therapy room as clean and tidy, as only part of it would be seen by the client.

It became possible to work with clients who could not travel to the therapy room. This was helpful to those with mobility, time or financial difficulties. Some therapists began taking clients from outside the UK, although this did result in some of them experiencing problems with their accrediting bodies and insurance providers.

For other therapists, me included, the change did not feel so positive. I missed sharing the phenomenological space with my client, breathing the same air, experiencing the same smells, sounds and distractions, all of which could be noted and form part of the therapeutic material of the session. I have started to see the experience of working with a person face-to-face being described as IRL (in real life) as opposed to working virtually (IVL; in virtual life).

For some clients, particularly those who started therapy during the pandemic, I have found that sessions sometimes had more of an air of a business meeting, slotted between two online board meetings. I and other therapists experienced clients getting up to make coffee or clearly reading incoming messages which were no doubt floating across the tops of their screen. On an online platform we are reduced to floating disembodied heads, sometimes with strange unreal fantasy backgrounds. I am no longer engaged with another fully embodied being, and so, as a therapist I have less than one-third of what is normally available for me to work with.

I can no longer see the tapping foot which may indicate boredom, annoyance or anxiety, the meaning of which we would explore in the session. Hands are generally kept out of sight and so give no physical indication of the level to which the client is relaxed or stressed. Eye contact, which can be very important in therapy can be distorted by strangely positioned webcams, giving the impression that that I or the client are looking away from each other. The sense of the physical self is suddenly reduced and non-verbal communication more limited than when working face-to-face.

For my own part, I remain conscious that I am working. I do not change my usual working wardrobe for one of tracksuits or loose clothing. I do not adopt more formal top wear while wearing baggy trousers or shorts underneath the desk. My footwear has changed so that for most of my Zoom sessions I am barefoot. I do not attach any great symbolism to this, I just note it.

Of course, although our visual field is reduced, the words are still present, although at times they may be faint or distorted. The context of our meeting is changed. We are no longer seeing each other in the same space each time; clients may choose to be in different parts of their homes or offices for the sessions. I now see various aspects of people's homes; some sessions may take place in the marital bedroom or the room of one of their children or around the kitchen table. One supervisee described a client who lay in bed, glass of wine in hand for one session before the therapist made it clear that she was not comfortable with this. I can recognise the different interior design style of client's homes and must work hard not to be drawn in to wondering what the other rooms may look like … would they have wallpaper that matches the curtains? I wondered to what extent clients reflected on what they chose to expose, knowing that I would have none of this visual information if the session was taking place in the therapy room. I wonder to what extent they are knowingly offering this additional information about themselves and those closest to them. The freedom and responsibility inherent in the client actively and consciously choosing what they bring into the session and what they leave out seems to be weakened.

Although, for the most part it is I and not the client who is conscious of the extra material brought into the work by encountering the client's personal physical space, some clients do not have spaces they feel comfortable in. The reduced level of safety some clients feel may increase levels of uncertainty or limit their ability to be open and authentic. This is particularly true when clients are sharing the building with people who are important aspects of their therapy narrative. In IRL, in the therapy room, the client feels able to talk openly about the difficulties they may be experiencing in these relationships and to explore aspects of the other person's behaviour or perceived 'person-ality'. In virtual space, where there is always the possibility of being overheard or even having someone enter the room 'to collect something they left behind' or because they 'forgot' the client was having a therapy session (situations which were frequently reported by supervisees), this may cause the client to limit the content and authenticity of what they bring to the session.

This is intensified for clients who live in multi-occupancy or shared houses, and whose therapy may be required to take place within the four paper-thin walls that surround them all day. They may not know the people they live with, and even fear other people's assumptions and reactions if it became known they were in therapy. During lockdown, I had clients who preferred to have their sessions on their phones while sheltering under trees in secluded spots, sitting in their (or in one case a borrowed) car, or walking around their area.

These practical changes bring challenges for the therapist in how they will deal with distractions. The therapist may be working from home, with other people in the house who would previously have been out at work when clients were present. The therapist needs to bracket out the sounds of their house-hold going about their business elsewhere in the house while they are working; if someone drops something or there are sounds of distress the therapist must know how to deal with their concern while remaining focused on the client. Distractions can also come from what is happening in the client's room. I had one session where the client's cat appeared, climbed on to her head and remained there throughout the session. I struggled not to be distracted by the cat, while the client appeared unmoved by its presence. We acknowledged it was there and then sought to forget about it. In another session a figure passed across the room behind the client; I mentioned this to the client as

I was concerned about confidentiality and thought he may not know the person was there. He replied, "Oh that is just the maid taking the laundry from upstairs through to the washing machine." The concern about confidentiality was mine and not the client's. However, I believed it remained my responsibility to point out to the client that he could be heard.

It is impossible not to believe that the change in the way therapists had to work went beyond the environmental ones and impacted on the relationship between therapist and client. Whether due to the online nature of the work, or to the sensitivity created by the pandemic, one supervisee working in private practice reported perceived changes in the openness and authenticity of the material some clients brought. The therapist also reported changes in their own instinctual response to clients' dilemmas. Two examples were brought to supervision.

In the first, a client was having a particularly gruelling course of chemotherapy during which she had a Covid-19 vaccine injection and became so ill she had to be admitted to hospital. She was planning on having the second Covid-19 vaccination three or four weeks after chemotherapy sessions ended, so that she could go on holiday in August. In supervision, her therapist expressed concern about her rush to have a second jab given her condition and the rationale for having it, saying: "If she was talking about sky-diving shortly after chemo, I might be equally concerned and would want to explore her motivation and any risks with her." The therapist felt that due to the pandemic situation they had become cautious about how to respond, they paused any challenge "not knowing whether an honest concern could be misconstrued". The therapist felt increasingly aware of their professional body and insurance company monitoring their work for any unofficial, non-government sanctioned interventions and stopped short of their instinctive approach.

In the second scenario, they had a client who said he did not want to have the vaccine (or gene therapy as he called it) but took over a year to tell the therapist of his doubts and concerns about the pandemic and the narrative we were being presented with. He later told the therapist that he feared saying anything which might impact on their relationship. He was worried that even though the therapist had held everything else he had brought, this was one subject he could not be sure would not lead to the therapist rejecting him. Apparently, he had lost friendships for his views and had become circumspect in what he shared when it came to this subject. He was relieved to know that the therapist could understand his concerns (without agreeing or disagreeing with him) and would not reject him for his views.

The supervisee noted:

> It takes something quite significant to cause such a change in general awareness such that formerly well meaning, ethical and phenomenological practice feels risky for either the client or the therapist. It takes me

back to my work as a consultant for an international EAP provider where former eastern European block countries would refuse to use the free counselling service since free speech was still a novel (and highly risky) concept. For me this is the biggest concern for our profession and society. Are all views still okay?

We can see from the seriousness the supervisee gives to these concerns that he was not feeling safe within the current situation, and that this was impacting on his work and the openness of clients. Vos (2021:72) reflects on the different views which the pandemic highlights and writes of the pandemic as having a

> Janus face … on the one face, there are those arguing how biopolitics undermines the material, psychological and social conditions of individual empowerment, democracy and revolution. On the other face, there are those saying that the pandemic is motivating to reflect, criticise and rise against authoritarian governments.

Therapists and clients will be representative of both those faces. It is essential that therapists find a way of being comfortable with holding their authentic personal views, bracketing them, when necessary in their work with clients and remain open to the exploration of the clients' views, fears and hopes.

This therapist's experience was not mirrored by all my supervisees. A therapist coming from a non-existential orientation, who works psychodynamically in his private practice, and is CBT focused in his NHS work, reported very little increase in lockdown-related anxiety in the earlier stages of the pandemic with a slight increase during the second lockdown, which he saw as "probably due more to lack of faith in the government's ability to manage infection". It would be interesting to research whether the more focused content of CBT sessions may have resulted in clients staying to task and not broadening the focus of the therapeutic material. The same supervisee felt that people's activities were less severely affected over time than in the initial lockdown.

He reported very little change in his view of himself as he had been at work during the entirety of the pandemic and felt that the reduced ability to travel probably increased generalised resentment rather than anxiety. Despite not noting any real changes in himself, he said that his own uncertainty around the management of the pandemic related more to his distaste for individual politicians than it did to their ability to manage a pandemic and felt a mild anxiety that this pandemic was a harbinger of future problems. When considering changes to his own sense of freedom during the pandemic, he believed that, despite being an enthusiast of outdoor pursuits, the change in freedoms affected him very little in terms of restrictions to travel or access to the outdoors. Indeed, he "would possibly unhelpfully" compare our freedoms rather unfavourably with those of Scandinavia. It did not seem that, for him, there was an emotional or psychological reaction to the change in his external freedoms.

However, he did notice a difference in his lived experience of time, finding that keeping track of time had "definitely become more difficult during the pandemic with the somewhat paradoxical experience of time passing both more quickly and more slowly – a not uncommon experience". He did not link this to thoughts of temporality and stated that he was unaware of any real change to his attitude to temporality and mortality other than the passing of birthdays while lock downed.

Neither did he find that there was any significantly increased thought about matters of meaning, believing that he had neither found nor lost any meaning during this period, although he reported increased love of the outdoors, something which was already incredibly important to him. Rather than any changes to his beliefs and values he considered that these were reinforced by the pandemic. He described how the values relating to nature and its positive effect on us, and our place in it, increased from his already strong belief, whereas his somewhat negative view of international capitalism and our management of the natural world had been reinforced and his sense of resignation had likewise increased.

The coaching world

Many of the points noted above in relation to psychotherapy also exist in coaching. However, coaching often takes place online or over the phone, so the move to increased use of online platforms was less of a change. Even so, it came up a lot in my conversations with other coaches, who noted that, although used to working virtually, and having developed sets of practices to support best practice there was "a new quality to the experience of working on such platforms". In my conversations with a colleague Jamie Reed, he reflected on what he identified as two different elements of the phenomenon:

> Firstly, the experience of being on a video call, which is increasingly being experienced a, impersonal, sterile, flat, boring, like being watched … Secondly, the reflections of people on the impact of being on an increasing number of calls over time, leading to reports of feeling drained, exhausted, languishing and being like a robot.

This left Jamie with a series of existential questions. What is this gathering collective awareness teaching us about what it means to be human, what does it means to listen and to be in relationship? He described how he had been struck by the wisdom of Dame Evelyn Glennie in her 2021 interview with Mary Beard for the *Inside Culture* series on BBC 2. He reported how, as a profoundly deaf percussionist, Evelyn Glennie relies greatly on the resonance and the vibration her instruments make when she performs. As such, she listens, as we all do, with her whole body. She cites that only with live performances do we get the resonance that allows us to listen in this holistic way, so we can taste the sound, feel the sound, and touch the sound. In this way listening becomes visceral, multi-faceted and speaks deeply to how we experience and make sense of the world. An awareness that goes far beyond just hearing words as data points for understanding, and the basis for determining action, that can be all that is left on video calls. Glennie also pays particular attention to the importance of the journey the sound makes between the striking of the instrument, the recipient and back again. A journey that, with the predominance of video calls, has been profoundly interrupted. She chose to stop performing until she is free to do so live.

As Jamie pointed out, "for coaches, and clients, the choice to stop 'performing' is not necessarily there, with the realities of having bills to pay, organisations to serve, and people to support". Jamie draws on an existential coaching approach, based on the belief that "we exist in constant relationship, in relationship to ourselves and to others. An existence that is the basis for how we make sense of the world as humans." This belief causes us to "consciously and unconsciously seek, and need, embodied experiences of relationship and listening, because this is essential to our ability to navigate our reality, to do our jobs and to be human, not robots". Jamie's experience has been that when we always meet with others in a way that is predominantly remote, "we have not only changed the journey of our listening, we have also dramatically reduced the quality of the relating that is possible and the quality of our experience of being human. An experience that, over time, is exhausting." He noted that, although used to working online, this tiring phenomenon may not even initially be noticed, but instead slowly creeps in, contributing to the experience of online sessions becoming increasingly dissatisfying and potentially damaging over time.

As coaches often use online platforms, Jamie suggests that it is too easy to have a

> lack of awareness of what a rich multi-dimensional experience listening is, and how essential this experience is to us as humans, and that without a sufficient amount of this experience, we are seeing the impacts on well-being and performance that are now being reported.

He calls on coaches to remain fresh and to

> raise our collective awareness of the importance of relationship and embodied listening, as an essential part of what makes us human, and that we balance our use of video conference with direct contact with others, as well as with other practices that build connection to ourselves, such as meditation and solo walks in nature.

In my own practice, which is focused on business, executive and leadership coaching, even though previously 60% of sessions would have been via Zoom there has still been a clear difference in having to use this as the sole way of working during the pandemic. Previously, I would work with clients who I had only encountered in their offices. We would sit in a fairly neutral office and meeting spaces, chosen for their sound proofing and privacy; even when sessions were online this would be the environment I saw them in. The content of the coaching before and during the pandemic was focused on their 'professional self' and, although this did not mean I was not sometimes made aware of their family and domestic circumstances, and that the core challenges in their professional lives were intimately connected with their personal life and their holistic sense of meaning, it was not our starting point.

Now my clients were working from home. Many had returned to families outside the UK. As with psychotherapy clients I was given access to their home. This was often a challenge to preconceptions and assumptions which I had not known I held. Many of my clients are very successful and, in my judgement, earn high salaries (for which they work exceptionally hard). In my fantasies they live quite affluent lifestyles and have comfortable, spacious homes. Although true for many, I saw clients living in very cramped conditions in central London apartments. Many were working from one end of the kitchen table while their partner worked at the other end. Children were in the same room playing, glued to screens, or attempting to do homework. Open space living suddenly looked less attractive. In 'normal' times they tended to spend little time in the home, working long hours, children at school and after school clubs, and family time was focused on holidays, which were no longer possible. The boundary between personal and professional was broken and finding a way of living holistically became a central challenge for many. Even those who were not surrounded by families no longer had access to quiet spaces for their sessions. On one session with a client in Goa I was frightened by a terrible sound which suggested that her home was being broken into by an angry gang; this turned out to be the monsoon rain!

In the following chapters authors write about their existential approach to their work during the pandemic. In some cases, they draw on the material brought by clients to reflect on the lived experience of the pandemic through the client's eyes. Where client work is included, changes have been made to anonymise the information.

References

Price-Robertson, R., Bloch-Atelfi, A., Snell, T., Day, E. and O'Neill, G. (2020) Reflections on Psychotherapy and Counselling from Covid-19 Lockdown. *Psychotherapy and Counselling Journal of Australia* https://pacja.org.au/2020/06/editorial-reflections-on-psychotherapy-and-counselling-from-covid-19-lockdown/.

Vos, J. (2021) *The Psychology of Covid-19: Building Resilience for Future Pandemics.* London: Sage Swifts.

Chapter 6

Birth, death and isolation
Motherhood during a pandemic

Claire Arnold-Baker

In December 2020 *The Washington Post* asked its readers to sum up 2020 in one word. The top three responses were, *exhausting*, *lost* and *chaotic*, other words used were *relentless*, *surreal* and *limbo* (Goren et al., 2020). These words perfectly described the experience of the most recent pandemic, a mix of our lives being turned upside down but also each day being repetitively the same. A blend of living in fear and living in boredom; two opposing feelings that are hard to assimilate. The Covid-19 pandemic has been an extraordinary time in all our lives, and across the globe no one has escaped its reach. But even when it feels like we are living in either fear or in limbo, everyday life continues and, in this unsettling time, babies continue to be born.

Pregnancy and the postnatal period are vulnerable times for women generally. Having a baby is a life-changing experience and the perinatal period is dominated by significant challenges on various physical-social-psycho-spiritual dimensions, which often result in women experiencing an existential crisis (Arnold-Baker, 2020). Yet when this experience also takes place during a pandemic, it has the effect of magnifying the existential dimensions that are prevalent during this time and intensifying the emotional and psychological aspects of becoming a mother. This chapter aims to draw out the existential themes that have emerged for mothers during the Covid-19 pandemic and how they have had an impact on their lives.

The main existential themes to be explored are mortality, natality and maternity; isolation and relatedness; freedom and choice; anxiety; and uncertainty. While the majority of women have found it a difficult and sometimes challenging time, there were also some positive, if somewhat unexpected, experiences that emerged. The existential themes explored in this chapter came to the fore through my work as an existential therapist with mothers during the pandemic. I worked with a variety of women at different stages of pregnancy and postpartum, yet there was a commonality of experience, which I will draw out in this chapter. A commonality that was captured by other mothers, whose reflections were gathered for a writing project culminating in the book *Born in Lockdown* edited by Emylia Hall (2021), who brought together the voices of 277 women who had had a baby during lockdown. I will draw on

DOI: 10.4324/9781003255765-9

quotes from these mothers to illustrate the themes that had become apparent through my work during the pandemic. It is hoped that these reflections will help both practitioners and mothers alike to gain a deeper understanding of the challenges that pregnant women and new mothers have faced and will potentially face in the future. I will also point to how we can learn from those lockdown experiences to move towards better ways to face maternity for both parents and potentially society as a whole.

Mortality, natality and maternity: the physical dimension

It will be unsurprising to find death, or mortality, to be an existential theme to emerge for people during a pandemic. The very nature of the pandemic has meant that many millions of people worldwide have died from the Covid-19 virus. Death, then, has come to the forefront of everyone's consciousness in a way that it does not normally happen in our everyday lives. The enormity of the situation and how little was known in the early stages meant that the concept of death moved from being something that happens to someone else to something that might happen to me or someone close to me. The pandemic, then, had shaken us from our everyday mode of being, as Heidegger (1962) stated, of being *tranquillised* from death and instead we have been confronted by the possibility of our own mortality and nonexistence.

Birth and death are the temporal markers that highlight the beginning and end points of each person's existence. The only certainties that we face in life are that we are born and then we must die, yet the date and the nature of our death is always unknown to us. Much has been written about death by existential philosophers such as Heidegger, and how mortality (the state of being mortal) impacts our lives. Heidegger (1962) believed that when we became more aware of our own mortality, we were in a mode of *being-towards-death*. This mode of being has the effect of individualising our lives; we begin to think of ourselves as unique individuals and to see our lives as a whole, with a beginning and an end. It may lead to us questioning our lives or making more authentic choices that are good for us as an individual; but it also has the effect of throwing us back into life, giving it a sense of urgency and purpose. In contrast, relatively little has been written about the impact that natality (the state of being born) has on our lives (Stone, 2019). Rather than individualising existence in the way mortality does, natality highlights the unavoidable relatedness of human existence, which in turn creates in us a sense of vulnerability, as our survival and our experiences are dependent on other people (Stone, 2019). Both ends of life's continuum, therefore, confer differing existential structures to our existence which are brought together in the experience of maternity.

Birth, death and motherhood are all corporeal events which ground us in the physical dimension. A woman's first experience of motherhood – pregnancy – is an embodied one and this corporeal experience continues through the birth and postpartum with breastfeeding and the mother facing a changed body. These corporeal events are biological in nature and concern the very tenets of existence: life and death. As Parker noted, a new mother must grapple with the fact that she is both the source of life but also the potential death for her child as 'she is responsible for keeping alive a child unable to fend for itself outside the womb' (2005:12). This is echoed by van Deurzen, who stated: 'Mothers ... having given birth, understand exactly how serious life is and how close it is to death, the fear of which is always at the horizon when you have a newborn baby in your arms' (van Deurzen, 1998:33). Although the mortality rates for mothers of seven in 100,000 in 2017 (Data World Bank Organisation, 2019) and babies (Office for National Statistics, 2019) in the UK is low, the fact that mothers and babies still occasionally die during child-birth adds a level of vulnerability and fear to the experience for mothers. This is also exacerbated by the medicalisation of birth which has contributed to the sense that childbirth is a high-risk event (Milnes, 2021).

The mother is not just confronted by the possibility of her own death and that of her baby's during childbirth; the nature of becoming a mother also brings the life cycle into sharp relief. De Beauvoir (1997) noted that when a woman becomes a mother she moves along the generational ladder, from daughter to mother. She recognises how her place in the life cycle has moved, seeing the passage of time in action and how, as a result, she comes closer to her own mortality as a result of this. The mother's own mortality becomes an issue for her as she worries about who will take care of her children or what will happen to her children if she dies.

Motherhood, therefore, always holds the tensions of the possibility of new life and an awareness of mortality which makes mothers intensely aware of the fragility of life (Prinds et al., 2013; Arnold-Baker, 2015). When this experience takes place during a pandemic, however, this tension is emphasised further, and women become concerned not just for their own safety but for the safety of their babies.

Conceiving and being pregnant during a pandemic

The way in which the issues of mortality and natality, of life and death, were manifested in women during the pandemic was through a preoccupation with the *safety and risk* pole of existence, which in turn led to worry, anxiety and fear. The physical dimension (van Deurzen, 2010) is dominated by this pole of existence, where the following questions are raised: Where is our safety? Whom can we trust? Are we healthy or ill? The experience on this pole of exist-ence was also determined by the stage that women were at in their mother-hood journey. The decreased fertility rate in 2020 (Census, 2020) indicated that, despite initial thoughts that there might be a baby boom due to lock-down, many women contemplating starting a family had decided to postpone getting pregnant, until such time that they felt safer, and the pandemic had receded. However, this was not possible for all women. Many women were already pregnant when the pandemic hit and others felt the pressure of time, either because of their age or because they had suffered miscarriages or fertility issues which meant that a delay in trying to conceive was not an option for them. For those wanting to conceive during the pandemic it became a mission of trying to plan for the unknown. It was a case of trying to second guess at what stage the pandemic would be in nine months' time when they would be giving birth. Or, for those who had had miscarriages in the past, what would it be like in the next 12 weeks. The questions most prevalent for these women were 'will it be safe?' and 'will I get the help I need when the time comes?' Women were left feeling out of control, unable to influence their environment or know what the future may bring; it was hard to make choices when so much seemed to be down to a matter of chance.

The paradox that emerged for perinatal women during lockdown was that they felt relatively safe in their own homes. This was an environment that they could control. Home became a protected space for both themselves and their unborn babies. The risk was felt to be greater in hospitals and being in contact with medical professionals, as this is where the sickest members of the public were being looked after. Women were concerned about a number of issues related to this. The first related to the availability of resources. There was a concern that, when they needed help, it might be at the highest point in infection rates, which would then impact whether the hospital would be full and whether that would lead to people being turned away. This led to concerns about where they would be able to birth their babies and also the impact that that would have on their own health and that of their babies.

Related to this would be the scenario that the hospital would be open but there would not be a full contingent of staff working in the maternity units which would impact the care that they received. These two concerns focussed on whether there would be people and resources available for them to enable a safe delivery or to ensure that, if they were miscarrying, they could get the urgent help they needed to ensure their own safety. For those women grappling with fertility issues, the concern was whether these appointments would still go ahead, as some clinics had to close during the first lockdown as staff were redeployed to other wards.

The second area of concern for women was related to the possibility that the mothers themselves, or their babies, might contract the virus while they were in hospital. The fear and anxiety were palpable in these women. For those women who were in the final stages of pregnancy their worry centred on what would happen in the hospital; wondering how they were going to be able to focus solely on giving birth, while still feeling the need to be vigilant towards a threat they could not see. It felt like their attention would be divided between tending to their bodily experiences in giving birth, while at the same time being confronted with the possibility that they may be breathing in the virus. Being told to take a deep breath took on another meaning at that time. As one mother described: 'Nobody was exempt; not the Prime Minister, not you. We were all learning to fear the air we breathed' (Hall, 2021:14–15).

Questions that arose for women who were about to give birth centred on safety. How safe would the hospital be? Could they trust the medical professionals? Would their priority be on looking after the pregnant woman or would they be preoccupied with what was happening with the Covid-19 pandemic? Other concerns centred on the practicalities of the birth; would their partner be allowed to attend; would they be allowed to have the birth they planned for or wanted? There was a general feeling that giving birth during a pandemic increased the level of anxiety women felt about the birth process and added a new dimension. These women were being confronted with additional worries and concerns that were not previously present and were not conducive to giving birth.

Giving birth during a pandemic

> I never believed in things like heaven and hell until I gave birth and found myself in both at the same time.
>
> (Hall, 2021:18)

For the majority of women, the thought of giving birth is often felt with trepidation and anxiety about what will happen and how the birth will proceed but at the same time excitement and anticipation of finally meeting their baby. This experience was highlighted by the quote above, and this paradoxical situation can lead some women fearing birth because they will feel something might happen to either them or their baby. In a pandemic the normal ways in which women were able to trust what was happening to them and those that were helping them was removed. The health professionals became anonymous strangers, masked and covered, with only their eyes showing. For some women, one in five according to the charity Pregnant Then Screwed (Summers, 2021), they were also required to wear masks during labour, not just afterwards on the ward. This took place despite official advice from the Royal College of Midwives published in 2020 stating it would be inhumane to do so. In the early stages of the pandemic the situation was rapidly changing, which meant that there was sometimes confusion over what the official position was. The result, however, was to make women feel more vulnerable and more fearful.

> Never known fear like it. The unknown in the unknown by the unknowing. Constantly trusting the eyes of strangers. The masks, the masks! Have we met before? My world reduced to looking through rectangles. All the scared eyes of women in labour must merge into one long scream.
>
> (Hall, 2021:19)

For many women the pandemic meant that their birth plans had to change. Baptie et al.'s (2020) survey of 485 parents found that 90% had changes to their maternity choices, with 51% stating that they had had to change the way in which they wished to birth their baby due to the pandemic. A number of women also opted to 'free birth' at home as it was felt the safest option for them (ibid.). For many women the experience of giving birth in a pandemic was one filled with risk and fear, the opposite of what is needed for birthing women as it changes the physiology of the labour birth, resulting in negative, often traumatic, experiences (Milnes, 2021).

The fear and risk did not end after the baby was born and mothers were left wondering how they could protect both themselves and their baby from the virus:

> Focusing on the weight of this tiny person on my chest I slow my breathing, listening to his own little breaths and soft sleeping sounds, earnestly trying to commit them to memory. In the wee hours, in this perfect moment, I have never felt my own mortality so keenly. I silently will time to stop.
>
> (Hall, 2021:33)

Yalom (1980) describes how fear, anxiety and death are all interconnected. Often when we think about death, we either think about it in terms of what the experience will be like, or how others will react or respond to our deaths. We are less likely to think about our nonexistence, of not 'being' anymore, as this produces a fear or a dread that is not located in a particular experience or situation. The existential anxiety that is created is not an anxiety of something in particular; it is a general anxiety about ceasing to exist. This in turn generates a sense of helplessness as there is nothing for the person 'to do' or no way of avoiding what will ultimately happen to us. Yalom proposes that the fear of nonexistence needs to be transformed from 'a fear of nothing to a fear of something' (Yalom, 1980:43) and in this way we can find ways to protect ourselves. This is also true for the pandemic; the virus is an invisible force that can strike us down and there is no way of knowing if it will and how badly we will be affected. It becomes a 'Sword of Damocles' that has hung over us all, but over mothers in particular who are more likely to be existing in an ontological mode (Yalom, 1980) and more aware of the basic tenets of existence (Arnold-Baker, 2015).

Isolation and relatedness: the social dimension

Whereas the physical dimension of maternity in the pandemic was dominated by the *safety and risk* pole of existence for mothers, in the social dimension the focus was on *isolation and belonging;* and these two dimensions became interconnected. One way of ensuring people's safety was to isolate everyone from each other to stop the spread of the disease, which meant that other people became a risk and a potential source of infection. Normally we would feel safer with those closest to us, our families and friends; people who were unknown to us would represent a greater risk. However, in a pandemic the opposite is true. Although we may feel safer with those people we know, they still present a potential risk. But it becomes harder to distance ourselves from the other in the same way we would be able to do with a stranger. Therefore, in a pandemic our ability to assess the risk posed by others becomes disrupted.

Not only does a pandemic mean that we are unable to distinguish who we are safe with, it also meant that we were faced with a sense of isolation and separation from other people. The other became someone to fear or avoid. It highlighted our vulnerability and dependence on others as an onto-logical aspect of our natality (Stone, 2019). We are social creatures, *being-with,* as Heidegger (1962) states, and we are always in relation to other people. Isolating from each other, therefore, becomes extremely difficult. Our comfort and support comes from others. In fact, our first experiences of existence were being held, comforted, supported and taken care of by others, notably our own mothers. Motherhood and giving birth, therefore, is inherently social. It has always been a social experience that involved family and others. In fact, it is the intense support, both emotional and physical, that is provided to birthing mothers that sets us apart from other mammals (Rosenberg, 2012). Therefore, the lack of social and bodily contact, of not being able to hug or touch another outside of the household during the pandemic, felt alien and unnatural.

It is around the concept of isolation and belonging that existential thought is divided. Yalom talks about existential isolation as referring to 'an unbridge-able gulf between oneself and any other being' (1980:355) which is in direct contrast to Stone's (2019) position that a fundamental aspect of our exist-ence is our relatedness with others. Yalom draws on the concept of indi-vidual responsibility as that which highlights our separateness from others. Responsibility, he claims, 'implies authorship: to be aware of one's author-ship means to forsake the belief that there is another who creates and guards one' (Yalom, 1980:357). There are two issues here. The first concerns respon-sibility, which is framed as individual responsibility, the responsibility we have towards ourselves as individuals (Sartre, 1943). While this is indeed an ontological aspect of human existence there are times when we are wholly responsible for another. Motherhood is one such time, but so are other situations where we take on responsibility for another in a caring role. The second element of Yalom's description of existential isolation is that another cannot create us as we have the freedom to create ourselves and indeed it is our responsibility to do so. However, Stone (2019) argues that we never create ourselves in a vacuum and that there is always a sense of inheritability that we can choose to take on board or reject. Therefore, the existential iso-lation that Yalom describes, which causes dread and powerlessness, I would argue comes from being related to others and fearing being disconnected and separated from them, rather than recognising that we exist solely in isolation, separate from the world. We do not fear it because we are fundamentally separate, we fear existential isolation because we are fundamentally connected to others and not to be is unbearable. Even discussing a concept such as isolation requires the concept of the other from which to be isolated.

Therefore, in relation to the pandemic, being physically isolated from others, at a time of high risk and uncertainty was extremely challenging for many. The lockdowns that happened during the pandemic demonstrated the toll that being alone can take on an individual's mental health (Jones, 2021). It highlights the importance that others provide in terms of support, safety and comfort. Previous research has already demonstrated the importance that the support of others has on the new mother and her ability to cope with the transition and demands of early motherhood (Price, 1988; Stern, 1995; Arnold-Baker, 2015). Collins et al.'s (1993) research concluded that women who received good social support experienced a better progress through their labour. A lack of support is often one of the contributing factors of postnatal depression. The mothers' experience of others present during childbirth can also contribute to the birth being experienced as traumatic. It is therefore important for women to feel supported both in pregnancy and during the birth and postnatal period. Baptie et al.'s survey showed the need for emotional support and acknowledgement of what it had been like to be a pregnant woman during a pandemic: 'I feel there has been a lack of appreciation for how frightening these times are for pregnant women' (Baptie et al., 2020). Mothers were left feeling 'alone' 'abandoned' and 'forgotten' (ibid., 2020).

It was into this milieux that mothers faced the possibility of giving birth without their partner present to support, reassure and advocate for them, which increased the fear and anxiety.

> Devastated. Frightened. Powerless. Helpless. Shocked. I was having an elective c-section due to previous birth trauma. To have my support taken away 2 days before I went into theatre and be told I had to do it alone feels like it is the hardest thing I have ever been asked to do.
>
> (Baptie et al., 2020)

For some mothers, their partners were able to attend for the final stages of the birth and then had to leave afterwards. These moments after the birth were captured by Hall (2021:25):

> The anxious wait in lockdown, the strict rules, the Covid swabs and no visitors. The lonely hours in hospital cradling you in my arms, waiting to go home. On quiet wards with no visitors, no balloons or flowers, just spaced out beds.

The quote above shows how the overriding feelings at that time were anxiety, fear and loneliness. These experiences also led to a sense of sadness and loss. Mothers experienced the loss of the way in which they wanted to birth their babies, but also the loss of support, of being able to share their experiences with others. Becoming a mother can be challenging enough at the best of times but during the pandemic it felt much harder, with some mothers grieving the life that they once had:

> no-one told me it would be like this. After seven years of trying, eight miscarriages, countless referrals, examinations, tests and procedures. Then it happened: twins. No-one told me how sad I'd feel. To finally get what I wanted. How isolated I would be. How I grieved my old life.
>
> (Hall, 2021:40)

The sense of being isolated did not end when the mothers returned home. Although the mothers had the support of their partners, they were unable to introduce their new babies to family and friends. For some mothers who were separated from their family by a big distance this was especially difficult, particularly if they were not able to see their own mothers. The mothers were again faced with a sense of loss. They were unable to socialise with others, sharing the excitement of having a baby, but also gaining the emotional and physical support they needed:

> Sitting on the edge of the bed I catch my reflection, wet hair, at least I managed a shower. Baby in arms. Figuring it all out. No one to pop by to celebrate, to hold or even meet this tiny bundle.
>
> (Hall, 2021:33)

> My heart broke a little bit when I saw my parents "meeting" their granddaughter for the first time; a sheet of glass separating my little girl from the loving arms that I knew ached to hold her. It's not how things are supposed to be.
>
> (Hall, 2021:39)

This important ritual was not possible for many mothers, nor were other elements of being a new mother. As the weeks went past many mothers wondered how old the baby would be before they met others outside their household. Some mothers defied lockdown, but the majority followed the guidelines even though it had a detrimental effect on them. But this sadness and loss also extended to family and friends who were also missing out on meeting the new arrival.

Many of the elements that mothers who had just had a baby came to rely on, such as help with breastfeeding, health visitor appointments, baby groups, meeting other mothers at a similar stage, were all affected by lockdown. There was confusion over the restrictions – when you could exercise with another outside does that number include the baby? Similar issues arose when lockdown restrictions eased, but groups were limited to six; it meant that mothers were not able to socialise with all of their NCT group at the same time.

As the months went by mothers worried about the impact that a lack of socialisation would have on their baby. The questions mothers were concerned about were whether it would affect the baby's development. One mother described the paradox as 'I can't decide if it's worse that the world is missing out on you or you are missing out on the world' (Hall, 2021:36).

Precious time for the family

There were upsides to the lockdown. Pregnancy felt easier being locked down and working from home. There was no anxiety about trying to keep the pregnancy a secret and women were able to rest, not having to commute to a place of work every day. For those women who had had previous miscarriages, it felt safer to be at home so that, if something happened, they would be able to respond more easily. Women were able to find their own pace during their pregnancy, which enabled them to prepare for their birth.

After the birth lockdown meant the mothers' partners were more available as they were now working from home. This was also an advantage for the partners too; fathers were able to be more present, more hands on in those very early stages as they were physically available to hold, change or feed the baby in between work or meetings. There were no more commutes to get home at the end of the day and so partners were available for bathtime or bedtime. This had a huge impact on both the mother and the father. Mothers felt more supported to have their partner close by in the early months after giving birth. The fathers were able to become more involved as they were more available to share in parenting and created closer bonds with their babies. Being locked down together meant that the parents and children were able to bond with and support each other. Mothers felt less that the burden of responsibility for the baby fell on their shoulders. While mothers mourned the loss of being able to see people after the birth, it did free them from the expectations of entertaining. Mothers were able to just focus on what they needed to do without worrying about other people and, especially for first-time mothers, this was helpful to enable them to find their bearings as a new mother.

Facing the unknown

Pandemics have the effect of throwing us into the unknown. There is always an element of the unknown in life as we never know the outcome of our choices and actions or what might happen to us. But often we are able to predict or have a sense of the direction of our lives. In a pandemic this feels

impossible. Mothers felt unable to plan, whether that was a plan to get pregnant, what might happen at the birth or what the situation might be like afterwards. There was no way in which mothers felt a sense of control over their
lives. Everything seemed subject to chance. This inevitably caused a great deal
of anxiety for women. It triggered health anxiety in some women and inflex-
ibility in others who were not able to see other possibilities due to a fear of
the unknown. The future became too open, too many possibilities presented
themselves and it felt impossible for women to know what to plan for as the
situation kept changing. The work with mothers at that time was to help them
to sit with this uncertainty, and to focus on what they could control, which
was how they would be able to respond to whatever life threw at them. It
was important to help mothers to be able to recentre themselves, to ground
themselves in the present and to recognise their own personal resources and
strength.

At times of risk and isolation it is important to help clients rediscover what
makes them feel safe and how they can reach out to others when they are
feeling isolated. Facing anxiety rather than avoiding it, or getting caught up
in continuous thoughts, enabled women to also face their fears and transform
them into actions. It enabled them to feel less helpless and powerless and at
the mercy of the situation that they found themselves in. Often those mothers
seeking therapy during the pandemic had had traumatic birth experiences
where they too had felt predominately helpless and powerless. This sense of
powerlessness comes from feeling unheard, or when the situation feels out
of control, where their choices feel limited or not possible. Mothers were
encouraged to review their expectations and to hold them lightly so they
could be more flexible in light of what they might face.

Conclusion

One of the main themes to emerge during the pandemic for mothers concerned
safety and risk, of life and death and of sickness and health. Home became
the mothers' sanctuary, their safe space and somewhere that they felt in control and in charge. Outside of the home represented risk and it was into this
riskier environment that they were being asked to give birth. This was at odds
with what women needed at that time; they needed a safe and trusted environment to be able to focus totally on the process of the birth. For some women it
meant birthing without their birth partner, and this also further eroded their
sense of safety and trust. This sense of aloneness and isolation was a second
major theme of mothers' experiences of the pandemic. Motherhood can be
an isolating experience in normal circumstances, but it was made harder when
the mothers were unable to socialise with others, share their experiences and
introduce their babies to their family and friends. This led to a great deal of
loss and sadness and in some cases made the experience feel overwhelming.
The final theme was uncertainty and again this is a normal part of the

motherhood experience – particularly for first-time mothers who enter into a new realm of existence with the birth of their baby. But when this takes place in a pandemic the sense of uncertainty and the unknown becomes more acute. This led to feelings of powerlessness and helplessness in mothers, of feeling that they had little or no choice and no ability to plan. Their expectations were continually challenged. The overriding emotion at this time was anxiety which led to fear and feeling overwhelmed by the situation.

However, the experience was not all negative and it is the positive elements of the pandemic that also need to be considered in the perinatal period, which could have further implications for how we approach maternity as a society. Mothers reported feeling more relaxed working from home during pregnancy. Not having to commute removed a lot of stress for women and they were able to be both productive and physically rested. The logistics of attending appointments became easier and any issues during the pregnancy felt more manageable. After the birth, even though the mothers felt bereft at not having the support of other family members, particularly their own mothers and others, they found the continuous presence of their partner past the usual two weeks' paternity leave incredibly supportive. Not having lots of visitors after the birth actually enabled the parents to settle into life with a newborn in their own time and in their own way. For the mothers, having their partner available while they worked from home meant that they did not feel so alone and holding the whole burden of the responsibility for the baby. Partners were available to give the mothers a break during the day or to be involved at the end of the day when normally they might be commuting home. Some mothers commented on how they might not have been able to cope so well without their partner being around all the time. It was not just an advantage for the mother either; the partners also benefitted from the experience. They were able to be more involved in the early stages of their babies' lives and feel more like a co-parent from the beginning. It meant that partners bonded quickly with their baby and were able to offer emotional support to the mothers.

If we are to learn anything from the pandemic about how we respond to maternity, it is that women need more support. That if a woman is allowed to work but also physically rest it reduces her stress which will have an impact her birth experience. Recognising the importance that birth partners have in supporting women in labour is also essential and, afterwards, the ongoing support of the partner past the usual two weeks' parental leave means that both parents and baby benefit. The pandemic has also shown that working from home, where possible, is as effective as being in a place of work. The pandemic has highlighted that if mothers, and partners, are able to slow down and move into a new rhythm it will help them settle into this new mode of being. That creating a sanctuary of their home provides a supportive, safe space to ground mothers as they go through the transition that having a new baby brings. It also brings into focus how isolated mothers normally are and how little emotional support they are given at a time where they feel *not at home* in their lives. The expression 'It takes a village to raise a child' is worth considering. How has our society devalued motherhood and abandoned mothers when they are at their most vulnerable? How can we make changes that will support new parents, and that will ease their stress and isolation so that they have full capacity to raise their child? These are the urgent questions the pandemic has raised.

References

Arnold-Baker, C. (2015) How Becoming a Mother involves a Confrontation with Existence: An Existential-Phenomenological exploration of the experience of early motherhood. Doctoral thesis, Middlesex University/New School of Psychotherapy and Counselling http://eprints.mdx.ac.uk/18278/.

Arnold-Baker, C. (2020) *The Existential Crisis of Motherhood*. London: Palgrave MacMillan.

Baptie, G., Baddeley, A. and Smith, J. (2020) The Impact of Covid-19 on Women's Maternity Choices. *Make Birth Better* https://static1.squarespace.com/static/5ed8a1b746cc235b44a50be1/t/5f61f513c456f529e2d774b8/1600255254237/The+Impact+of+COVID-19+on+Women%27s+Maternity+Choices.pdf.

Collins, N.L., Dunkel-Schetter, C., Lobel, M. and Scimshaw, S.C.M. (1993) Social Support in Pregnancy: Psychosocial Correlates of Birth Outcomes and Postpartum Depression. *Journal of Personality and Social Psychology*, 65.6, 1243–1258.

Data World Bank Organisation (2019) Maternal Mortality Ration (modeled estimate, per 100,000 live births), United Kingdom. *Data World Bank Organisation* https://data.worldbank.org/indicator/SH.STA.MMRT?locations=GB [accessed 6 August 2021].

De Beauvoir, S. (1997) *The Second Sex*. London: Vintage.

Deurzen, E. van (1998) *Paradox and Passion*. Chichester: Wiley.

Deurzen, E. van (2010) *Everyday Mysteries*. London: Routledge.

Goren, E., Kulkarni, S.S. and Vongkiatkajorn, K. (2020) The *Washington Post* Asked Readers to Describe 2020 in One Word or Phrase. Here's What They Said. Washington Post www.washingtonpost.com/graphics/2020/lifestyle/2020-in-one-word/ [accessed 3 August 2021].

Hall, E. (ed.) (2021) *Born in Lockdown: 277 New Mothers. One Shared Story.* Mothership Writers.

Heidegger, M. (1962) *Being and Time*. Trans. J. Stambaugh. New York: SUNY Press.

Jones, A. (2021) 'My thoughts became poisonous': the Toll of Lockdown When You Live Alone. *The Guardian*, 20 February www.theguardian.com/lifeandstyle/2021/feb/20/my-thoughts-became-poisonous-the-toll-of-lockdown-when-you-live-alone [accessed 29 August 2021].

Milnes, S.E. (2021) Has the Pandemic Reaffirmed What Women Want From Maternity Services? *MIDRIS Midwifery Digest*, 31 March, p. 293.

Office for National Statistics (2019) www.ons.gov.uk [accessed 6 August 2021].

Parker, R. (2005) *Torn in Two: The Experience of Maternal Ambivalence*. London: Virago Press.

Price, J. (1988) *Motherhood: What It Does to Your Mind*. London: Pandora.

Prinds, C., Hvidt, N.C., Mogensen, O. and Buus, N. (2013) Making Existential Meaning in Transition to Motherhood: A Scoping Review. *Midwifery*, 30.6, 733–741. doi: 10.1016/j.midw.2013.06.021.

Rosenberg, K.R. (2012) What Makes us Human? Answers from Evolutionary Anthropology. *Evolutionary Anthropology*, 21, 182–194.

Sartre, J.-P. (1943) *Being and Nothingness*. London: Routledge.

Stern, D. (1995) *The Motherhood Constellation: A unified view of parent-infant psychotherapy*. London: Karnac Books.

Stone, A. (2019) *Being Born: Birth and Philosophy*. Oxford: Oxford University Press.

Summers, H. (2021) UK Women Forced to Wear Face Masks During Labour Charity Finds. *The Guardian*, 14 May www.theguardian.com/lifeandstyle/2021/may/14/uk-women-forced-to-wear-face-masks-during-labour-charity-finds [accessed 27 August 2021].

Yalom, I. (1980) *Existential Psychotherapy*. New York: Basic Books.

Chapter 7

Relatedness and relationships in the time of Covid-19

Luci Moja-Strasser and Michael Worrell

This chapter grew from the dialogue maintained since the start of the pandemic. We were engaged in a process of 'supervision' that included wide-ranging discussion of the context of current experience both professional and personal. Our chapter is written as an aspect of our ongoing discussion, necessarily incomplete, the writing of which folded into and arose from this dialogue. Our conversations throughout this time were conducted over zoom, less due to the pandemic, and more to do with the fact that Lucia lives in France and Michael in London.

Luci

We all have a story to tell about our experiences of the pandemic and lock-down. The memories of these experiences that we recall in the now, in the present moment, are a recollection of these experiences. These recollections represent with more or less accuracy how they related to these events and experiences. All is about relatedness.

From an existential perspective, we are not fixed, and neither is our memory. We are in constant flux: 'Those who step into the same river, have different waters flowing ever upon them' (Heraclitus para. 12, trans. Freeman, 1962). The world is in constant change. The world is one unified whole (the river), which is constant. Here is the paradox; our mind has the ability to change throughout our lifetime. It is the basis of all adaptation, memory, learning and unlearning. In the case of a traumatic experience, which was the case for many people during the first lockdown, the plasticity of the memory was a very useful tool. The ability to remember and to forget, is what makes us human. However, certain emotions being so strong, the recollection of these events remains very vivid and might appear as fixed.

The president of France announced solemnly one day, during the first lock-down, that "We are at war with the Covid 19 virus!" On many peoples' mind was the question: How can we be at war with 'an invisible' and unknown enemy, the origin of which appears to be so full of contradictions? Here we are, pure science fiction.

DOI: 10.4324/9781003255765-10

The next thing we were communicated was that 'We have to live with the virus!' The suggestion as to having to live with the virus, was not very long lived. We were very soon after showered by a great number of restrictions that sometimes were very conflicting in themselves, such as being allowed to leave our home only under very strict control, not further away than a 1 km area. Parks were all closed. Going outside, we could be often stopped by the police and checked if we had in our possession our identity cards plus, more importantly, a document created by the Internal Ministry that we had to fill in every single day if we were leaving our domicile, with information about our name, date and place of birth, our present address and the reason for going out. The form had five boxes with acceptable reasons for leaving home. Only one of them could be ticked: visit to the doctor; going to the chemist; buying essential food; seeing a therapist; or going to certain working places.

People who had a dog, or those who were doing some physical exercise, were privileged: it meant still the restricted 1 km area, but on top of the one hour allowed. The form had to be signed and dated and marked with the exact time of leaving home. The curfew in the first three months started at 7 pm; after those few months it was prolonged to 9 pm. Some people who lived during World War II were saying that the document we had to carry reminded them of what it was like living during Nazi occupation.

Forced to be locked down and isolated in France, I wonder Michael, what was your story of the lockdown?

Michael

I find that now quite hard to recapture. It is all entwined with my experi-ence of separating from a long-term relationship and quite soon moving to live alone. I find it hard to describe the lockdown in a way separated from this very personal and unique experience of relationship breakdown and separation. I recall withdrawing and isolating myself even further than that dictated by the government. At the same time, I experienced myself as also part of this worldwide occurrence that we were all thrown into. The image that stays with me most is of deserted London streets. Oxford Circus com-pletely empty. I continued to do some face-to-face therapeutic work in the city, partly out of necessity and where psychotherapy was arguably seen as an 'essential service'. I travelled through the public transport system with my NHS ID as well as a letter from my health trust certifying that I was a 'key worker'. I was never once asked for these documents.

Isolation

I managed to catch Covid-19 fairly early, but late enough into the pan-demic that I had a clear suspicion of what the sudden rising temperature I experienced might mean. An individualised rapid global warming throwing my precariously balanced weather system into chaos. Testing was not available at this time, but I immediately removed myself to a bedroom and closed the door and did not emerge for a week. The sudden experience of being isolated, of being sent to isolation and ethically required to isolate, was unnerving. It was short-lived since everyone else in my household developed Covid-19 shortly after, meaning that the isolation was suddenly unnecessary. Both my children developed Covid-19 symptoms. They both had a high temperature but seemingly were able to shrug this off in about 30 minutes with no loss of essential service to computer gaming. As I think of this time now, I also recollect the scraping, scratching sensations in my chest and the sense of heaviness and lethargy as well as the creepy experience of feeling like there was a definite inhuman 'other' that had invaded my physical-psychological being, at that time somehow visualised as something to do with a wretched, malevolent, diseased bat.

During my short time of isolation, I deluded myself into thinking that I had the opportunity for reflection. Perhaps virally compromised, I also experienced the strange sense of 'fellow feeling' towards a well-known British politician who seemingly had developed Covid-19 at the same time as I did. I followed his condition in the media and noted that he was sent to hospital at the same moment that my own symptoms temporarily worsened, and I experienced a brief experience of anxiety and concern that I perhaps may become very unwell. This politician is an individual whose views and general demeanour is normally one that would lead me to engage in such grumpy middle-aged man behaviours such as shouting at the TV. And yet here I was experiencing a sense of concern and compassion toward this individual who I would usually regard as the most complete embodiment of absurdity, inauthenticity, and bad faith (I suspect psychoanalysis has better insults than existential therapy?). What on earth was wrong with me?

Luci

Covid-19 and the subsequent lockdowns imposed on us, not just illness, but various restrictions that disrupted life as we were used to it, we had come to consider to be 'normal'. The normal became what we had to live with in the moment and accept it as such. Several of my clients asked the question, when are we going to go back to normal? It was difficult for some of them to accept the thought, what if there is no way back and we have to accept this, as being the 'normal' … what then? This made some of my clients angry or anxious. Only a few could see that maybe, in that moment, there is no way but to go with the flow that has been imposed on all of us.

One of my clients, who was terribly affected and traumatised by the lockdown, had had suicidal ideation, but never expressed this openly. She asked me one day: "What is the purpose of living on earth, under these conditions?" I responded to her: "This is a very provocative question. Let us look at it together. What purpose could you give to this life? But before that, can you tell me, where else, besides this earth, you could be living?"

The biggest factor in reclaiming our health and our lives remains connection, despite all that was trying to prevent this. Personally, the lockdown deprived me of feeding my heart, my cells, my brain, and my soul, with the care, the love, the fresh air, the nutrients, the movement that it takes to truly thrive.

Every day I have a choice to open my heart to the world and to other people; to care enough to also take care of ourselves. It is always a risk to open my heart, as I can fail and be hurt. It is noticeable that some people hide from the world and others. When one lives alone, the confinement is the ideal opportunity to hide from the world and others and, as a result, fall into depression.

I found the means to nourish my soul and not to lose my sanity. I found two ways of doing this. One was by starting practising Qigong online, for approximately ten hours a week. This opened new doors for me, as each moment could be an opportunity to increase my wisdom, in the sense Jaspers (1951) talks about practising philosophy. Qigong is a philosophy of life, which is not about possessing knowledge, but becoming 'A true lover of wisdom, who is in search of knowledge as opposed to someone who considers himself wise, in possession of knowledge' (Jaspers, 1951:12).

The other way was that I decided to benefit from the 'free time' and returned to regularly practising the piano, three to four hours a day. It is a paradox that with the lockdown we lost our freedom; at the same time, I had more time to invest in something that really mattered to me.

We are all looking for belonging. Seeking truth and spirituality. Great energy supporting creativity! Self-love has transformative powers. The more I love myself, the more my intuition can become stronger; intuition which is vital in any creative process, including music and to a large extent therapy.

Michael

'All is about relation' as you say! Our written dialogue here is a result of an ongoing weekly dialogue we have had via Zoom since the start of the pandemic. I must remind us both, however, that this dialogue also arises from and is a continuation of the dialogue we had face to face over 20 years ago now, when you were my supervisor during my existential therapy training. As I think you would remind me, the past is always an aspect of the present situation. My seeking you out at this time was at least in part an attempt on my part to 'refind' and 're-search' my own relation to existential therapy at a time where I felt very much at sea and disconnected. I was drawn to speaking to you as someone I had experienced as being very 'rigorous' (maybe also a bit strict and scary?) in the application of phenomenology. I felt I wanted to re-experience this challenge and to think through the implications of this for my practice, of couple and relationship therapy. Of course, one cannot really re-experience anything and I have found I found it both encouraging and deeply therapeutic that, in addition to the expected phenomenological rigour, you have brought to our conversations both compassion and a delightful irreverence and humour. 'Heidegger-schmeidegger!' has become an essential liberating conception for me over these months.

Luci

My experience of working with you, Michael, really has taught me a lot and enriched my way of supervising, as I felt that your openness, humanity and warmth was an example that gave me a new dimension onto what it really means to have a meaningful supervisory relationship.

Michael

I too kept some hold on sanity and worked against my isolation through starting to offer Zoom karate classes to kids and adults. Martial arts training has been part of my life for years and the lack of going to train with people has been something that I have found hard to tolerate. I am embarrassed to recall it! Am I so shallow? I felt enraged about not being able to go to the gym and not being able to train martial arts! So, I offered twice weekly Zoom classes from my lounge room. To keep the younger members of the club engaged, this soon evolved into story-telling competitions and drawing – the usual rather stern martial arts attitude slipping a bit in favour of some humour and warmth. All of this was at the expense of one of the other instructors, particularly known for his sternness and shouting, suddenly transformed into a superhero who has many odd weekly adventures. This went on for a year, before we eventually, slowly, and cautiously resumed training face to face. We are now shouting at one another and throwing punches rather than telling the strange tales of 'Sensei L'.

Relatedness

This fundamental principle of relatedness is at the heart of what we try to 'attend to' as existential therapists and supervisors. Recently, there have been some challenges to this emphasis on relatedness, with the suggestion that this has become dogmatic and somehow covers over the experience of difference, individuality and aloneness (Bazzano, 2021). Personally, I remain unconvinced by this challenge. However, this pandemic, and the imposition of repeated 'lockdowns' and 'social distancing', if anything seems to highlight the existential dilemmas of relation–separation, connection–withdrawal in a highly stark, anxiety-provoking fashion. As a global 'limit situation' how could it do otherwise? Jaspers defined 'limit situations' as being unavoidable 'essential situations' that arise from finite human existence. In limit situations, according to Jaspers:

> Everything is in flux, in a restless movement of being questioned; every-
> thing is relative, finite, split into opposites; never the whole; the absolute;
> the essential. We cannot bear the stark confrontation with the limit-situ-
> ations; therefore, they almost never enter into our living experience in
> total clarity.
>
> (Jaspers, quoted in Friedman, 1964:100)

The very existence of the virus and its manner of spread arises from our relatedness to others and our relatedness to nature and the world. And our response of withdrawal, lockdown and distancing serves to highlight our equally fundamental experience of separateness, uniqueness and aloneness. In the early days of the pandemic, this was frequently rather comically brought home to me by the experience of seeing someone, who on initial glance looked frail or unathletic, manage a form of 'backwards long jump' in response to my unexpected, unwelcome and potentially contaminating presence.

While, following Spinelli (2015), the experience of being separate, isolated and at a distance can be best understood as being grounded in and arising from a more fundamental 'relatedness', an 'ontological' aspect of being, at an 'ontic' level, the way that I have experienced this global boundary situation is the way in which 'I' experience this, reflective of the unique context in which I find my existence.

Virtual relatedness

Luci, what has been your experience of relating via the mediation of the internet?

Luci

I will try to briefly respond to your question. Basically, I do not think that there is an essential difference between working in person, face to face, or working on Skype or Zoom. What leads me to believe that? I have been living and working in Paris for the last 11 years. Most of my clients were not living in France. One could say that maybe I got accustomed to this way of working. Obviously, that is possible, but I would not accept that habit is the decisive factor in my interactions with my clients. It would be a very simplistic way of trying to understand my work.

As I do both, working face to face as well as working on Skype or Zoom, I would like to emphasise that in either situation what remains the focus is the person or persons who are in front of me. At the ontological level, at the ground of our being, what emerges is care, which represents our attitude towards the world and our clients. For me, in any therapeutic encounter, be it face to face or virtual, what is essential is presence and what and how we, my client and me, convey meaning to one another. Schneider also asserts that: 'Presence informs the therapeutic alliance, through the communication of attention, concern, support and availability' (Schneider, 2015:305).

I do not know if this answers your question. Sometimes I have more appreciative feedback from my online work than from those I meet face to face.

Michael

My experience has been that the sense of relatedness as well as of separation, aloneness and distance has been accentuated. This question of 'remote' therapy and 'virtual' sessions seemingly points towards a sense of distance and disconnection, a sense of the virtual as not being 'real'. I must confess that, in addition to my maintenance of a hostile stance towards the appearance of certain politicians on TV, I have maintained a sceptical stance towards the possibilities of online therapy, seeing this as in important respects inferior to and a poor substitute for 'real' embodied face-to-face therapy.

I have now conducted a lot of therapy via online platforms, as well as conducting all-day workshops and supervision in the same way. Speaking to many of my colleagues I have noted that they too have experienced this form of therapy as both meaningful and whatever one might mean by terms like 'effective'. During sessions I have often been struck by how intense the dialogue seems and how affected I have been by what has occurred. This is seemingly enhanced by the fact that I am presented with a constant 'close up' of my client's face throughout the session in a way that is not the case in face-to-face therapy. I have learnt to switch off my 'self-view' so as not to be distracted by the uncanny appearance of me watching and listening to me looking at and listening to the client. I note that some of my clients do not do this and seem often to look at their own image as they are speaking to me. I recall one of our sessions, a session where our dialogue became more 'therapeutic' than 'supervisory' in nature and in which you commented that I had not been looking at you for a while. I was very much aware of this in our session and yet afterwards I thought 'but was there the actual possibility to look at you?' I was looking at a screen as were you. We were in a dialogue made possible via 'digital representations' of ourselves. And yet the conversation was real and dire.

Many of my clients have remarked that they find the online therapy sessions meaningful and important and much to be preferred to making the time to come in to face-to-face therapy. I am now doing both face-to-face and online therapy and have clients who switch from one to the other and back again as contingencies change. As much as the online platforms appear to offer new possibilities, I am also acutely aware of what is lost. I am interested in your experience of how sessions end? I have noted that many of my clients have adjusted how they start the sessions, allowing themselves some settling in via adjustments to the image and sound and furniture. The end of sessions, however, often seems very abrupt. The face-to-face experience of getting up off the chair, moving with the client to the door of the therapy room, perhaps pausing a while silently before sitting to reflect, all of this is missing and instead the session is 'switched off' and Zoom asks me to 'rate my experience'. I too am suddenly present again to the room in which I am sitting alone, the client's presence fading much more swiftly than had the session been a face-to-face one. The 'trace' of the session somehow fainter. I can no longer smell my clients! A therapeutic anosmia.

Couple relationships

> Happy families are all alike; each unhappy family is unhappy in its own way.
>
> (Tolstoy, *Anna Karenina*)

Luci, one of the issues that lead me to seek out your wisdom was that of couple therapy. I know you have an interest in working with couples phenomenologically and I have developed a practice over the past ten years in which I see couples. I have found the demand for couple therapy to have greatly increased during the pandemic.

The first issue is again that of delivering couple therapy online. This has at times felt more like a digital home visit. I have felt invited into the couples' environment in a way not possible when couples come to the therapy room. This has been at times hilarious and at times troubling. I have become very interested in how the couple will choose to set up the online session, where they will sit and how. Nothing new for systemic family therapists in this but much greater degrees of freedom for the couple it seems. I am aware that various bits of guidance have been put out about how to help clients set up online sessions to ensure confidentiality and safety. While not wishing in any way to dismiss these concerns and guidelines, I have also found that there is value in just seeing what the couple themselves will do. As a result, I have had one couple set up the session such that when I 'tuned in' I was apparently seated at the dinner table as they were having pizza and red wine. I felt that if I just reached forward I could take a slice of pizza.

Luci

I would have been reaching out for a glass of wine!

Michael

As I had previously worked with this couple face to face for many sessions, I felt the freedom just to laugh out loud and mime reaching for the pizza. This couple later repositioned their laptop so that they were seated on a sofa. Unfortunately, the laptop fell and, as I was concentrating intently on the screen, I had the distinct experience that I was falling and spinning! Very unnerving! A recent couple chose to have their session in bed, fully clothed but sitting up in bed. At this point I felt the need to go and find those guidelines but was interrupted by their dog who ran straight towards the male partner and gave him a black eye with his nose. These sessions have felt extraordinarily real if very much less under my control! Some couples, certainly the ones who are more in distress, have chosen to have their session using two separate devices, even if they are in the same house – their separateness and conflict expressed in the need to have the added space of having a couple therapy conducted three ways virtually. In each of these cases I was aware that I could have possibly provided 'more structure', giving guidelines for where and how the session can be set up. And yet it seemed to me that something would be lost by too much structure, especially since we are dealing with the artificial limitations and structure of the online platform.

The pandemic and lockdowns have also affected couple relationships in myriad ways. I have had couples, who I previously saw face to face, who were in bitter, ongoing and, seemingly, intractable conflict, contact me to say they no longer needed sessions. Wondering whether the lockdown had exacerbated their difficulties to breaking point, I have instead been informed that lockdown has improved things greatly; the sources of conflict have been removed and the relationship is experienced as much richer and rewarding!

Other couples have entered therapy due to the direct impact of the pandemic. This has included couples where one partner has been hospitalised and ventilated and where the other has also been highly traumatised by the experience – isolation, uncertainty and the possibility of loss bearing down upon them while they anxiously awaited by the telephone for daily updates from nursing staff. Once the ill partner has recovered, there have been sessions exploring the change in role dynamics, self-identity and hopes, fears and anxieties about the future as well as the impact of 'long Covid' and the high level of uncertainty that this entails.

Still other couples could be characterised as 'lockdown couples'. This is where the relationship was at its very early stages and where a decision had to be made: do we not now see each other for however long or do we make the decision to move in together and see what we can make of this? Clearly, I have gotten to see the couples where at least one of them has felt that the decision made in haste has led to a range of unforeseen and unwanted relational consequences. In one of these situations, the couple sessions did not go ahead and instead one of the individuals chose to see me in her car in the underground car park where she lived. The impression gained here was one of great distance. I felt that the client could have been in the Middle East some-where, with the possibility of armed conflict going on outside the car park. Several days later I looked out my lounge room window only to see this client walking along the street … where am I again?

What are your views and experience of this Luci?

Luci

The pandemic has affected all strata of society and relationships, couple relationships not an exception. From the examples you gave above – couples who are not willing to face up to their difficulties and try to resolve them – then anything is a good excuse to opt for ending the relationship and to run away. Working with individual clients or couples, it is important to having clear boundaries and a framework that the clients need to be informed about at the start of the relationship. Accept them and agree with them. Of course, nothing ought to be rigid and each situation needs to be taken into consideration.

You Michael, the therapist, you need yourself to agree, but not only with your head but also with your heart! You need to feel at ease and clear about what you demand and what you cannot compromise on. Some people like your clients who had their pizzas and red wine in your presence, I think they have stepped over the boundaries, but you might think it was OK. This is what I meant when I say you need to know where you can or cannot com-promise with their behaviour even when they step over the mark. From a phe-nomenological perspective everything can be explored, either in the session with you clients or in your individual supervision.

Michael

Luci, wonderful! As always in the times when our conversation could be understood as supervision, you manage both to support, encourage and challenge me, all in the same moment! I guess I am not all that clear as to whether I felt comfortable or whether in fact feeling uncomfortable was in some way important and challenging in these situations. I hope the people who have chosen to read our conversation, now to be temporarily interrupted and yet also continued, will have gained something, even if that has been to disagree with everything we have said! Right now, here in the UK, lockdown is officially over. We are in incredibly uncertain times. Walking around outside it seems as if half the people are wearing masks and are acting cautiously and the others are acting as if all is now 'normal'. I, for one, find myself now more uncertain than I was when we were in a clear lockdown.

Conclusion

Existential phenomenological psychotherapy is a philosophical practice. We both adhere to this practice, though we might be influenced by other ways of thinking about therapy. Phenomenology is the basis of working with our clients. The lived experience of human beings invites for a form of qualitative enquiry that focusses on how the phenomena is experienced at the time it occurs. Our dialogues allowed both of us to stay with our respective experiences without trying to interpret them or impose our own assumptions and values on the experiences presented. It is for the reader to ascertain if that was so. Listening, which is the key for dialogue, was what allowed for our respective narratives to unfold.

To finish, we would like to share with you the wisdom that comes from Pyrrho of Ellis, a pre-Socratic philosopher, who was the founder of ancient Scepticism. He is drawing our attention to some very important points for reflection (Moja-Strasser, 2016:51):

1.   Approach the phenomena undogmatically.
2.   Human senses do not give us truth or lies.
3.   We can know things only as They appear to us, not as They are.

References

Bazzano, M. (2021) *Re-visioning Existential Therapy: Counter-traditional perspectives*. London: Routledge.

Freeman, K. (1962) *Heraclitus of Ephesus Fragments in Ancilla to the Pre-Socratic Philosophers*. Oxford: Basil Blackwell.

Friedman, M. (ed.) (1964) *The Worlds of Existentialism: A Critical Reader*. London: Random House.

Jaspers, K. (1951) *Way to Wisdom*. Chelsea: Book Crafters.

Moja-Strasser, L. (2016) Considering the Epoche as an Attitude Rather Than a Method. *Existential Analysis*, 27.1.

Schneider, K. (2015) Presence: The Core Contextual Factor of Effective Psychotherapy. *Existential Analysis*, 26.2, 304–312.

Spinelli, E. (2015) *Practicing Existential Therapy: The Relational World*. 2nd edn. London: Sage.

Chapter 8

Existential resilience and Covid-19

What existential coaching can offer

Yannick Jacob

It often takes what Jaspers (1919) refers to as a 'boundary situation' – a time during which we are forced to acknowledge uncomfortable truths about life as we find ourselves faced with something no longer deniable – to bring us back to seeing the world how it is rather than how we would like it to be. The outbreak of SARS-CoV-2 in 2019 and its subsequent pandemic in the years 2020 and 2021 is such a boundary situation on a global scale. It reminded us that endings, change, absurdity, paradox, dilemma, and other existential themes are existential givens, inescapable aspects of the human condition, weaved into the fabric of the human experience.

The big questions and how they emerged during Covid-19

As learnt from previous chapters, existential philosophers have long used philosophical methods of inquiry to explore questions concerning our existence and human lived experience. Wong (2010) proposed six dimensions of existential questions, many of which surfaced during this pandemic and subsequently found their way into the spaces that coaches create to help their clients navigate their lives and careers.

1. Who am I? What defines me? Who am I when everything is stripped away from me, and I am reduced to a naked lonely soul? Is there anything unique and special about me?
2. How can I be happy? Why am I bored? Why am I so dissatisfied with life? What is the good life? Why is happiness so elusive? Is this all there is to life?
3. What should I do with my life? How should I then live? How could I live in a way that my life counts for something? What is my calling? To what should I devote the rest of my life?
4. How do I make the right choices? How do I know that I am making the right decision regarding career and relationships? How can I tell right

DOI: 10.4324/9781003255765-11

from wrong? What do I know what is the responsible thing to do in complex situations with conflicting moral demands?

5. Where do I belong? Why do I feel so alone in this world? Why do I not feel at home on this planet earth? Where is my home? Where do I belong? How can I develop deep and meaningful relationships? Where can I find acceptance?
6. What is the point of striving when life is so short? Why should I struggle to survive when life is transient and fragile? What is the point of building something only to see it swallowed up by death? (Wong, 2010:2)

The nature of existential questions is that there are no universal answers, if answers at all, and this uncertainty, together with the paradoxes and dilemmas they often reveal, can cause anxiety.

Coming face-to-face with existence: CoViD-19 as a boundary situation

Covid-19 and its global impact highlighted our connectedness with others. Whole countries mandated their citizens to not leave their homes unless necessary, health care systems were overwhelmed, economies tanked, entire industries collapsed, and many people lost loved ones to the virus. Many existential themes suddenly became prevalent, and it was impossible for most not to acknowledge them. Among them were death, endings, isolation, (lack of) freedom, the collapse of meaning structures used to hold our lives and careers in place, as well as absurdity in the face of trying to make sense of the emergence and subsequent global consequences of this virus.

While some were thrown into the midst of the crisis and found themselves busy fighting to survive or helping others survive, others were forced to pause as they locked down, socially distant, not being able to work or engage in social interactions, often with more time on their hands than they knew what to do with and faced with many of the thoughts and questions that they had previously distracted themselves from by means of working, socialising or other events now unavailable to them. Many relationships suffered due to a growing divide exacerbated by political views, misinformation, conspiracy theories, and opinions on the safety and necessity of vaccinations. Whether people had to take urgent action facing the crisis head-on or were stuck at home, existential themes revealed themselves powerfully, and those who had previously come to terms with the fragility of life, and perhaps even embraced some of its givens, were the ones who adapted much more quickly to 'the new normal'.

Resilience

Resilience has been a buzzword in the psychological literature for some time and, with the emergence of positive psychology in 1999 as a branch of science dedicated to producing empirical data on what is *right* with people and hence focusing research efforts on the topic of resilience, we have learned a great deal about this important concept.

Resilience constitutes the ability to adjust to change and bounce back from misfortune or adversity. It has been defined by the American Psychological Association (APA) as '[t]he process of adapting well in the face of adversity, trauma, tragedy, threats and even significant sources of stress, such as family and relationship problems, serious health problems, or workplace and financial stresses' (APA, 2021). The business standards company BS 65000 conceptualised resilience as 'the ability to anticipate, prepare for, respond and adapt to events – both sudden shocks and gradual change. That means being adaptable, competitive, agile and robust' (BS 65000, 2014). Both definitions highlight that resilience can be acquired.

In physics, resilience points to 'the capability of a strained body to recover its size and shape after deformation caused especially by compressive stress' (Merriam-Webster, 2021b) and is often seen as a quality, given that materials are not prone to the kind of change we can produce in human beings. This means that while in the world of physics resilience tends to be a given, people can learn to be resilient, either as a coping strategy to learn and apply in times of crisis, or as a skill set to be acquired in anticipation of future adversity. In the psychological literature too, we can find evidence pointing towards resilience as a trait (Leys et al., 2018). We may conclude that part of what makes people resilient is a skill set that can be acquired and part is due to personality traits and biological factors. This argument can be extended to existential resilience. Recommended resources for learning more about resilience are Waldman & Jackson (2017) and Ungar (2020).

Existential resilience

In considering existential resilience it helps to distinguish between different levels of adversity as to carve out why and how *existential* resilience comes into play. Given that existential themes and questions concern all human beings and that sooner or later we will all have to face them, everybody benefits from fostering existential resilience. The earlier we accept and come to terms with them, the less shocked, surprised or unprepared we will find ourselves when they come to the fore.

Adversity has been defined as 'a state or instance of serious or continued difficulty or misfortune' (Merriam-Webster, 2021a). Commonly this may refer to losing a job, partner, ill health, or continued challenges with relationships or performing at work. Existential resilience kicks in when existential themes are at the root of the adversity. To illustrate, being made redundant can be a painful experience as we may be concerned about our financial situation, social status or struggling to find a new job at the same or higher level in a crowded and competitive work environment.

Existentially, losing a job may represent a significant ending, which may shake the foundations of our relationship with endings in general, sweep the proverbial rug from underneath our assumed solid professional structure that had provided a clear path, provided meaning in our life and a network of social relations, many of which tend to dissipate when leaving a work-place. As a result, we may not just lose a job, but the belief that we are safe in our professional structure, faced with the reality that endings may come suddenly and unexpectedly. 'What else might end suddenly?', one might ask, falling deeper into uncertainty, expanding the impact of this event onto other structures that had previously felt solid.

The fallout from the Covid-19 pandemic showed us that relationships that seemed solid may crumble when circumstances change drastically, that families, well-established companies, even entire industries, can find them-selves struggling to survive within a couple of months due to unforeseen circumstances. We tend to live comforted by the illusions that we are safe and sound, shielded by what we have built, often over several decades, not wanting to consider the possibility that ecosystems are fragile and even the soundest structure may crumble under certain pressures or when even a single small part is being disabled or removed. Facing this reality is uncomfortable and causes anxiety. Avoiding acknowledging such possibilities can help us to feel much better, but only until such a possibility turns into a reality, at which point we may need some time to process and adapt to the new situation. An existentially resilient person will have come to terms with such possibilities, perhaps even embrace them as the kind of fact that adds to the excitement that life brings. They will have a healthy relationship with the uncertainty of living, acknowledging but not dwelling on the anxiety that such an awareness produces.

This applies to all the existential themes, and our existential resilience may be triggered into action by seemingly insignificant reminders of our human condition or the sudden collapse of several important structures at the same time as commonly experienced during an existential crisis.

Seven assumptions underlying existential resilience

Existential resilience is hence based on several assumptions that help to dif-ferentiate it from resilience in the context of more general challenges. Vos (2015:62) lists the following six:

1. **The 'existential givens' are universal.**
    All human beings can experience 'universal givens of existence' such as freedom of choice and inevitably facing limitations and challenges in life.
2. **They show up in everyday life and evoke symptoms.**
    Individuals can immediately experience these givens in their daily life, but this awareness often evokes existential moods, such as death anxiety,

existential guilt, isolation, urgency, nausea, absurdity, boredom, and meaninglessness.

3.   **Denial and avoidance protect us from such feelings. Becoming aware can be a shock.**

Individuals often defend themselves against these givens and moods, via denial and avoidance; however, they also have the ability to become aware of the fact that they are denying and avoiding these existential givens; this awareness often comes as a shock when a traumatic undeniable event happens like 9/11 or facing a cancer diagnosis.

4.   **Denial and avoidance due to our need for meaning, certainty, structure and autonomy.**

The denial and avoidance of the existential givens and moods seems driven by existential needs, such as the human needs for meaning, certainty, structure and freedom in life.

5.   **We can learn to accept the givens and hold the paradox of living.**

Depending on their existential skills and life experiences, individuals can learn to accept life's adversities and uncertainties, and to develop a dual awareness of both the need for denial/avoidance and the given reality of life's challenges.

6.   **Lack of adequate coping strategies leads to distress, pathology and need for therapy.**

Distress, psychopathology and a wish for professional help are often the result of ineffective existential coping styles, such as rigidly denying the existential givens, moods and defence mechanisms. For instance, the need for psychotherapeutic help in cancer patients can be explained by their underlying existential needs and skills. The same arguably applies to professional help such as coaching.

The author of this chapter proposes a seventh assumption:

7.   **We can learn to embrace our existential givens.**

We can go beyond accepting the existential givens and embrace them as 'the stuff that makes life worth living', the significance in the stories we tell, and the essence of what makes us 'human'.

This important seventh assumption opens the doors towards working to not just increase existential resilience, but working towards better wellbeing, life satisfaction and happiness in the face of the existential givens and other types of adversity. Developing a growth mindset (Dweck, 2006) with regards to existential challenges, and an appreciation that they are not just inevitable, but a distinctly and characteristically human aspect of our existence, may help us to transcend some of our suffering by repositioning ourselves towards the givens and hence changing our relationship with existential anxiety from something to be avoided at all costs, to a meaningful human experience. Once embraced, an encounter with our human condition through the existential givens will still elicit anxiety, but our new relationship with this experience allows us to reassess it as part of being human, a feeling that constitutes aliveness, in relation to which we may evaluate times of bliss, perhaps even a teacher that points us towards something important, and hence we may appreciate and value the feeling instead of suppressing or distracting ourselves from it.

Practical ways to foster existential resilience

There are numerous ways in which we may nurture existential resilience across several levels and which coaches may use as a framework for working with clients both during and post-pandemic. The following section aims to introduce a few of them.

Level 1: Drawing resources from past crises and finding meaning in suffering

An excellent foundation for existential resilience is to explore times of adversity and existential crises from the past and to look out for signs of post-traumatic growth (PTG; Tedeschi & Calhoun, 1995; Calhoun & Tedeschi, 2006). The five dimensions of PTG are:

- embracing new opportunities – both at the personal and the professional front
- improved personal relationships and increased pleasure from being around people we love
- a heightened sense of gratitude toward life altogether
- greater spiritual connection
- increased emotional strength and resilience.

In a coaching setting, we may invite our client to share a story of how they have risen from an (existential) crisis. Individually we may think back to such a time, write about it, or tell it to a friend. What we are listening out for, wanting to identify and bring into our awareness are aspects of the story that point towards elements of growth following adversity. From an existential perspective we may add:

- a stronger and more authentic sense of identity
- a more solid, yet flexible, worldview and set of beliefs of how the world functions
- an appreciation that life can be fragile but also that we have the resources to rise from crisis
- an understanding that life and living operate in waves and that ebb and flow are part of existence's weather conditions, which can be quite extreme at times

- a clearer picture of our ideology, values, personal philosophy and deep-seated beliefs
- a broader perspective on life and existence in general and our place in it
- a clearer sense of purpose and what provides meaning to one's existence.

Bringing into awareness that we have, in the past, emerged from challenging situations stronger than we were before and that indeed that 'what does not kill me makes me stronger' (Nietzsche, 1889:8), can provide solace in times of crisis and act as a reminder that we may have more resources to deal with crisis than we may have recognised. This forms the basis of a narrative that is positive, constructive and meaningful and can help us move through the next crisis, rather than becoming paralysed. 'We must imagine Sisyphus happy', writes Camus (1955:123) about the seemingly meaningless struggle of a man condemned to repeat the same task over and over again. We recognise that the struggle itself offers meaning to our existence and that, once we find value in engaging with whatever life throws at us, we can find ourselves content even during times of hard work or even suffering.

Level 2: Recognising existential themes in everyday living

Reminders that death, meaninglessness, isolation and freedom are part of the fabric of existence are all around us – if we pay attention to them. If we can acknowledge and accept the givens when they reveal themselves in smaller scale and with some discomfort, we will be better prepared when they come in larger sizes and with heavier impact. If we instead distract ourselves, push them out of our awareness, or look the other way, we will be unprepared and shocked once we can no longer ignore them. All major existential themes regularly make themselves known in our day-to-day existence.

Endings are everywhere. Nothing in life lasts. People are always in the process of becoming. Change is inevitable and necessarily involves the end of what was. Relationships end. Work projects end. Weekends, meetings, books and movies end. Various *dead*lines are looming over us. Birthdays mark that we get older. Our phone batteries die. All of these act to remind us of temporality and that, sooner or later, we too will die, and our embodied human experience will end, regardless of whether or not one believes in any form of afterlife. Every such reminder, uncomfortable as it may be, is an opportunity to welcome this fact into our awareness. Having come to terms with the small and seemingly insignificant endings, we are more likely to have made our peace with the concept of endings, and hence less likely to be thrown when encountering larger-scale endings down the road.

Absurdity is a regular occurrence as we navigate our lives and careers. A boss, parent or teacher may pass on senseless tasks. We watch the news, and the world seems chaotic. We might be in a job that feels devoid of all meaning. We see history repeating itself and no one seems to learn. The 'other side' of the political spectrum seems blind to the realities of the world which are so obvious to us. We invest years, even decades, into raising children, nurturing relationships, or building businesses, only to see them end in the shortest amount of time. People invest time in the weirdest of hobbies for no apparent reason. Humour thrives on absurdity, and we laugh to mask our discomfort with the concept. If we accept, even embrace, the fact that meaninglessness and absurdity are part of our existence as it presents itself gently and without the stakes being very high for us, we might not be so surprised when there comes a time something happens that we just cannot wrap our heads around. If we entertain the idea that some things might not make any sense, then it will be much easier to consider not having to make sense of all things all the time, and to be more at ease during a time adversity hits us for no apparent reason.

Existential isolation points to the fact that nobody can truly understand what it is like to be you. As much as we try to let other people in on our experience, our thoughts and emotions, nobody can really understand what we are going through, even if they had experienced something similar. Human beings are simply too complex and unique. Every time we are misunderstood, or someone assumes about what is going on for us, it is a reminder of this fact. Every instance of interpersonal conflict demonstrates that others are different and that, existentially, we are alone in the world. It is easy to ignore or suppress the bigger picture when such differences are not grave and do not cause much discomfort; but recognising the small differences and misunderstandings as symptoms of our existential isolation prepares us for facing times where we feel completely alone and misunderstood by the world.

Freedom tends to be valued and desired by people. It is commonly attributed to autonomy, a key pillar of psychological wellbeing (Ryff & Keyes, 1995). Existentially, however, freedom carries a dizzying quality as every choice we make excludes other possibilities, often with no way of knowing whether the choices we make are the 'right' ones or what would have happened if we chose differently. Every choice, no matter how big or small, carries this fact. When we tune into our experience closely, we may recognise the anxiety that accompanies our choices. To illustrate, some people despair over their restaurant menus, others over decisions about their next mobile phone, or trying to pick the best cereal in the supermarket, or what to wear to a party. When the choices seem small and insignificant, it is easy to suppress or distract ourselves from feeling uncomfortable in the face of the inherent uncertainty regarding the implications of our actions. But choosing to recognise that every choice has the potential to alter our lives forever, and that we can never be 100% certain about the outcome, will prepare us for making important decisions with more ease, and provide a level of comfort when things do not work out as we wish they had. It can of course be comforting to tell ourselves that we did not have a choice in the matter and hence to push responsibility away from us. But taking responsibility (the inevitable flip side of freedom) for our involvement, not only when things have worked out well, is a crucial foundation for taking ownership of our actions (or lack thereof).

A few practical steps can help us recognise existential themes in everyday life and at times of crisis.

- Engaging with stories that highlight the challenges of being human. Most great stories highlight the big themes, but many pieces of art and culture shine a light on the 'everyday mysteries' (van Deurzen, 1997)
- Meditating, particularly the type of meditation during which we sit in silence and the aim is to simply 'be there' (German: *da sein*), is an ideal way to get a taste of what emerges from your existential depths. Sitting with our thoughts and feelings without distracting ourselves allows the existential discomfort to surface, but in a relatively controlled environment. It allows us to face the experience that often emerges during particularly existential moments in our life, but without the urgency of a crisis. Consider it inviting existential anxiety over for tea, to encounter each other in a relaxed environment.
- Noticing language that points to Bad Faith (the Sartrean term for denying our responsibility) such as 'I have to ...', 'I can't ...', or 'I'm not able to ...'. When you hear such language, take a moment to challenge this assumption to see if it is not merely a matter of priorities, and whether you might be able to take responsibility for your situation and own your choice in the matter (even if it means you are choosing to not make a choice).

Level 3: Befriending paradox and embracing the human condition

An important step in coming to terms with our existential human condition is learning to hold paradox. It can be difficult to wrap our heads around the concept of 'both, and'. There is a natural comfort in 'either, or' and most people find comfort in the simplicity of black-or-white thinking. Beyond the complexities of shades of grey, being human entails living with paradox. We may both like *and* dislike a person at the same time. We want to rebel against deadlines, which restrict our freedom, *and* we appreciate them to help us get things done. We want to be part of a group to induce a sense of belonging, *and* it is also important to preserve our individuality, to be unique and special. We want to have clarity on the consequences of a particular course of action before we choose a path, *and* we enjoy the excitement of not-knowing. We try to avoid uncertainty, *and* we enjoy venturing out into the unknown by learning new things.

Recognising the paradoxes inherent in the human condition, and how they add energy and excitement to our lives, allows us to sit with this challenging experience, rather than to try and fight it to somehow create a world that is free of paradox and dilemma. Accepting, and perhaps even embracing, that being in the world with others is a condition that is not always clear-cut and neatly distinguishable in good or bad, right or wrong, happy or sad, enables us to appreciate the complexities of being human, to even look forward to such moments to 'spice up our lives'. After all, the stories we tell almost always involve at least one, usually many, of the existential themes, challenges and dilemmas. Finding ourselves in the midst of such a story has the potential for enormous personal and collective meaning – *if* we choose to (and find ourselves able to) create such a narrative in the face of considerable suffering. Chances are that when we put the work in to explore our human condition and its givens during a time we are well able to cope with life, we will be much more likely to have access to such resources once the next crisis lands.

On a practical level, it is important to make space to face our human condition. Beyond engaging with existential(ly-themed) literature and stories, create time and space to reflect on your own life. Journaling regularly is a great way to reflect. Talking to a professional (such as an existential counsellor, therapist, or coach) is an ideal way to lean into the discomfort that life inevitably offers, but in a safe environment. Being deeply listened to by someone whose aim is not to rescue you from your human condition and its discomfort (as many well-intentioned friends, parents or partners might) helps us to notice and acknowledge life's many trials and tribulations, big and small, and to come to terms with the reality of our existence. Discomfort and anxiety are natural experiences, and often they are excellent teachers that help us to recognise what is important to us. Through a process of regularly facing (instead of distracting ourselves from) life's subtle challenges, we foster the courage to face our human condition, and hence build existential resilience.

Level 4: Trotzdem – Feel the anxiety and do it anyway

There is no cure for the existential condition. The only way to escape existential anxiety is to stop existing, or to continuously distract ourselves. The latter can work for some time, but stops with the inevitable boundary situation, at which point we will be facing the harsh realities of living, but unprepared. Engaging in the above outlined activities will help us to anticipate challenging times and to build resources; however, it will not stop them from occurring. Therefore, a key attitude to develop to foster existential resilience is to act *in spite of* (German: *trotzdem*) anxiety and discomfort, to get used to taking action despite not feeling certain about the outcome or in the face of dilemma. If none of the options seems best, bear the uncertainty, and choose anyway. If you are nervous about how a presentation will go, do not let that stop you. Your mind is telling you that you should not try; check if there is any *actual* risk or danger and, if it is existential anxiety that is in the way, do it anyway! Fear has a clear function and should be taken seriously, but getting accustomed to acting in the face of discomfort is a useful skill that may allow you to continue moving forward in the face of a crisis instead of letting anxiety and uncertainty paralyse you.

At a practical level we may start by imagining situations that make us feel uncomfortable, but which we have already vetted as not actually dangerous (such as telling someone we like them or asking for a promotion). Focusing on the feeling that arises and allowing ourselves to experience it helps to get accustomed to the discomfort. Re-evaluating the experience as excitement (usually a positive connotation) instead of nervousness (usually seen as negative) helps, but even if it continues to feel 'bad', imagine you are doing it anyway. Moving from imagination to the real-world scenarios, starting at a small scale, will start to build the *trotzdem* muscle and help us to keep moving in the face of adversity.

Existential coaching as fertile ground for building existential resilience

Considering the above, existential resilience stems from both a skill set in times of crisis and adversity, as well as from a general attitude to life and existence. An ideal way to foster existential resilience is to work with an existential coach during a time when crisis and adversity is not an imminent threat or has already occurred. Van Deurzen and Hanaway (2012:xvi), to frame the practice, write:

> Existential coaching is a philosophical method for helping people to live more effectively … [It] focuses particularly on existential issues such as freedom, responsibility, authenticity, meaning, purpose, paradox and dilemma. It helps a person to get more of a perspective on the way they live and to ask some new and more profound questions about life. There is room for philosophical debate and contemplation but ultimately it is an approach with an entirely pragmatic objective: to help people to live their lives with greater deliberation, liberty, understanding and passion.

When we engage in conversations with a professional steeped in existential philosophy, we will be invited to consider our personal philosophy and worldview as well as our relationship with the existential givens through explorative and creative dialogue, and in the process foster resilience against the inevitable future run-ins with the existential givens. Hanaway (2018, 2020, as cited in Jacob, 2019:93) suggests that, among other benefits, clients who seek existential coaching can expect that they will be

- encouraged to speak up for themselves and the values they hold and will not be treated as if they fit into a pre-established model
- invited into a creative dialogue where they take charge of their own exploration and are helped to think in new ways about making choices and decisions in their lives

- helped to formulate with clarity who they think they are, where they are, where they want to go in their life
- shown how to probe a little further and deeper and to challenge their assumptions about their lives, themselves, other people and the world they live in
- given the opportunity to tackle the conflicts in their lives and understand not only how they contribute to creating some of these but also how to face up to conflicts and surpass them
- invited to consider dialectical principles and the way in which they make more of the paradoxes of human existence, using the ebb and flow of their lives to create movement for themselves
- enabled to recognise their own ideology, in the form of their unspoken assumptions, their prejudice, their values, their most deep-seated beliefs and their predictive framework of human existence
- taught new methods for tackling some of the distortions that have obscured their vision and they will increase their capacity for widening their perspective on their life
- helped to take a broader and wider view of human existence in general and gain greater understanding of how life and the world actually work
- engaged in debating their personal philosophy and will feel tested and challenged, but also helped to arrive at a more wholesome and complete view of the world
- encouraged to abandon old destructive habits and replace them with new and more creative ways of proceeding in life, by reengaging with a meaningful purpose and project, which will make them feel passionate and enthusiastic about what they can contribute to the world
- examining their physical embodiment, and be helped to observe and note the habits that break them, so that they can break these habits instead
- discovering how emotional and interactional patterns create constant friction with other people around them and get better at resolving such conflicts or using the energy of those frictions to move on
- considering their self-image and their personal sense of who they are; they will become more able to become who they are capable of being and want to be
- improving their vision about the life they live, and the life they would like to live. They will do so by understanding first of all their own beliefs and values, but also by finding out more about human existence, its challenges, purpose and internal lawfulness.

Going through such a process as part of a series of conversations will help clients to build a solid worldview and philosophy, flexible enough to allow new circumstances to be integrated and to bounce back quicker when adversity arises. We may still fall, but we will accept falling as an inevitable part of life, and we will know what to hold on to and how to get back to solid ground.

Chances are that less severe adversity will not shake us to an extent that we enter freefall, but merely stumble, pause, readjust, and move on with our life within the new circumstances. Existential coaching is a space which invites us to pause in the midst of often hectic lives to make sense of what is happening around us, to consider how we live and work, and to ponder some of the big questions before we can no longer ignore them. It allows us to consider how we navigate this human condition and to counter the paralysis during times when it is crucial to keep moving.

Conclusion

The Covid-19 pandemic has been an existential boundary situation on a global scale. Beyond the physical threats of ill health and the collapse or pause of important structures, it acted as a powerful reminder that death, freedom, isolation and meaninglessness are inescapable characteristics of the human condition, and that such givens can occur suddenly and in bulk, often resulting in pulling the metaphorical rug from underneath our illusion of stability and structure. Resilience, the ability to adapt to change and bounce back from adversity, is a valuable skill in times of crisis as well as an attitude towards existing in general. Existential resilience includes the ability to navigate through existential crises and creates resources to help us avoid paralysis as to keep moving in the face of existential calamity. There are practical ways in which we may foster existential resilience through explorations of past challenges, recognising existential themes in everyday life and through learning new coping strategies. Existential coaching presents a fertile ground to nurture existential resilience due to its defining characteristics grounded in existential philosophy and equips people to better deal with life's inevitable existential crises, including the effects of similarly inevitable future pandemics.

References

APA (2021) Resilience. *Dictionary of Psychology* https://dictionary.apa.org/resilience [accessed 4 September 2021].

BS 65000 (2014) *Guidance for Organizational Resilience*. London: BSI Group.

Calhoun, L.G. and Tedeschi, R.G. (2006) 'The Foundations of Posttraumatic Growth: An Expanded Framework', in L.G. Calhoun and R.G. Tedeschi (eds), *Handbook of Posttraumatic Growth: Research and Practice*. Mahwah, NJ: Lawrence (pp. 3–23).

Camus, A. (1955) *The Myth of Sisyphus: And Other Essays*. Trans. J. O'Brien. New York: Vintage Books.

Deurzen, E. van (1997) *Everyday Mysteries. Existential Dimensions of Psychotherapy*. London: Routledge.

Deurzen, E. van and Hanaway, M. (2012) *Existential Perspectives on Coaching*. Basingstoke: Palgrave Macmillan.

Dweck, C.S. (2006) *Mindset: The New Psychology of Success*. New York: Random House.

Hanaway, M. (2018) *Existential Coaching Skills: The Handbook*. 2nd edn. Guernsey: Corporate Harmony.

Hanaway, M. (2020) *The Handbook of Existential Coaching Practice*. London: Routledge.

Jacob, Y.J. (2019) *An Introduction to Existential Coaching: How Philosophy Can Help Your Clients Live with Greater Awareness, Courage and Ownership*. London: Routledge.

Jaspers K. (1919) *Psychologie der Weltanschauungen*. Berlin: Springer.

Leys, C., Arnal, C., Wollast, R., Heidi, R., Kotsou, I. and Fossion, P. (2018) Perspectives on Resilience: Personality Trait or Skill? *European Journal of Trauma & Dissociation*, 39.1, 22–28.

Merriam-Webster (2021a) Adversity. *Merriam-Webster.com* www.merriam-webster.com/dictionary/adversity [accessed 4 September 2021].

Merriam-Webster (2021b) Resilience. Merriam-Webster.com www.merriam-webster.com/dictionary/resilience [accessed 4 September 2021].

Nietzsche, F. (1889 [1990]) *Twilight of the Idols: or How to Philosophize with a Hammer*. Trans. R.J. Hollingdale. New York: Penguin.

Ryff, C.D. and Keyes, C.L.M. (1995) The Structure of Psychological Well-Being Revisited. *Journal of Personality and Social Psychology*, 69.4, 719–727.

Tedeschi, R.G. and Calhoun, L.G. (1995) *Trauma & Transformation: Growing in the Aftermath of Suffering*. Thousand Oaks, CA: Sage.

Ungar, M. (2020) What Works: A Manual for Designing Programmes that Build Resilience. *Resilience Research Centre* https://resilienceresearch.org/files/WhatWorks-Ungar-WebVersion.pdf [accessed 4 September 2021].

Vos, J. (2015). An Existential Perspective on Resilience: An Overview of the Research Literature. *International Journal of Emerging Mental Health*, 17.2, 62.

Waldman, J. and Jackson, P.Z. (2017) *The Resilience Pocketbook*. Alresford: Management Pocketbooks Ltd.

Wong, P.T.P. (2010) What Is Existential Positive Psychology. *International Journal of Existential Psychology & Psychotherapy*, 3, 1–10.

Chapter 9

'It's been a good pandemic for me'

Working with coaching and psychotherapy clients, with a focus on clients with a diagnosis of pure obsessive compulsive disorder

Monica Hanaway

My private psychotherapy practice is based in Oxford, and I am fortunate in having a very diverse and interesting caseload. As a coach I focus on leadership, business and executive coaching and work with clients across the globe. All my work is informed by existential philosophy.

Psychotherapy

Pre-pandemic, my psychotherapy work was face to face. I have written in the introduction to this section of the book that I am not a fan of the use of online platforms for psychotherapy, but in the spirit of Winnicott (1949), I was willing to try to offer a 'good enough' experience for my clients and me, and so, during the pandemic, moved reluctantly to working via online platforms or telephone sessions, depending on the client's preference.

I have always had a busy practice, and this continued throughout the pandemic. At the start of the pandemic, my work as a trainer stopped and this freed up more time for client work. A few clients put their therapy on hold for a while. These included nurses and doctors who were exhausted and distressed by their workload, and what they were experiencing. Although, it would have been impossible to continue with the in-depth personal therapy they had been involved in, I offered irregular sessions at their request, focused on their need for support and on providing a safe place for them to address the traumatic situations they found themselves in. This had a personal impact on me as I could not cut myself off from the realities of Covid-19, with medics distressed at what they saw: overcrowding, people being treated in corridors or ambulances queued at the hospital entrance. The reality of people dying without their families, and medics trying to compensate for this by taking on the role of doulas for the dying, while at the same time trying to continue to treat the living, were weekly narratives.

My psychotherapy waiting list grew to a point where I was forced to close it. I had begun to take on clients from across the country, who I had yet to meet in

DOI: 10.4324/9781003255765-12

person, and who I expect I may never meet. As with many other therapists, my experience of these 'Zoom' clients was that the quality of the therapeutic relationship took longer to develop. Those coming from a business background were often 'fitting in' their therapy between Zoom business meetings. They did not have the preparation time nor the immediate reflection time which they would normally have while travelling to and from their therapy, and I found that it took them longer to move from the professional to the personal. I was aware that work emails were often running across their screens and although they would never have had their mobile phones on during a face-to-face session it was not unusual for some clients to forget to turn them off. If their 'boss' phoned they would find it hard to ignore the call as they were 'working from home'.

Even those not struggling to continue to work were having to cope with 'offscreen distractions', such as children and pets, people at their door or even family members bursting into the room when they were speaking to me; they would not have had to cope with any of these if they were in the therapy room. The sense of the therapy room providing a safe and confidential space was threatened and working online felt to me like 'making do'. Some clients were more able to ignore what was going on around them, whereas others felt very unsafe and told me that they censored the material they brought to the sessions, fearing they may be overheard, or because they felt bad speaking about someone who was elsewhere in the house. It was not unusual for a client to begin speaking in a barely audible mumble, indicating that they needed to speak about their relationship with someone they feared might overhear the session. A client living in a shared house chose to have his sessions in all weathers while sheltering under a tree in a nearby park. Despite trying to get as far away from others as possible, he seemed to be a magnet for dogs who often wandered over to him and interrupted our sessions until their owners claimed them. Another client borrowed a friend's car to sit in for her sessions.

Clients spoke of missing the time walking or driving to their therapy and returning home after a session. Pre-pandemic several clients would go from their face-to-face sessions to the small café at the end of my road to provide a space before going back to their hectic lives. They recognised how important this time was for reflection. During the pandemic I encouraged them to build in the time to take walks before and after online sessions and, when it became possible to do so, to start taking that coffee time again rather than going straight from an online psychotherapy session to online business.

My clients are all long-term clients and so I saw changes in their therapeutic material from pre-pandemic, through lockdowns to the present day. In the early days of the pandemic there was very little mention of Covid-19. The first mention came with the worries of one client about his young son who had heard that there were now cases in the UK. He began obsessive handwashing to the point that his skin was sore and was showing signs of not wanting to go to school in case others were 'not washing their hands properly or might breathe on him'.

On a family outing in March 2020, the family were driving near Milton Keynes when the son had a panic attack as he had heard that 32 people with confirmed cases of Covid-19 were in the town. He did not want the family to drive anywhere near as he feared to do so would mean they would all die. For the boy, a world which had seemed safe and certain suddenly became dangerously uncertain. For the first time he became focused on temporality and the reality of death and loss. My client, an anesthetist, spent quite a lot of his sessions focused on his worries for his son and, through gentle reassurance and authenticity, over many weeks, managed to reduce the son's existential anxiety.

The father had not initially been too worried about the virus and believed the necessary plans were in place in the hospital where he worked; however when the reality of the situation became clear he had to stop his weekly sessions due to the intense workload caused by the virus, with his skills required particularly for those very ill patients who were being put into induced comas. As he was in constant contact with Covid-19 patients, and two of his team had contracted and died from the virus, he was concerned about passing the virus on to his family. As a result, his family moved to stay with family in the countryside. His usual pattern of relatedness with family and colleagues was disrupted. He now spent his working life in full PPE (personal protective equipment) with virtually no opportunity to speak to colleagues about anything other than the immediate professional concerns of the moment. He reported that 'time had lost all meaning and he was struggling to know the date and day or even whether it was morning or afternoon'. It has been reported that nearly half of NHS critical care staff have suffered PTSD, depression or anxiety during the pandemic (Grover, 2021; Vos, 2021). Some early work is underway to offer therapeutic support to this group, but it is anticipated that it will only be when the pandemic lessens that the full extent of this need will become apparent.

The original reason for him coming to therapy had been to improve his relationship with his wife and 'to gain a better understanding' of himself. He felt these concerns had to be put on 'the back burner for the time being'. We continued with occasional phone sessions when there were particularly traumatic events but hope to resume weekly sessions when it feels safe and appropriate to do so.

Early in the first lockdown, a new client suffered what he described as 'a breakdown' (later to be renamed as 'an awakening'). He described himself and his partner as very happy, well suited, and settled in their relationship and, like many people during the pandemic, they chose to add to their household by getting a longed-for puppy. It was the arrival of this pet which precipitated the client's rapid decline into depression, guilt and self-loathing. He liked the puppy, yet felt overwhelmed by the sudden responsibility and loss of freedom which comes with owning a pet. He disliked himself for having those feelings. Just as the lockdown had limited everyone's freedom and called for us to consider others, to social distance, and wear masks, the new puppy brought many existential issues to the fore, which the client had previously suppressed. For the client it posed the question who he was, and what really mattered to him, what was the meaning of his existence and how he could relate to loss of freedom and increased responsibility.

He had believed himself to be happy in his 'settled' existence and for the most part he was. However, he had been caught unprepared for the existential concerns which arose and which, he came to see, he had suppressed for some time. By nature, he was quiet, quite shy, responsible, and gentle, but in a previous relationship he had been able to explore a more adventurous side of himself, travelling in quite dangerous countries and 'surviving by chance'. He had happily moved on from there into his current relationship and a more risk-adverse way of being, focused on buying a bigger home, and he and his wife becoming established and successful in their careers. In the past he had worked in a very 'sexy' job, which he found people to be interested in; but hehad chosen to move to work which was socially important and in which he was highly respected and doing well. At the same time, he was surrounded by very successful family members who seemed to do well in everything, including sport and finding the best houses in which to live. He often negatively compared himself to others.

Over time, he had felt restless, but could not justify why. He became aware of his age (mid-30s) and for the first time acknowledged to himself that life was short, and we can never know how long we have. This more philosophical thinking was at the beginning unnerving for him, but he gradually began to value it. He wanted to enter mindfully into the immediate future in an authentic way, expressing all his ambiguities and staying true to his values.

He and his wife began to discuss whether they would like to have a family. The home they were in began to represent 'settling for something' and although it was something 'nice', for the client there was a feeling that something was missing. Children seemed 'the obvious answer' to them both, although both acknowledged a certain degree of ambivalence towards the idea. Their first step towards parenthood was the acquisition of their puppy and, through his reaction to this, my client discovered that he was not yet ready to abandon the adventurous side of himself which desired the freedom which was sorely lacking in lockdown. In discussion both he and his wife realised that they had assumed children were the next step in life but had never stopped to question whether they wanted them. The uncertainty of the pandemic made them stop and consider their options in a future which could not be planned out with any certainty. While my client began to enjoy the possibilities which uncertainty presented, his wife longed for security. Instead of looking for a next house where they expected to 'spend the rest of their lives', my client suggested that they rent out their current house or sold it and put the money in the bank while they had an adventure. He explained to his wife that uncertainty had become attractive to him. He needed a meaningful project which allowed him to feel free but had no wish to abandon his work or to financially risk their future in any way. With the move to home working, he could carry on in his job from anywhere. From this new authentic speaking out he and his wife were able to openly discuss their desires, their different reactions to uncertainty and to find a way which worked for both.

As lockdown continued clients brought more dreams than usual. Several, who were locked down with other people (these included students in student accommodation and those in multi-occupancy houses), brought dreams which were concerned with suffocation, and often ended with the client waking struggling for breath. This seemed to indicate a growing awareness of their embodied vulnerable state and their 'suffocating' physical closeness to others at a time when we were warned to isolate ourselves. This was coupled with their loss of personal freedom, meaning they were unable to escape from other people's presence. Others mentioned that they had been concerned about what they were hearing in the news and on social media, where those dying of Covid-19 were described as choking to death. Clients particularly concerned about their uncertain future reported dreams including sensations of falling into a void. In some cases, the void was described as full of unseen dangers and monsters which were impossible to avoid as you could not see them, and so they could catch you unawares. Even clients whose dreams were not populated with clear references to the pandemic reported an increase in remembered dreams early in the lockdown which they described as having brighter colours and being more vivid then pre pandemic dreams. All these dreams seemed to lessen as the lockdown went on.

I had three clients with suicidal ideation who were considered to be at great risk pre-pandemic. During lockdown, all three stopped speaking of their desire to 'end it all' and embarked on healthy activities aimed at keeping themselves safe from dying of the virus. It is one thing to believe you hold agency for your own life, and can choose to end it at any time, and quite another to think it may be taken from you by a virus you cannot control. Their freedom to choose to die seemed at risk, and so they fought hard to remain alive. It is too soon to know whether the desire to preserve their lives is a long-term change that has replaced their desire to die.

'Pure obsessive compulsive disorder' clients

As lockdown started, I was working with three clients who had been diagnosed or had self-diagnosed as suffering from pure obsessive compulsive disorder (POCD). As an existentialist, I do not diagnose people as having disorders; but if this is a label they have taken onboard, it becomes part of their worldview and is part of the therapeutic material.

POCD often manifests as intrusive, inappropriate and shameful thoughts on which the person will ruminate. The thoughts are often themed and commonly will be concerned with existential fears, sexual thoughts, sexual perversion, worries about events which happened (or might have happened in the past), fears of doing something illegal or over concern for absolute honesty. Such thoughts make the client very anxious, and they become caught in a circle of anxiety, with the action of trying to repress the thoughts resulting in them focusing on them even more.

One of my clients with reported POCD had a long history of mental illness and, since the age of 17, had several admissions to psychiatric hospitals. She came to therapy following a 'psychotic episode' and was extremely fearful for her future wellbeing.

She had seen and experienced inappropriate behaviour of different kinds from her father, who had also sexually abused her as a child. In her teens, she had nearly died due to an eating disorder and reported that from 'a young girl' she had suffered constant troubling and intrusive thoughts. She was married to a very loving and supportive husband who had known her from school-days, and they had embarked on IVF treatment with the hope of starting a family. This desire for a baby meant she was eating well and exercising regularly but not to excess. She held down a good job and she was highly respected by her boss who knew of her difficulties. However, her boss was the subject of one of her recurring thoughts in which she stripped naked and shouted abuse at him during a business meeting. Such thoughts distressed her.

However, for my client, the worst of her suffering was the constant thoughts about death, which she only told me and her husband about. The fact that we shall all die in her view made life not worth living. 'If we die anyway, what is the point in living'. She constantly spoke in sessions of the inevitability of killing herself. During our work together we challenged her belief that she was the only one who had such thoughts, and in one session she laughed when I told her that if she was Head of Philosophy at Oxford University, she would be paid good money and be well respected for giving time to contemplate the meaning of death! We explored how to live authentically with thoughts which may be difficult for others to know about.

Shortly after, she became pregnant. Even the thought of her child growing up without her did not entirely stop the overwhelming paradoxical fear of death and the desire to die 'to get it over with'. As the pregnancy developed, the thoughts did recede a little. Previously she had suffered from social anxiety and avoided social or new situations. During our work together she became more social and took an increasing interest in her environment, sharing some of her thoughts with others who did not react as though she 'was mad'.

As the time of the birth drew nearer, she was much improved, when the psychiatric system suddenly remembered her existence and panicked about her ability as a mother. She was called in for several meetings and assigned specialist workers. This threw her into a panic, and intrusive thoughts of physically or sexually abusing the baby started to be a regular element of her obsessive thinking. She withdrew from the social circles she had built. Eventually, the psychiatric services acknowledged that she had been doing well in therapy and that their interest seemed to have a negative impact on her. As a result, they agreed that she just continue with the therapy, and they would reassess her after the birth. The negative thoughts continued but at a much-reduced level. She described her pregnancy as the most 'peaceful period of her life', resulting in the birth of a very healthy little boy.

Shortly after this we had the first cases of Covid-19 in the UK, and I was concerned about how the constant record of daily deaths would affect my client. Paradoxically, it proved to be an essential part of her recovery. She no longer felt different as 'everyone is worrying about dying'. Her worry became acceptable and authentic, and she felt better placed than most people to deal with it as she was very used to death anxiety. The pandemic empowered her and increased her self-esteem. She became the leader in setting up social meetings, initially online and then in person. She said that she had learnt 'not to be afraid of her thoughts, whilst not being overwhelmed by them'. We ended the therapy as her son was approaching his first birthday and she had returned to work, albeit from home, and received a promotion. The thoughts did not disappear, but she saw them as part of her authentic self, a self which she no longer feared. This allowed her to risk being in relation to others, as the concern that she may be rejected disappeared with her acceptance of herself.

Another client with diagnosed POCD started therapy at the start of lock-down. He had just finished his final year at university. He had done quite well academically and had enjoyed a full social life, being a member of a band, which seemed to be on the first steps to national recognition. However, he had started to suffer disabling dizzy spells in social situations and, when lockdown happened, he returned home to live with his divorced father. Their relationship seemed a good one and his father suggested he seek help with the dizziness. He had many medical investigations which failed to find a cause and decided to explore whether there was a psychological reason. In the therapy, he recognised that these dizzy spells seemed to arrive when he was feeling anxious in social situations and the dizziness was often accompanied by worrying thoughts.

As we started working together and built trust, he confided that, although presenting as a well-mannered and caring young man, he feared he was 'a very unpleasant person'. Over time he began to tell me of the thoughts that plagued him. After any social situation he feared that he had 'done something awful' which he could not remember. These concerns were very different from his actual behaviour. His most consistent fears were that he may have insulted someone, verbally, physically or sexually. These kinds of behaviours were ones he abhorred and there was no evidence at all that he had ever behaved inappropriately. People who he feared he had insulted showed no signs of not wanting to engage with him and always seemed pleased to see him, but this did not set his mind at rest. His disturbance was added to by the fact these behaviours were the opposite of his values and beliefs.

He held very strong liberal moral beliefs, placing the needs of others and the requirement to behave ethically towards people high on his list of priorities.

He believed in a mindful freedom and the necessity to take responsibility for his choices and actions. In his case he also felt responsibility for things he may never have done. This heightened sense of responsibility was problematic for him.

His worries caused him to drink heavily when out with friends, increasing the likelihood that his memory of events would be poor. It also meant that when drunk he was not capable of taking responsibility. His dizzy spells also meant that at times he was reliant on others to take responsibility for him. He longed to belong to a group of friends but also feared that he 'would do something' or 'they would come to know something' which would make them hate and reject him. And so he held a lot of ambivalence about his relationships.

The return to the parental home took away these fears as he no longer had access to his friendship group from university. He felt a greater sense of acceptance at home and realised that he had been trying hard to live an inauthentic 'rock star' lifestyle which did not fit with his values. The lockdown provided the opportunity for him to step away from the 'false self' he had created. He began to consider what he wanted to do in the future and to make plans for post-pandemic life.

At the same time, he realised that his dizziness had started shortly after his parents' separation. The separation had come as a shock. He had believed his parents, who had met as children, would remain together throughout their lives. In therapy he was able to acknowledge his authentic feelings about the separation and the difficult he experienced in his parents not living up to a moral and philosophical code they had brought him up to respect and in which he had trusted. The certainty this 'code' had given him was taken away from him at the same time as his world changed with the ending of his studies and the start of the pandemic. He could no longer look to his parents for certainty but had to take his own 'leap of faith' and address who he was as an individual, rather than as part of a family, part of a friendship group or even part of a band. For this client the pandemic gave him time to reflect on the life he had been living. He focused on issues of authenticity, freedom and responsibility and his relatedness to others, both positive and negative.

The third client with a POCD diagnosis also saw benefits to their being-in-the-world from the pandemic. With everyone's anxiety raised and the provision of a 'valid' and universal worry, their sense of isolation decreased. They could not find a way to blame themselves for Covid-19 and indeed seemed to worry less about catching the virus than most of my clients. This also appeared to herald a decrease in their usual negative ruminations.

Coaching

Many of my coaching clients are high achievers and in most of our pre-pandemic sessions presented as confident, in control and professional. Their reasons for coaching were often focused on their desire to move to the next level, which called for them to identify their strengths and perceived weaknesses and take action to address the identified gaps in their skills and knowledge through the coaching or through further training. As I make it clear that I operate as an existential coach, we would also cover areas linked to existential themes, but these would be centred on the work environment. I give a fuller exploration of the importance of existential themes within the business world in my books on leadership *The Existential Leader* (2019b) and *An Existential Approach to Leadership Challenges* (2019a). The most common existential themes which came up during the lockdown periods were those of authenticity, freedom and responsibility, and uncertainty.

Although there were fewer practical changes in my coaching work, as much of it was already online (although usually from their workplace or a neutral space), with some coaching clients there were changes in the material for the sessions. The contextual changes meant that I was given insight into their home situation and often into tensions which had not formerly been apparent. Previously, there would have been very little discussion of their home circumstances or their relationship with their partners and other family members. This could not be avoided when these individuals occasionally made an entrance into the room the client was using for their coaching session. I experienced the level of support or frustration the client's work created in their partner and saw the struggle of trying to maintain a high level of professional integrity and performance while children were begging for attention. How this increased familial relatedness impacted on their professional self became part of many coaching sessions.

For some, this immersion in family life was an unwelcome challenge, whereas for others it brought delight and made them question some career decisions they had made. One very successful female executive felt 'she did not know her children' and experienced this as a great loss. She had employed nannies for the younger child while her older child attended boarding school. She had believed that these arrangements were her only choice if she were to maintain her freedom and reach her potential. In her professional life this had worked, but in her personal life she now felt herself to be a stranger from her own family. Her relationship with her husband was also strained, as previously they had both been so busy that the only times they had together were well organised and planned social events, usually with lots of other people. Now they had to get used to being together 24/7 and sharing a workplace. During lockdown she realised that her relationship with her husband had lost the depth that was there in the beginning and that he too felt like a stranger. Together, they decided to start couple therapy. The need to give greater priority to relatedness, particularly with members of her own family, came as a surprise.

She also began to consider whether her professional identity and her professional way of being-in-the-world were examples of Sartrean 'bad faith' (1943) and living inauthentically. She was known as being forthright and had been accused of bullying. For the first time, she questioned why she behaved in this way and how others might perceive it. She recognised that she had mirrored the behaviour of people who had been hard on her during her early professional life and, without considering there may be another way of 'leading', she had copied what she had seen.

She started to engage with uncertainty. Perhaps, post-pandemic, she might have a different life. This currently remains the focus of our coaching work: can she stay in her job and attempt to change the culture while at the same time forming a deeper relationship with her family, or did she need a more radical change? If she were to leave her post what would happen to that part of her which sought the adrenalin rush her post currently provided. She recalled that before giving so much time to work she had enjoyed outdoor sport, particularly whitewater rafting and committed to trying out some outdoor activities with her family when pandemic restrictions allowed.

Other coaching clients also used the pandemic opportunity to reflect on their choices. One client returned to Poland to look after her sick mother and, while there, decided to get married to her long-term partner and remain in Poland and retrain in a different professional field. Another decided to leave a successful media career, move from London to the countryside and set up a business renting yurts. One client returned to Spain, something he had been contemplating for a long time, but the twin pressures of Brexit and Covid-19 showed him that the 'certainty' he had felt in his UK job was not a given and that settling for security and stability 'was a mug's game if it failed to fit with your values or make you happy'. He also saw that life could suddenly alter, or indeed stop, and that waiting for the 'right moment' to act was a gamble he was no longer willing to take, as he could not 'guarantee living to see that moment'.

Very few of these clients wanted to return to the same high-pressure world which the pandemic had altered. They either wanted to alter their professional way of being or take a new path entirely. Most felt a deeper understanding of the issues people who worked for them experienced daily, and believed they would respond more empathically to any family difficulties employees might have in the future. Several expressed a desire to redesign the work environment, and/ or the structure of the working day to provide more meaning for themselves and others.

It is too early to say how the pandemic experience has affected clients in the long term and whether decisions to make radical changes will bring the peace and happiness hoped for. However, the pandemic has given clients the opportunity to step back and reassess their decisions, to own their freedom to change things, to accept the responsibility for previous actions, and individual thoughts, and seek a more considered and authentic way of being.

References

Grover, N. (2021) Nearly Half of NHS Critical Care Report PTSD, Depression or Anxiety. *The Guardian* www.theguardian.com/society/2021/jan/13/nhs-icu-staff-ptsd-severe-depression-anxiety?CMP+Share_iOOSApp_Other.

Hanaway, M. (2019a) *An Existential Approach to Leadership Challenges.* Abingdon: Routledge.

Hanaway, M. (2019b) *The Existential Leader: An Authentic Leader for Our Uncertain Times.* Abingdon: Routledge.

Sartre, J.-P. (2000 [1943]) *Huis Clos and Other Plays.* London: Penguin Classics.

Vos, J. (2021) *The Psychology of Covid-19: Building Resilience for Future Pandemics.* London: Sage Swifts.

Winnicott, D.W. (1949) *The Child and the Family.* London: Tavistock Publications.

Part 3

The business world and other communities

Existential issues for businesses, communities and organisations to consider post-pandemic

As seen in the previous chapters, living in pandemic times has created challenges for individuals. However, the challenges are not just for individuals, but also for communities and working environments.

Communities have changed as a result of the restraints of lockdown. For many, who pre-pandemic left their homes in the morning, travelled to their workplace, and then returned, tired, to their homes, the division between the time spent at home and the time spent in the 'office' shifted. Home was now also office, and the community in which their home existed took on more significance.

This could be negative or positive. Many communities started up WhatsApp groups, initially intended to support people who were isolating or needed practical help during lockdowns. This new way of relating to a mix of people, some of whom were well-known to each other and shared values, and others who people may have chosen not to get to know well, presented its own challenges. For those who like their privacy, receiving daily updates on the minutiae of their neighbours' daily existence was unwelcome, as was the unspoken expectation that they would respond with small details of their own.

Over time, these WhatsApp groups morphed into more social groups, focused round lost pets, and furniture and equipment that people were offering free. People got to know their neighbours, and creative ways of raising community spirits were introduced. My own road enjoyed a jazz pianist giving concerts in the road, while everyone listened from their own front gardens. It became apparent that social distancing proved harder for some than others and this did create some tensions, as did the level to which people adhered to the regular use of masks and other lockdown rules. We learnt new ways of relating, reassessed priorities, and discovered our own levels of tolerance.

It was not just communities who faced existential issues during the pandemic but also businesses. The place for existential thinking in the business

DOI: 10.4324/9781003255765-13

world may not be immediately apparent. I have been working for many years as a coach and consultant, to develop an applied existential approach relevant and accessible to the world of business. The pandemic has caused businesses and organisations to change the way they function. We have seen heartbreak and loss, with many businesses failing to survive; but the pandemic has challenged businesses to take a fresh look at what is 'normal' and invites them to use the opportunity to make positive changes which take account of the existential needs of those working within them. I am hopeful that if we can learn lessons from the pandemic the world of work may be more centred on the existential needs of the people working within it.

Although, there are opportunities for improving things for the better, there is also the possibility for things to be made worse. One client reported that during the pandemic her employers had decided to take the opportunity to close the office in which previously several hundred people had worked. They now expected everyone to work from home and even expressed the opinion that as people no longer had to travel to the office it may be possible for them to work longer hours. The employers refused to offer any extra money to contribute to the costs of home working, such as electricity, heating, suitable office furniture etc. For my client, who lived alone in quite an isolated place, work had provided her with most of her social contacts. She would regularly go to the pub or a restaurant after work with her colleagues. She felt bereft of friends and of her professional identity with the change in her working situation.

In the following chapters, the authors step outside of the psychotherapy and coaching space to look briefly at what existential thought can add to business, community and other settings during times of crisis, including during and following the pandemic.

Chapter 10

East of Eden

An existential view of the pandemic

René Märtin

In the crisis triggered by the pandemic, human beings show their vulnerable side. It becomes clear through the global images of the suffering of the many people who have fallen ill or lost loved ones who have died. It does not matter whether we know this from our own experience (e.g. through the illness of relatives, or experiences from the workplace), because all this is also explicitly transmitted to us through the media. It shapes our awareness, how we think about it, and how we want to deal with it personally.

The pandemic confronts us with four essential 'givens' of the human, as Yalom (1980) describes them in his classic *Existential Psychotherapy*: mortality, freedom, isolation and meaninglessness. These themes are brought to us by life; they are unavoidable – and thus one cannot avoid dealing with them. Besides all the freedom, self-determination and creative power we have as human beings, we can never protect ourselves from the inevitable. All four categories come under the existential burning glass in the pandemic; we see clearly how every life is challenged by these questions. What is the meaning of human life if man must die? How should we deal with the meaninglessness of our own existence? How can we live with the constant possibility of death? Against the backdrop of the pandemic, the fear arising from these questions becomes our constant companion and drives us to act. We have two options: to let ourselves be driven to substitute actions that promise short-term satisfaction and thus distraction. Or we face the certainty of death and take responsibility for shaping our life. For only in this way do we have the possibility to give meaning to our life out of a free decision. This requires consent and insight, as the Psalmist puts it: 'Teach us to remember that we must die, that we may be wise' (Ps. 90:12). The pandemic presents us with precisely this challenge. Consent is to be given to the reality: that we must die is allegorically equivalent to the fact that we do not dwell in paradise. There is no eternal life, neither endless peace nor lasting health nor absolute material security. Beyond these certain uncertainties, there is no other form of certainty or security, nowhere and nowhen. In principle, our lives are always at risk. But some idea of paradise is strongly rooted in human beings; no one likes to deal with their own

DOI: 10.4324/9781003255765-14

finitude. Therefore, let us remember as wordless and senseless as Cain slays his brother Abel in the field in the old biblical story of fratricide, so unexpectedly and absurdly does the catastrophe come upon us. In this sense, it is wise to realise that we are already, to remain in the metaphor, 'East of Eden' (Gen. 4:16). From an existential point of view, this means taking limitations as incentives to take responsibility in and with what we have. It is also important to come out of the victim role and to adopt a creator attitude.

Mortality: 'remember that you will die'

In everyday life, we are rarely confronted with death. The pandemic, however, makes us aware of our own finiteness. As with the catastrophic epidemic of the plague in Europe from the mid-fourteenth century, a central existential thought is reinforced – every report, every narrative, every experience is a whispered *memento mori* (remember that you will die). The ancient Roman ritual of the slave who stood or walked behind the acclaimed commander in the triumphal procession, holding a gold or laurel wreath over the head of the victor while admonishing him incessantly with these words, can be understood as the *ostinato* of the pandemic.

The ancients understood the existential dimension: death is the 'eternal equaliser'. We are all destined to an end of our existence. That this is absolutely part of our existence is expressed in the second whisper of the slave: *memento te hominem esse* (remember that you are a human being). Existence and death are irrevocably intertwined foundations of life. The more distant we imagine ourselves to be from this fact, the easier it slips from our consciousness. This is reinforced by increasing individualisation, accompanied by an almost infantile egocentricity, the extreme intensification of which can be seen in the permanent narcissistic display in social media. This 'fear of insignificance' (Strenger, 2011) makes people believe, on the one hand, that they are immortal and, on the other, that their own uniqueness manifests itself. The third whisper of the slave becomes more important here: *respice post te, hominem te esse memento* (look around and remember that you too are only human). The continued presence of death on the horizon, the face of suffering and dying in the pandemic, and the omnipresent threat to life and limb, suddenly becomes visible to all.

Three things must be noted here from an existential point of view. First, we are mortal beings. Secondly, death is part of existence, indeed, it defines existence. And, thirdly, this fact unites all human beings. Our mortality is the defining element of our lives, it marks the span of life, the uncertainty of its occurrence always resonates unconsciously and 'disciplines us to live' (Frankl, 2004). However, many perspectives play a role: not only the loss of life, but also the loss of freedom, strength, courage and hope, being trapped in our own physicality, the transience of the body, health, etc. In existential work, it therefore takes courage to make this fact a topic.

Freedom (and responsibility)

From an existential point of view, human beings are not merely the result of inner-psychic processes, or environmental influences, but are beings who can create themselves in what matters in life. Kierkegaard emphasises that we are free in our choices and therefore dependent on ourselves. In the knowledge of this freedom, the necessity of having to make a choice, we remain in search of the meaning of life. The German theologian Dietrich Bonhoeffer, anti-Nazi dissident, and key founding member of the Confessing Church, emphasises (1986–1999) our freedom to act responsibly; responsibility and freedom are corresponding concepts. Responsibility presupposes factual – not temporal – freedom, just as freedom can only exist in responsibility. Whoever knows about his or her freedom also knows about his or her responsibility. Jean Paul Sartre (1993; 2007) radicalises this relationship between freedom and responsibility. We are condemned to freedom, we cannot escape our fate, and therefore bear responsibility for all actions in the world. The assumption of absolute responsibility is the consequence of total freedom. What happens to us, happens to us through ourselves, and we can neither be grieved by it, nor rebel against it, nor resign ourselves to it. This is exactly what many existentialists say: Life has specific tasks in store for every human being that want to be solved. If we succeed in answering these life questions in a meaningful way, we experience meaningfulness. This is also where values come into play that are important to us, that we orient ourselves by and that help us cope with life. They are not just a theoretical or even metaphysical instance but want to be realised. That is why we are urged to actively create this life.

In this self-responsibility, our life is thus about recognising a central task in life in seeing our possibilities and shaping this life according to our convictions, reflections and decisions. This is precisely what the pandemic calls for. In the crisis, the acting human being shows himself, and in the existential work important traces can be laid here.

Isolation and the experience of it

Quarantine, distance, isolation, being alone – these are defining conditions in times of pandemic. The social consequences of self-imposed or externally imposed isolation are striking. We are social beings. In evolutionary terms, humans have organised themselves in small groups with a few handfuls of individuals. This environment has been relevant to human survival; as a loner, we have hardly had any chance of survival. Among other things, this may lead to people who are isolated quickly feeling cut off and lonely, and thus anxious and depressed. We are a being dependent on relationship in four ways: we are, , according to Hanaway and Reed (2014), in relationship with the *Umwelt* (physical), with the *Mitwelt* (social), with the *Eigenwelt* (psychological/personal) and with the *Überwelt* (spiritual/transcendental). Isolation fundamentally threatens this 'harmony of four-tones'; in the end, we remain alone in all decisive questions. We are in danger of being lost to ourselves, to others, and to the world. This 'four-tones' is also intertwined in the experience of isolation and loneliness and clearly shows how fundamental it is for human beings to overcome them. Isolation is experienced existentially in four ways; sometimes one existential theme is stronger, sometimes the other, but they always influence each other, they basically cannot be separated from each other. These four themes are found in the many situations provoked by the pandemic, in which isolation, loneliness, being alone and even loneliness can be found.

Isolation – 'noisy loneliness': In the pandemic, isolation is caused by the external situation, mainly by the quarantine imposed by authorities, but also by otherwise enforced distance (home office, ban on group-related activities, etc.). Sometimes people decide to self-isolate, but this can also harm the person in the long run. The longer the isolation lasts, the greater the distance from the environment. Through the (forced) retreat into the private sphere, one's place in the world begins to waver. Growing insecurity and increasing fear are serious consequences. Despite the isolation, however, the *Umwelt* is still there. Because it is essential for our existence, and still perceptible, it makes itself felt; life asks in this specific way, 'knocks', also penetrates medially into our own seclusion – and wants an answer. An isolation experience of a 'noisy loneliness' arises. Existential work can pick up here and bring the world into dialogue.

Loss of relationships – 'raging aloneness': At a distance, people move away from the usual relationships at work, in their private lives, in their leisure time. Distance work and video conferencing do not change this. Isolation grows. A vicious circle. But because we are human beings and depend on being able to be with others, the longing for relationships grows – the joy in life, in work, in our own hobbies, etc., on the other hand, can decline. What initially feels depressing on some days can lead to a deep depression. Despite the loss of relationships, the people around us, the *Mitwelt*, still exists. In the depressive mode, being alone seems more and more painful the less authentic relationships are possible. Above all, this longing for relationship expresses itself in an isolation experience of 'raging aloneness'. In the distance to the other, we remain unfulfilled and go empty. In existential work, the counsellor is therefore called upon with his or her own capacity for relationship.

Identity problems – 'resonance less silence': In isolation, even the desire for exchange and reflection at eye level is not fulfilled. At the same time, a certain discretion increases. Who likes to admit that they need exchange? And even more so in a professional context, e.g. in the context of online meetings. Needs are suppressed so as not to trigger false conclusions about one's own competences (in times of New Work and distance work, surely everyone should be able to organise and lead themselves optimally, some would say …). Communication and information deficits, lack of feedback and reassurance, misjudgements and misunderstandings, loss of integration are all developments that attack our self-image. Uncertainty about the own person ('Who am I? Who am I in this situation? What happens to my roles? Am I allowed to be like this?') leads to a noticeable restlessness. This, combined with neurotic, especially schizoid, behaviour, can be clear indications of significant identity problems that the isolated person is struggling with. This is exacerbated if a distorted self-image was already prevalent before the isolation forced by the pandemic. This may be especially true of the narcissistic personality type who may experience a crisis because the stage is missing. Identity, selfhood – the personality has its space in the *Eigenwelt*. Lack of engagement with others, insecurities in self-image, lack of feedback and reassurance lead to an experience of isolation, which can be described as 'resonance less silence'. When no one responds, one's own response becomes impossible. Existential work is therefore about clarifying the question of identity. Especially the aspect of authenticity.

Existential emptiness – 'oppressive infinity': If during life there is increasing isolation, loss of relationships, insecurity in the own identity and an inner, existential emptiness arising from perceived meaninglessness, then isolation and the loneliness associated with it unfolds its threatening potential in full. If one fails in giving meaning to one's own life again and again, the result is an experience of isolation in which the absurd gains the upper hand: the 'crushing infinity and strangeness of the cosmos' (Malraux, 2009) penetrates the emptiness left in the *Überwelt*. This is the basis of the *horror vacuum* – we must be afraid of this blank space if we do not fill it ourselves with meaningful life in the time of our existence. This is a particular challenge in pandemic times. In existential work, therefore, the question of a meaningful existence is significant.

Meaninglessness and absurdity – catastrophes have no meaning

The paradox for human being is that because of death, life must be meaningless, but we can wrest meaning from life through our actions. The pandemic has no meaning. Any attempt to wrest meaning from the catastrophic consequences of the pandemic must fail. Like death, the pandemic is proof of the absurdity of life. The experience of the absurd as the utterly contradictory points to a contradictoriness that is constitutive of existence as a human being yet can be resolved neither logically nor ethically. Living in an antinomic structure that sabotages the pursuit of meaning and happiness from the outset becomes an ordeal for the individual, who is forced to search for a niche in the meaningless for the realisation of their idea of a successful self-design. For Malraux (2009), absurdity means the futile attempt of the ego to come to terms with itself and the world – whereby the ego feels the immutability of a situation that exceeds human powers and to which it is thus at its mercy. We should also add the aspect of the inevitability and 'planlessness' of a situation and consider a discrepancy between 'being' (the sobering reality) and 'wanting to be' (the overly high expectations of life).

From an existential point of view, there is a side of the crisis that we should look at critically; it sounds a bit paradoxical, but the point is that many people are suddenly experiencing a sense of meaning in a certain way.

The coronavirus is the product of a mutation, i.e. a purely biological phenomenon, not intended by anyone (as far as we know), a pure product of chance. Human beings, however, cannot stand the idea of chance. We insist that there is a reason and, if possible, a meaning. If we can make sense of the virus, we can cope better with the impositions. Meaning creates resilience. The need for meaning can be explained by evolution: When the going gets tough, those who are supported by meaning have the best chances of survival. Nietzsche put it this way, as Frankl mentioned in *Man's Search for Meaning*: 'He who has a why to live for can bear almost any how' (2004:109). We are tremendously adept at creating the meaning we need. The coronavirus only has the sense we give it, and so at present one can hardly save oneself from offers of sense. Thanks to the pandemic, we finally manage to get off the hamster wheel! We use the lockdown to meditate, to clean up, to talk to each other. We discover a solidarity among neighbours that we hardly dared to believe in anymore. We make the best of it, and we talk about it, incessantly. And that is precisely the problem. For this form of meaning production is practised above all by those who have the privilege of a home office, gladly with a fixed salary. The more precarious the living conditions, the more difficult this self-therapy becomes. Even with small children, things look different in the home office, not to mention families in which the weaker, smaller ones fear violence. Old people's homes, prisons, refugee camps or slums in any form – here the crisis cannot be sold as an opportunity, the very thought would be cynical. Excluded from the middle-class discourse are also those poorly paid hard workers whose systemic relevance we suddenly discover.

We should look at this critically in existential work. One important thing is to establish a connection to reality and to work out the difference between 'being' and 'wanting to be'.

'Get up Abel': from victim to creator

We need to also see these issues in the context of free will. We are not free from conditions, whatever they may be. But we are free to create everything possible to us in our own way. It is about how we deal with the free space, with the creative leeway that we have. It is about taking responsibility and creating our lives in the face of, and despite, the pandemic. The fratricide quoted at the beginning makes Abel the eternal victim in the story. He himself had no choice; Cain killed Abel abruptly and without a word. From a passive attitude, isolation, and powerlessness in the face of the catastrophe, a feeling of abysmal inability to do anything can easily arise. During the pandemic, many people were covered with the heavy cloth of passivity and the dark poison of pessimism spread inside. They needed an encouraging counterpart in counselling, but, once again, they also need to be confronted with what they can do themselves, the challenge to take their lives into their own hands and to create their own existence. In the current debate and development of society, the 'silent victim' attitude is joined by the 'loud' one. These take to the streets, protest against measures, carry the riots to government palaces, indulge in conspiracy theories, refuse to vaccinate and enter into sinister alliances. They all have one thing in common: they see themselves as victims and chant the same. They are not above comparing themselves to the victims of the Holocaust. And is there a more extreme victim attribution than that reference to the Shoa?

In many places it is becoming visible what society has not succeeded in doing before. The vehemence of the protests, the insistence of the conspiracy theories and the aggressiveness in everyday interaction (especially in the social networks) can also be summed up simply by Sartre (1993, 2007): The failure of communication is the beginning of all violence. Jaspers writes about the background to this:

> The stubborn pride of man, who wants to be only himself, repels communication. He wants to identify the world with himself and knows only the will: to possess the world. He listens out of curiosity and greed for humanity, cannot bear to show any nakedness or to be put in the position of the inferior. With people he does not seek the relationship of solidarity, he wants to conquer them and have them as his own.
>
> (2008:91)

During this, the individual human being, like society, needs a great 'nevertheless'. It never ceases to amaze us how those who have experienced and survived one of the greatest 'catastrophes' in the history of mankind are particularly committed to this 'nevertheless'. It is no coincidence that it was the Auschwitz survivor Frankl who intensively pointed out how important it is to create one's existence, to give meaning to existence even under the most adverse circumstances and, above all, to move from being a victim to becoming a creator. The Jewish poet Hilde Domin, a contemporary of Frankl, tried to develop a specific faith from the same impulse. This consists in the conviction that we can nevertheless have trust and confidence. This trust is a resistant trust. It is a trust that does not sweep suffering and guilt under the carpet and that, in addition to the memory of what has been suffered, also knows the memory of the help received. Catastrophes cannot be compared. However, the memory of the solidarity experienced is essential for dealing constructively with the experience. For her, as for Frankl and others, the essential key to coping with the terrible lies in the conversion from victim to creator. Domin describes herself as a child of Abel. A child of Abel who fights for a world of fraternal justice, who has accepted her fate. Without her Jewishness, she would not have become a *poet of nevertheless*. She sees her poetry as a kind of vaccine against inhumanity and for freedom. Poetry, she says, is a great ringing of bells. Poems address the innocence of every human being. To the area in us that is not obscured by compromise and herd instinct. With her poem 'Abel steh auf' (1970), which was highly controversial at the time, she takes a radical path. In this poem she appeals to Abel, to the victim, to stand up again, to give the perpetrator, Cain, a second chance. Cain is not to commit the manslaughter again, but to subordinate his actions to the motto that he is his brother's keeper ('get up / so that Cain says / so that he can say / I am your keeper / brother / how can I not be your keeper'.) (2003:28) In this way, Abel's appeal falls into the arms of catastrophe and interferes with the seemingly inevitable story. It seems essential to interrupt the silence in the field. To come into action. To counteract what inevitably threatens. Whoever switches to the mode of the creator at this point discovers the manifold possibilities life offers to counteract the pandemic: whether as a stable crisis manager, energetic optimist, creative communitarian, or high-handed activist. The crisis has brought forth different 'creator types' who actively involve themselves in world affairs and thus also become role models for others.

Living solidarity, entering dialogue

We often do not understand that through alienation from the other we are becoming increasingly alien to ourselves, we do not *see* ourselves in it and consequently cannot *understand* ourselves in it. At this point, it helps to look beyond oneself. Existence is always directed towards the other. Camus describes, especially in his key philosophical novel *The Plague* (2000b), that the focus on the central values of solidarity, friendship and love is what makes overcoming foreignness and hostility, understanding, togetherness and meaning possible in the first place. Solidarity alone would be enough for a successful dialogue. In an existential sense, the goal should be to encourage people to show self-determined, self-responsible solidarity, and to promote solidary behaviour. In addition to that, being oneself essentially requires communication with other people. In existential communication from person to person, people come close to each other and *deliver themselves to each other* (Jaspers, 2008). They overcome their fear of the foreign, of otherness, recognise in the other person a human being like themselves and, on this basis, engage in a conversation that remains open in attitude to what arises in dialogue. In dialogue, a movement arises, a dynamic that guides the participants towards a (common) third that was not 'there' before. The requirements of existential communication formulated by Jaspers in this regard generate borderline experiences that can lead to existential experience. And the readiness for dialogue grows to the extent that it is recognised that, in principle, the other person's life is the same as one's own. Out of this 'solidarity of mortals' (Burkert, 1985; Castoriadis, 1997), the authentic exchange about the questions of life and what answers we want to give to them can succeed.

Those who overcome themselves and stand up for others, who stand in solidarity with them, experience self-efficacy. Experiencing beautiful things, especially in difficult and dark times (nature, art, music ...) strengthens the ability to love and give. There is no life without suffering, isolation, meaninglessness, and death. But suffering can also be viewed from an existential perspective. 'One must imagine Sisyphus happy' (2000a:89), Camus writes as the final sentence in the *Myth of Sisyphus*. To imagine Sisyphus as a *sufferer* is absurd: 'he too concludes that all is well ... The struggle itself toward the heights is enough to fill a man's heart' (ibid.) Nor is it a question of what life does for us, or what we do for life. But whether our life is worth living. Life optimisation and progress do not help in the pandemic. Only quality and density of life. This is how the existential concept of achievement is to be understood. To have a fulfilled life, to live a valuable life, even in the face of the existential challenges of a pandemic, means to give meaning to one's own life, again and again.

References

Bonhoeffer, D. (1986–1999) *Ethik, Dietrich Bonhoeffer Werke (DBW), Band 6.* Gütersloh: Gütersloher Verlagshaus.

Burkert, W. (1985) *Greek Religion.* Cambridge, MA: Harvard University Press.

Camus, A. (2000a) *The Myth of Sisyphus.* London: Penguin.

Camus, A. (2000b) *The Plague.* London: Penguin.

Castoriadis, C. (1997) *World in Fragments: Writings on Politics, Society, Psychoanalysis, and the Imagination.* Redwood City, CA: Stanford University Press.

Domin, H. (2003) *Ich will dich, Gedichte.* Frankfurt: S. Fischer Verlags GmbH. English translation of 'Abel steh auf' by Meg Taylor and Elke Heckel. http://hildedomin. megtaylor.co.uk/.

Frankl V.E. (2004) *Man's Search for Meaning.* London: Random House.

Hanaway, M. and Reed, J. (2014) *Existential Coaching Skills. The Handbook.* Henley: CH Group.

Jaspers, K. (2008) *Philosophie. II.: Existenzerhellung.* Berlin: Springer. English translation by the author.

Malraux, A. (2009) *Man's Fate.* London: Penguin.

Sartre, J.-P. (1993) *Being and Nothingness.* London: Simon & Schuster.

Sartre, J.-P. (2007) *Existentialism Is a Humanism.* London: Yale University Press.

Strenger, C. (2011) *The Fear of Insignificance: Searching for Meaning in the Twenty-first Century.* New York: Palgrave-Macmillan.

Yalom, I.D. (1980) *Existential Psychotherapy.* New York: Basic Books.

Chapter 11

Existential challenges for business leaders post-pandemic

Monica Hanaway

The Covid-19 pandemic has regularly been referred to as an 'existential crisis'. Although it is often unclear exactly what the writer means by this. It is certainly true that the pandemic experience has brought existential issues such as uncertainty, anxiety, time and temporality, meaning, authenticity and relatedness more to the forefront, not just for individuals but also for organisations. It is true to say that for some businesses and organisations the pandemic has indeed been a crisis, and one which they did not survive. This is a crisis on an organisational level but also on a personal level for all those people who had expected to continue to work within the organisation and now find their daily existence very different.

We have seen people who felt secure in their jobs finding themselves furloughed or made redundant. Often their jobs did not just provide them with a financial reward but also gave them a meaningful project, a sense of (misguided) certainty and security, and a professional identity. It was not their choice to make a change in their professional life at that moment; many were totally unprepared and found themselves at sea, feeling lost, losing a sense of identity and status, and struggling financially.

Others retained their jobs, but for many the circumstances and environment in which they worked was radically altered. They were told to work from home, which at first may have felt quite an attractive proposition until they encountered the reality of sharing a kitchen table with one's partner, instead of working at their own desk, in their own office. This was often accompanied by sharing space with their children who would normally be at school, but whom they were now expected to home school.

The impact of the pandemic changes to individual working lives is coupled with practical organisational challenges. Projected projects, incomes and developments were no longer possible. Some industries were not able to function at all, while others had to change the way they worked to align with the need for social distancing and other pandemic needs. This was not always negative in terms of the availability of professional opportunities, as we have seen in the increase in jobs for delivery drivers etc. We should also note the government's call for 'creatives' to retrain as 'techies'! These practical changes

DOI: 10.4324/9781003255765-15

do not consider the existential challenges. If we are fortunate, we choose our professions because the work has meaning for us and is compatible with our values and beliefs. No doubt we could all do jobs other than the ones we are currently holding; but without meaning, or where there is a clash in values, we are likely to experience existential anxiety. In the chapter by the musician Laurence Colbert (Chapter 2), we see the challenge presented by the removal of work which he was passionate about, and which formed part of his self-identity.

If we are going to be required to consider the meaning of our work, on both the individual and organisational level, we have considerable challenges ahead of us. Priorities will need to be addressed. The nature and pattern of work has always changed and evolved. Each decade presents new challenges and opportunities. We have moved from the industrial age to the information age. Post-pandemic a company may find that its intangible assets, such as intellectual property, winning brands, innovative ideas and, most importantly, talented staff are now equally, if not more, important that its hard assets. If people are recognised as the most important asset moving forward, then businesses can no longer ignore existential issues which have all come into sharp focus during the pandemic. I intend to merely highlight a few existential areas which business leaders need to address. I welcome a deeper debate. We shall certainly need to engage with new ways of understanding and being in the world in our professional as well as our personal lives in the years to come.

Existential themes

The business world, with its five-year plans and milestones, and the conventions of an office based 9–5 business model, has been severely tested by the pandemic. Most plans assume that, although things will change, there are some core elements of stability. Who would have thought that highly desirable business properties would be closed and shuttered and standing idle for months on end? The fact that many businesses have survived, with staff working from home, is something which has surprised many, and raised questions as to how businesses may look in the future.

It has been an anxious time for business leaders and unfortunately the impact of the pandemic has resulted in many established businesses going under and many people losing their jobs. This has been an emotional experience for many people. For some, it has meant the loss of the identity they invested in their work status. It has caused individuals to question who they are without their professional label, and perhaps to question for the first time their authenticity, self-identity and set of values and beliefs. Some have felt trapped and mourned the loss of the freedom they believed their salaries afforded them. Without the security of work, they may have felt they were unable to fully carry out their responsibilities to themselves and their families, and so felt disempowered, vulnerable and afraid. Many may previously have sought their sense of purpose and meaning in the workplace and, without their daily schedule, had to consider what really was meaningful for them. The not knowing when or whether they would return to their previous positions has brought them truly in touch with uncertainty and caused anxiety.

Their sense of time may have shifted. Some have felt liberated to be away from tight schedules. They have stepped back and looked at their previous lives and questioned whether they ever wish to return to cramming themselves in overcrowded rush-hour tube trains to get themselves to a building where they would remain throughout the day, before heading home on another overcrowded train. They have used the opportunity of home working to embrace the freedom to go for a walk, or to eat at times of the day to suit their own rather than other people's schedules, leaving them to wonder whether they wish to, or even can, return to the time structures and restraints they had previously accepted. However, it is important to note that while the lack of rigid time structures may have felt liberating to some, others may have experienced the loss of structure as frightening. Many found it difficult to take on the freedom and responsibility to structure their own time; they missed colleagues and the ease of immediate consultation and feedback. The uncertainty of how long they might be expected to continue working in this way presented problems for those enjoying the experience and those struggling with it.

Existential thought does not allow much space for certainty, but we can be fairly sure that the day offices reopen, and people return to the workplace, it will not be 'business as usual' or a return to 'normal'. Both the people and places will have changed as a result of the Covid-19 experience. This experience has meant that people have had to engage with existential issues they may previously have avoided. Leaders need to focus their attention more on these existential challenges if their businesses and organisations are to flourish post-pandemic. Let us look briefly at some of the implications of these issues.

Anxiety

Existential awareness and the acknowledgement of the inevitability of living with uncertainty produces an anxiety, which can be pervading and never ending. This can be made manageable in the workplace by an authentic existential leader. Such a leader cannot take away existential anxiety, but understands that often people find it too hard to acknowledgement existential anxiety and transfer it onto multiple smaller anxieties which seem more manageable. This action is a guard against the feeling of being out of control which uncertainty brings. Leaders who understand are able to 'read between the lines' and not get bogged down trying to address multiple small anxieties, but rather seek to understand and explore the level of existential threat and anxiety an employee is experiencing.

We can become anxious if we feel we do not understand or agree with the values of an organisation we are part of. The pandemic has afforded us time to consider our values and beliefs and may have drawn a person's attention to discrepancies between their personal values and those of their organisation. Leaders may need to reassess the organisation's values, beliefs, mission statements and policies in line with the greater understanding and new priorities the pandemic may have highlighted. This is helped when there is transparency regarding organisational values and an open discussion about what they mean for all in the organisation, resulting in an understanding of what is meaningful. To authentically engage with these issues, leaders must ask themselves several questions, aimed at reducing unnecessary anxiety.

Anxiety is often caused by lack of clarity and through experiencing requirements or behaviours which contradict stated values. During the pandemic people may have become detached from the world of work or may have had the time to reflect on their work experiences, both positive and negative. Leaders need to ask:

- Are our organisational values and ethos still valid after what we have learnt in the pandemic?
- Are our values clear to everyone?
- Do organisational behaviours match our values?
- Is it ok for people to question whether what they have been asked to do is the most efficient way of doing it? They have often had to make these decisions on their own during the pandemic and may have questioned why previous things had to be done in a certain way.
- Are we wanting people to maintain the pre-pandemic status quo? What are the losses and gains in maintaining the status quo, in business terms, and in terms of existential anxiety?
- How can 'anxious' individuals be enabled to embrace the potential for change the pandemic offered?
- Am I personally anxious about change?
- Can I offer a new vision?
- People may be more willing to speak their minds; how will I respond?
- Others may be so afraid of being without work that they will be afraid to say anything they feel may jeopardise their employment. How does the organisation encourage an open and transparent ethos which encourages debate?

If people are clear and believe that the organisation is consistent and coherent in the way it defines and practises its values, anxiety is reduced. People know what they have joined, they know the company values and whether they match their own, and so existential anxiety is decreased. In times of change, such as returning to work after lockdown, there will inevitably be change;

business leaders must ask how they can make any changes exciting and creative for themselves and their staff. One challenge for the existential leader is how to give clarity and encourage creativity, remaining authentic, in a time of uncertainty.

Anxiety is also reduced when people know exactly what is being asked of them. To gain satisfaction from their work they need to know how success is measured. The pandemic may have made some of the previous ways of working and the projected goals no longer relevant. The organisation may decide this, or an employee may return from lockdown questioning why things are done in the way they are, or even why certain things are done at all. Doing meaningless work helps create anxiety. Days are passing without a sense of meaning, adding to already existing existential anxiety.

In addition to the more organisational questions posed earlier, business leaders need to recognise that not just their organisation but their own selves have been alerted through their pandemic experience. It may be worth considering some more personal questions, such as,

- Am I anxious in my organisational role?
    - Is this different from pre-pandemic?
- Am I aware of the anxieties of those around me?
- Am I trying to rescue others from anxiety?
    - If so, am I doing it in a way which disempowers them?
- Am I expecting others to take on anxieties which I should deal with rather than pass on?
- How am I making work meaningful for me and for others?
- If anxiety comes from a dissonance between values, am I clear about my personal values and those of the organisation?
- Do my values differ from those working in the organisation?
    - If so, how will I address that?
- What have I personally learnt from the pandemic experience?
    - If I ignore that learning, will it lead to anxiety?

Uncertainty

People may have consciously encountered real uncertainty for the first time during the pandemic, bringing with it feelings of powerlessness, making it difficult for them to connect with their essential freedom. During the pandemic, we have been required to live with uncertainty, to an extent which may have felt unbearable. Surviving this uncertainty can bring with it a greater understanding and belief in personal freedom and responsibility for self. No company or organisation can address our existential uncertainty, but it can be held in mind when making plans. The 'certainty' their previous job seemed to promise with its long-term plans and pension provisions may have proved uncertain, and the false belief in the security it represented may provide people with a rationale for taking more risks in the future and possibly placing authenticity and meaning higher than security. Of course, the taste of uncertainty may have proved so painful for some that they will attempt to seek out more certainty going forward.

All leaders must consider the relationship with uncertainty that their returning colleagues bring with them, and how this will be effectively built into new ways of working. Leaders will need to identify those who have flourished without the previous constraints, and who may have newly identified creativity and an increased comfort with uncertainty which can serve the development of the organisation. To ignore this is to risk that people will become bored and seek stimulation in other more progressive organisations. Equally, there will be other people who are longing for a greater sense of certainty and security and leaders must also consider how they will address this.

It may be useful to ask a few questions:

- How can it be acknowledged that everyone's stance on uncertainty may have shifted due to individual pandemic experience?
- How does the organisation address the uncertainty inherent in temporality and time to create an authentic structure on which uncertainty can safely sit?
- How do I encourage myself and other people to take creative risks and engage in creative dialogue?
- Can I hand over control to others when appropriate and deal with the uncertainty of what they may do with that freedom?
- How do I respond to those whose experience has caused them to seek more routine, greater security and certainty?
- Is it authentic to try to offer certainty in an uncertain world?

Temporality and time

The general level of anxiety has increased as people have been brought into a more overt relationship with the temporality and vulnerability of existence. Some individuals may have faced the death of loved ones, often without the opportunity for a face-to-face goodbye. They may have authentically considered their own death for the first time. They may also be grieving other losses; they may have lost their job, relationship, plans or self-concept.

Time may have taken on a very different 'feel' as, stuck in lockdown, the days may have been hard to distinguish one for the other; it may have felt a long time since they have seen friends or ventured out to their workplace. Day has followed day, week has followed week, and we find a year or more of our lives has passed in a very different way from how we may have expected. Time may have been experienced as standing still, going very slowly or even racing by. The subjective nature of time will have been brought into sharp focus for many people.

Some people may be seeking longer-term security and looking for permanent contracts and stability, while others may have come to believe this is no longer a possibility and have come to embrace a more peripatetic and varied 'portfolio' style of work. Leaders need to consider how they will meet the needs of both views, which may require radical changes in how their organisation operates. They may consider:

- Is it necessary to return to the same pattern of regular hours or can greater flexibility be introduced?
- How can I show that the organisation understands the change people have experienced in relation to time and temporality?
- Is it possible to offer working patterns which will address the need for structure and regularity for those who need it, while offering a 'freer' alternative to those who have learnt to embrace their own management of time?
- How as an organisation can we deal with changing views on how long people may want to remain with one organisation when people have learnt that there is little in life we can rely on?
- How will the organisation respond to possible changes in priorities as Covid-19 has brought people more closely in touch with temporality and the shortness of the human lifespan?

Meaning

An enforced disengagement from the daily schedule, which people may never have given much time to considering before, has led people to need to engage more fully with the question of what is meaningful. Their previous occupation may no longer provide meaning and so they may question whether they wish to return to their old job or look for a new more meaningful pathway in life. Leaders will have to consider the place of meaning within their organisation, asking:

- How can the organisation address the human need for meaning?
- Can the organisation consider how meaningful the tasks we ask people to complete really are?
- Are people aware of how their work contributes to the organisation and the community?
- Has my own sense of meaning changed during the pandemic?
- Do I want business to return to how it was before the pandemic, or can I improve it to make it more meaningful for me and others?

Relatedness

Our way of relating to others has changed. Other people may be seen as potential threats to life, silently infecting us with a deadly virus. We no longer spontaneously greet people with hugs or kisses; we strive to keep at least two metres away. We have found new groups to divide into, e.g. those keen to be vaccinated vs anti-vaxers; mask wearers vs those who refuse to wear them; those who stick to the rules vs those who challenge or break them. How we work to remove the alienness of the Other when it is safe to do so will be a major task for workplaces on both a psychological and practical level.

While some people may struggle to feel comfortable relating closely again with others, other people will enthusiastically embrace the opportunity … possibly too enthusiastically. Learning to read the boundaries of other people's personal space may become an essential skill. As Spinelli points out we cannot avoid relatedness as it is present in 'all reflective experiences of relatedness' (2007:27). Even by seeking to avoid others we are highlighting the importance of relatedness and the inherent anxiety present in our desire to contain it.

Although productivity may have been maintained while working from home, the interaction with others and the possibility of spontaneous creative conversations has been lost. It is these unstructured conversations which often lead to the most innovative ideas. Without them, is there a danger that businesses become stuck with the status quo? Leaders must find ways to allow their staff to feel comfortable and to engage in creatively addressing the opportunities for change that the pandemic has provided.

There are several relational questions that leaders may usefully ask when considering their post-pandemic working practice:

- If more people are working from home, how do we address any feelings of existential loneliness that this may highlight for them?
- How can existential loneliness be addressed in my team? Each person will have a different desire and tolerance for intimacy, both psychological and physical. How can we work with individual needs to provide the best working environment for all?
- What importance is given to the company's relationship with
  - staff?
  - community?
  - environment?
- What difference has the pandemic made to me personally regarding my relationships within the organisation and my work life balance?

Authenticity

Being true to oneself and one's values and beliefs is an important element of existentialism. Our beliefs and values may have shifted during the Covid-19 experience and re-entering the 'new'/'old' life may present challenges to our authenticity. People may have expectations drawn from their pre-Covid-19 interactions which will need challenging and, in doing so, provide opportunities for creative dialogues and different ways of doing things. On a personal note, it has often been the shift in organisational values away from my own which has led to me leaving organisations.

I may need to ask myself some questions to be in a position to authentically respond to post-pandemic life. These may include:

- Who am I following my pandemic experience?
- To what extent am I remaining true to myself in returning to my previous position?
- What changes need to happen to remain true to myself and my beliefs?
- What factors are obstacles to my authenticity and how do I overcome them?
- Am I happy with the balance and appropriateness of what I disclose to others in consideration of any anxiety which may result?
- How do I create an organisation with authenticity at its heart?
- Do I hide behind my role and exist in Sartrean 'bad faith'?

Freedom and responsibility

The pandemic has been experienced by some as a loss of freedom. This is true in relation to what we may or may not have been legally allowed to do, but throughout we have retained the freedom to think and make our own decisions.

Some have experienced an increased sense of responsibility, particularly in relation to protecting the health and wellbeing of others. Businesses must address the increased awareness of these issues in a positive way. They must be ready for challenges to the old boundaries in freedom and responsibility, with some individuals seeking more freedom and others craving more structure and less responsibility and freedom. This presents a creative challenge for organisations and calls for an exploration of some questions:

- Does the organisation inspire freedom and courage?
- Do the organisation and its leaders take away freedom from others to defend their own freedom?
- What are the fears about sharing power and increasing the freedom of others?
- Where are the limits on responsibility set?
- How can people be encouraged to make full use of their freedom and responsibility?
- How will tensions between responsibility to the organisation and responsibility to self be handled?
- What level of responsibility is owed to staff who have been through a unique experience during the pandemic? Does it include:
  - their physical and mental health?
  - a financial responsibility beyond their work hours?

- training and development?
- The pandemic has, for some, increased the focus on global politics such as climate change; so to what extent does the organisation hold responsibility for the business environment, and the environmental impact of the organisation's products and services?

Values and beliefs

During lockdown, we have had the opportunity to reassess our values and to consider what is important for us in life. Business leaders have found themselves home schooling; people have got dogs and have been experiencing the responsibility, worry and joy of being a dog owner; some have been made redundant and can no longer rely on the daily structure of the working day. In whatever way Covid-19 has changed our existence, it is unlikely that we have not found ourselves questioning our values, beliefs and the priority we have given to some things over others.

Before the pandemic, many businesses shied away from conversations about values. In doing so they missed an important element, because people are looking for meaning and a correlation with their values in what they do every day. More than ever, it is important that an organisation identifies and clearly communicates its values. They must be more than sound bites which sound good or make a nice poster for the reception area. They must be clear, authentic, backed by organisational practice. It is worth asking:

- Have my values changed during the pandemic?
- Does this require changes in my professional behaviours and attitude to work?
- How can the organisation remain open to any changes in the values and beliefs within their team?
- Do the changes we have seen call for a change in ethos in the organisation?

Existential dimensions

We do not always feel the same, or act the same, in all contexts. We may choose to share different aspects of ourselves with different people, and in different contexts. As explained earlier, these contexts can be grouped into four dimensions of human existence – the physical (*Umwelt*), the social (*Mitwelt*), the personal (*Eigenwelt*) and the spiritual (*Uberwelt*). Readers coming from a business leadership background may see the connection between these dimensions and Deal's (Davies, 2003) four frames of organisational behaviour used in *Reframing Organizations* (Bolman & Deal, 2017), which consist of the structural, human resource, political and culture.

If an organisation reflects on these dimensions, they may offer relevant questions which may help in preparing for a post-Covid-19 world, or at least one in which the pandemic is under enough control for a resumption of business.

Physical/Umwelt

In the physical dimension, which is concerned with physical wellbeing:

- How does your organisation relate to the environment – workplace, landscape etc?
- How do you look after the physical needs of staff?
- To what extent will environmental changes need to be made considering the Covid-19 experience?
- How comfortable are people in their own bodies? Do they have an increased fear of illness etc?

Social/Mitwelt

In the social dimension, which is concerned with relatedness to others:

- How will social interaction and communication be encouraged?
- How will a sense of belonging and relatedness be developed?
- How will people be enabled to feel safe in their interactions with others?

Psychological/Eigenwelt

In the psychological dimension, which is concerned with emotional and mental well-being:

- How will the organisation take care of the psychological needs of staff?
- Do mental health/wellbeing policies and practice need revision?
- How will people's anxiety regarding travel to work, being with others, perceived loss of skills or confidence etc., be addressed?

Spiritual/Uberwelt

In the spiritual dimension, which is concerned with values, beliefs and meaning:

- Does your organisation show and develop its beliefs, values, meaning and purpose?
- Are these clearly evidenced in the mission statement and daily practice?
- Is there the potential to involve staff in a review of these, in light of the pandemic?

- If people have new foci of meaning (e.g. greater interest in the environment, development of meditative and other practices through lockdown) how will these be embedded in organisational thinking, planning and practice?

Business leaders may find it helpful to use these existential themes/givens and the 'existential dimensions' as a framework for preparations for reopening business. They may also need to consider whether there is a need for new training, support, and development initiatives across all levels of the organisation to provide safe places to discuss the changes individuals have experienced in themselves, and how these may set both challenges and opportunities for the organisation going forward. Some organisations already offer tailor-made bespoke in-house packages facilitating leaders in considering the relevance of existing values, structures and behaviours. Business-focused existential training courses are still hard to find, as are existential coaches and consultants, although these could provide real benefit to organisations post-pandemic.

In 2005, Boyatzis and Mckee wrote: 'For those bold enough to lead in this age of uncertainty, the challenges are immense. Our world is a new world, and it requires a new kind of leadership' (2005:1). This statement seems even more relevant following the challenges the pandemic has presented for organisations and industries, and should act as a call to action.

References

Bolman, L.G. and Deal, T.E. (2017) *Reframing Organizations: Artistry, Choice, and Leadership*. San Francisco: Jossey-Bass.
Boyatzis, B. and McKee, K. (2005) *Resonant Leadership*. Boston: Harvard Business School Press.
Davies, B. (2003) *The Essentials of School Leadership*. London: Sage.
Spinelli, E. (2007) *Practicing Existential Psychotherapy*. London: Sage.

Conclusion

The existential legacy of the Covid-19 pandemic

Douglas Adams (2002:102) warned us that 'trying to predict the future is a mug's game' but pointed out that it is increasingly 'a game we all have to play because the world is changing so fast'. Certainly, Covid-19 has brought home to us all the knowledge that there is very little, if any, certainty in our world. Although we cannot predict the future Price-Robertson et al. (2020) suggest that 'pandemics tend to produce broadly similar social outcomes: they trigger panic responses, challenge the sense of predictability and control offered by epistemological paradigms, and ultimately lead to changes intended to overcome "blind spots" in scientific and cultural understanding (Honigsbaum, 2019)'. These challenges are not necessarily negative and an exploration of them can lead to a more worthwhile and authentic future.

However, van Tongeren and van Tongeren (2021) suggest that the legacy of Covid-19 will be one of suffering, as our individual and cultural worldviews have been challenged by the pandemic experience. They believe that when one's cultural worldview is rendered ineffective, we are left to suddenly bear the full weight of existential anxiety (Vail et al., 2019). Cultural worldviews are seen as ways of seeking to answer existential questions. They help us to understand that suffering undermines safety-providing frameworks, 'leaving people prone to new questions, and fresh anxiety, resulting from contemplating existential realities. Indeed, suffering is an existential issue, as they must confront their core existential fears head-on' (van Tongeren and van Tongeren, 2021). In response, van Tongeren and van Tonqeren developed the existential positive psychology model of suffering (EPPMS), informed by existential and positive psychology, focused on human strengths, growth and reaching one's potential (Peterson, 2006). Although many people would wish to consider the two approaches separately, some recent writers such as Wong (2009) suggest there is a fruitful synergy between existentialism and positive psychology and propose a shift toward 'existential-positive psychology', addressing existential realities while working for the sustainable psychological growth of individuals, groups and societies.

If, as van Tongeren and van Tongeren suggest, the legacy is to be one of learning from suffering, or indeed learning how to suffer 'better' – with meaning

DOI: 10.4324/9781003255765-16

and learning, then an attribute which has been identified by many is that of resilience (Jacob, Chapter 8; Wong, 2009; Vos, 2021). I shall return to this later.

During the pandemic, every one of us has been confronted with existential questions which we may have sought to ignore or may have chosen to use as a springboard for taking a leap of faith into a different future from the one anticipated. The post-pandemic future offers an opportunity for us to stop and think and reflect on some personal existential questions and to face them with resilience, and perhaps even come to a point of welcoming the opportunities for creative change which they present. Some such questions are:

- Has my idea of meaning, and the places I might look for it, changed through my pandemic experience?
- How do I now feel about other people?
- In what way do I now relate differently to others?
- How have I dealt with the uncertainty of the past months and has this brought a deeper change in how I approach uncertainty going forward?
- Has Covid-19 brought me more in touch with my own vulnerability and temporality and what implications does that have for how I experience time and how I want to spend the rest of my time on earth?
- What level of anxiety have I experienced and are there ways to use this positively?

To address these questions and live in accordance with the answers is to live authentically; to ignore them is to live in Sartrean bad faith.

In the short film *In All of This Unreal Time*, which had its world premiere at the Manchester International Festival during the pandemic, the actor Cillian Murphy plays a man on an existential mission. His character engages in the kind of self-reflection described above. He is seen striding through the empty streets of an anonymous city at night during lockdown reflecting on shame, guilt and masculinity, while berating himself about how he has been living life and his treatment of other people and the planet. This may resonate with a journey that many people will have been on over the past year.

> 'I came out here to apologise. I find myself, at the midpoint of my life, in a dark wood, and now I'm here, in the forest of my mind, and every tree is shame, every living thing is a reprimand, and I realise, I must speak freely now, before I lose you.'

The film's writer, Max Porter, stated that he hoped "it would result in its audience confronting their religious, spiritual, political, physical relationships to the world around them".

Whatever our experiences the legacy of the pandemic needs to be heeded and used to build a more mindful future. This task can be aided through drawing on the existential elements referred to throughout this book.

Existential elements

Anxiety

Although existentialists may argue that anxiety is an inevitable part of human existence and that we should not try to eliminate it, but instead learn to live with it, the level of anxiety people have experienced over the past months has been far in excess of our more usual experience. It had been suggested that this would result in increased suicide rates, which currently does not seem to be the case. In fact, in Japan the suicide rate showed an initial decline (Tanaka & Okamoto, 2021). The cultural focus on individual success, the cause of much anxiety in Japan, may have faded into the background of concerns in the face of a global pandemic which affected everyone, and the sense of collective concern may have taken away from individual anxiety and despair. On a more individual level, we saw this in the response of the POCD clients I referred to in Chapter 9, where the more universal anxiety saw a lessening of personal anxiety.

We have yet to see if existential anxiety decreases or increases as we re-enter a more regular life. It has been suggested that it may worsen with the easing of restrictions. We will need to find a way of living with the knowledge that life is uncertain, as this is no longer a theoretical knowledge but a lived experience. As such we must find a way to be-with-anxiety and the knowledge it brings. Being open to the experience of an existential 'crisis' or 'reawakening' can be positive, guiding us to question the purpose and meaning in life and in our actions, in a new and deeper way. Johal (2021:161) wrote:

> the process of learning to live with this existential anxiety should possibly be framed as adaption rather than recovery. Adaptation means being able to constantly move as conditions change rather than trying to recover to some imaginary fixed point in time.

Johal is realistic in suggesting that such adaption will not all happen at the same time or in discrete ways but is likely to be a 'much messier adaptation' (ibid.). Increasing our ability to be more adaptable while retaining authenticity is one of our challenges going forward.

Authenticity

The questions of who we are and what is important to us have been considerations forced on us though our reduced freedoms during the pandemic. We may have found ourselves asking: now that the familiarity of life has been stripped bare, what is life really about? (Madison and Spinelli make this the focus of Chapter 5). We may have a more authentic acceptance of the fleetingness of existence and the importance of living authentically in each moment with passion and vitality. We may have reflected on own authenticity, but we have also been faced with the inauthenticity of people or organisations we may have looked to for truth. We have seen government policies and information change on an almost daily basis, with many paradoxes – such as 60,000 at a football match and borders remaining open when there was clear evidence of new variants originally confined to certain countries, while most of us were being told to continue to mask and social distance. We have learnt that, as Obi-Wan Kenobi told us in *Return of the Jedi*: "You're going to find that many of the truths we cling to depend greatly on our own point of view."

Individuals may have felt their authenticity limited by their context. However, some people have learnt that context and limitations offer us the opportunity to innovate and create. We have broken the daily rituals and structures. We have learnt that it is not necessary to go into an office 9–5 to be productive. We have learnt that people adapt when they cannot get to the shops. This new knowledge challenges us to ask why we have been doing things the way we have and to what extent past behaviours and rituals have been authentic and meaningful. For some, this will bring a radical change to their way of being-in the-world. This may be very practical changes, such as a career change or moving from the city to the countryside. Our legacy with regard to authenticity lies in acknowledging that our decision to return to the status quo or make changes has to be authentic and in full acceptance of the knowledge that we are free to choose.

van Tongeren and van Tongeren (2021) suggest it may require the formation of a new narrative that accepts and includes any suffering we have undergone, and an authentic consideration of how we know and see ourselves, our values and hopes. Acknowledging and owning our struggles as part of our narrative can be liberating and empowering, and allow us to integrate who we saw ourselves as being before the pandemic, and how we now view ourselves following our experiences and suffering.

Michael Rosen, as a result of contracting Covid-19, spent a long time in hospital, four weeks of which were in an induced coma. During this time he reflected on how a different 'self' emerged and continues to form out of the experience.

> I look at the word 'recovered'
> I want to change it to the word 'recovering'
> I am not sure that I will be 'recovered'
> As for that old self,
> He is the guy I knew six months ago.
>
> (Rosen, 2021:178)

This enhanced authenticity can lead individuals to find new and authentic meaning and purpose (McAdams & Janis, 2004).

Despite having to re-examine ourselves and find an authentic way of being in a post-pandemic world, Moustakis (1996:12) is hopeful that this is achievable, and points to examples where in the face of a crisis 'people found possibilities for reconciliation, resolution of problems, and recovery of authenticity and a true identity ... They found a way out of inauthenticity, anxiety and guilt, a way forward to actualizations of intentions and talents.' It is indeed possible that the pandemic experience may offer us increased freedom to live life more authentically if we can find a way of accepting that 'we can't escape the realities of our existence, we can face them with courage and learn to accept that there is much that is out of our control' (Existential Academy, 2020). We need to find authentic and open new and flexible ways to approach and work with what life throws at us

Meaning

Our existence as meaning making beings is important in existential thinking. It has been suggested that the pandemic has brought about 'a collective calamity for meaning' (van Tongeren and van Tongeren, 2021). Current research, so far, appears to show a decrease in meaning in life experienced by people from pre-pandemic (January 2020) to mid-pandemic (June 2020) (VanderWeele et al., 2021). This would seem to support the claim that meaning has been impaired by the suffering elicited by the pandemic. We are yet to see the downstream effects of lost meaning on mental health and social functioning.

Covid-19 has challenged many individuals' primary pathways to finding meaning, bringing a senselessness for many who struggle to come to terms with a seemingly random shared trauma and grief. As post-world war generations within Europe, we have not previously needed to develop a schema for such a once-in-a-generation event as the pandemic. The Covid-19 legacy requires us to find new meaning in a changed and uncertain world.

van Deurzen (2021:138–139) wrote:

> when meaning is robbed from us altogether and we lose our faith in politics, in humanity, or even in life itself, we face a tricky and difficult situation. It can take months, even years, to overcome such a complex and long-term grieving process. As is always the case in crisis, the capacity to learn something of value in the process of reconnecting our lives to a wider meaningful framework of reference is what will save us.

Pre-pandemic factors which provided meaning may have been many faceted. We may have found meaning through work or relationships. Covid-19 has altered these things. Following their pandemic experience, some people may be searching for new meaning without lost loved ones or professional identities as their job no longer exists, and so they need to find new avenues for making meaning. Trzebiński et al.'s 2020 research found that finding greater meaning in life was, not surprisingly, associated with less stress and anxiety during the pandemic. People who were able to find meaning reported better psychological health and wellbeing (Hooker at al., 2020) which may mean that experiencing this pandemic leaves us able to fare better in the long term.

One legacy of Covid-19 may be that mental health commissioners see the need to move away from more behavioural therapeutic models and give greater priority to more existential approaches which place the search for meaning at the centre of their work. Indeed, a meta-analysis of clinical work found that meaning-focused therapy was more successful than standard treatments, precisely because of the meaning provided by such approaches (Vos, 2016). The positive effect of such approaches has been found to improve health (Roepke et al., 2014), including among cancer survivors (Canada et al., 2016).

Yalom (1980) taught us that a harsh confrontation with existential realities, through the death of loved ones, or similarly through the range of existential challenges presented by a pandemic, may be *precisely* what is needed to jostle people into radical periods of growth and transformation, bringing about a new consideration of what is truly meaningful. Despite it being difficult to imagine that you can find meaning in situations that cause suffering, the Existential Academy suggests that there are things that can be done that may bring meaning, suggesting that reconnecting to nature can have a powerful effect on our sense of calm (Harkness, 2018). They also point to the importance of relatedness and suggest meaning can be found through helping others,

> through volunteering to deliver food and medicine to those self-isolating or giving a friendly call, can also give a sense of purpose in times of crisis. The meditative quality of arts and crafts are also a creative response to difficult times.

What is clear is that one challenge which we are presented with as part of the Covid-19 legacy is to reassess where we have found meaning and to find new meaning which fits within a better understanding of the uncertainty of the future.

Freedom and responsibility

Before the pandemic we may have bemoaned the perceived limitations in our lives without engaging with our own existential freedom to choose how we perceived these obstacles. The pandemic has given us a lived experience of existing at times when our freedom to physical action has been limited while we still needed to use our freedom to choose to navigate life amid conflicting (or confusing) information. This immediate encounter with existential freedom may have proved troubling to some who may have become overwhelmed by decisions about whether to travel, how to keep family members or friends safe, and how to conduct life and work within new restrictions. This vast uncertainty may have proved fatiguing and led to a sense of impotency, and yet we are never without some level of agency. I have previously referred to the works of Frankl and May, both of whom experienced very real limitations to their freedom, Frankl spending time in the concentration camps and May spending many years in the Saranc Sanitorium, New York, suffering from tuberculosis, which at the time was an incurable disease. Both these men used their experiences to take full freedom and responsibility for making meaning of these times. Hopefully our pandemic experience will have enabled us to become better acquainted with our freedom to choose how we respond to things and to the potential impact of our decisions on others.

In Chapter 2 Laurence Colbert offers a very practical example of such a choice. He describes confronting the experience of no longer, as a musician, having the freedom to tour or to play to live audiences. Despite remaining open to authentically experiencing that as a loss, he describes the resulting freedom of creating new online projects and experiences. He could have chosen to grief the loss of the known and take a position of impotency, but instead took on the leap of faith to explore new ways of using the freedom he did have.

Relatedness

People recounting critical incidents described feelings of

> being thrown, or tossed into a sea of doubt, confusion, and pain and forced to find their way out, alone. They have described their experience as forms of falling into a common bent of becoming totally absorbed in others and losing themselves in idel [sic] talk, uncertainty, curiosity, and chronic pain, in which life is controlled and dominated by others' social standards, needs and expectations.
>
> (Moustakis 1996:2)

The pandemic has brought our connectedness to others into focus. This may have been focused on everyday experiences but also on life and death experiences. Residents of care homes were not allowed family visits, people died alone because visitors were not allowed onto wards. The impact was not just on 'existing' people. Indeed, in Chapter 4, Cleo Hanaway-Oakley wrote of her relationship with her unborn baby and concerns about the ways the restrictions not allowing a father to be present at scans, or for the whole of labour, might affect the relationship between her husband and their baby.

Many people found it hard to be cut off from family, friends and work colleagues, while others have enjoyed lockdown as it provided a legitimate excuse to stay away from others. Other people may have come to represent a threat to our health, or even our life, and the comfort of being in the presence of others might have been replaced by a greater comfort with their absence.

This may leave some people with the legacy of continuing to avoid others and instead of asking, 'Is there a reason to do this online?' may move to 'Is there any good reason to do this in person?' One coaching client begged his employer to let him go into the office throughout the lockdown as he began feeling very depressed living alone in his small flat. By the time the office reopened he begged to stay at home as he had become anxious at the thought of being with others. Businesses and organisations need to consider that the workforce will not be psychologically unaffected by their pandemic experiences and returning to business requires more than looking at physical needs.

van Deurzen (2021:134) pointed to the importance of 'connectivity ... to our sense of safety, feeling at home and finding meaning', and poses the question of 'what happens to us, then, when that very connectivity becomes a threat to us and even a mortal danger?' Coming at the same time as Brexit, when certain sections of the government and media were intent on emphasising the separateness and difference of Britain and its people from its close neighbours, Covid-19 provided a fertile breeding ground not just for the virus itself, but for a move away from connectivity and commonality to a sense of distance and alienation. This may be a long-standing negative legacy of the pandemic, or may lead to positive and creative reflection, and a growing understanding that we are all just vulnerable human beings, and that collaboration is essential for human survival. Johal (2021) points out that, 'research shows that connecting, especially through collective action, can mitigate the impact of disasters on our mental health and sense of agency.'

Having understood, during the pandemic, that things we had previously taken for granted, such as touching things, being with other people and breathing the air in an enclosed space, can be considered risky, how will we meet the challenge to reconnect? No doubt that risk awareness will recede at a different pace for different people and our previous ways of relating may have changed forever. It could become second nature to recoil from shaking hands or kissing cheeks, instead offering a nod or a 'namaste' instead. On a positive note, we will hopefully be more mindful of other people's space and their ownership of their own bodies.

The pandemic may also have offered an opportunity to consider our relatedness to others on a global scale. Governments have needed to consider how open borders would remain and whether to share scientific knowledge and vaccines. Coleman (2021) expresses the hope that due to the 'extraordinary shock(s) that the coronavirus pandemic is bringing', major changes may be possible within American society. He speaks of the pandemic legacy as opening the possibility of breaking 'America out of the 50-plus year pattern of escalating political and cultural polarization we have been trapped in' moving towards 'greater national solidarity and functionality'. This would require what Coleman terms a move to the 'common enemy scenario', which he hopes will see the common threat of the pandemic causing us to look past differences and 'provide us with fusion-like energy and singularity of purpose to help us rest and regroup' (ibid.). The fruition of his hopes lies in the quality of relatedness at all levels that we can establish post-pandemic.

Time and temporality

With daily news updates of the number of Covid-related deaths, this pandemic has reminded us of our mortality, and made *death* salient. It has been hard to ignore the frailty of human life and the truth that we shall all eventually die. Before now, the practice of contemplating death was 'a challenge to the death-denying neurosis of our culture' (Lief, 2001:27). The pandemic has perhaps encouraged us in an opposite approach 'taking death out of hiding, examining it and accepting it as part of life' (ibid.), as in contemplating death we are, at the same time, contemplating what it means to be alive.

So, one legacy of the pandemic may be increased awareness of our own temporal existence, bringing a more intense love of life, with the commitment to make the most of each moment, or it may paralyse us with fear. Our existential freedom calls on us to accept that we have a choice here.

Many people have reported a change in their experience of time. With many people working from home or no longer working a 9–5 day we have been given the opportunity to ask why we have chosen to break up 'time' in the way we have. We are now challenged to own our own 'time' and chose the most meaningful way of relating to and using it.

Uncertainty

The totality of the pandemic experience has been surrounded by uncertainty. In these circumstances we have had to address the question of how much uncertainty we can bear. As a result, we may have found that we were able to bear more than we expected. We may even have come to find value and freedom in uncertainty.

The pandemic has left us with the need to develop a new understanding and relationship to uncertainty. No longer could we kid ourselves that anything is certain. This new relationship challenges human potential and raises questions about the 'old normal' and our previous professional and personal identities. It brings an invitation to play and be creative and, if we can learn to hold our fears, it presents us with a new and potentially exciting 'playing field'.

If we have a greater acceptance of uncertainty, it calls for us to develop greater adaptability. Vos (2021:132) writes: 'If we find the inner elasticity to start imagining ourselves and our lives anew, we can adjust to many more challenges than we ever thought possible.' If we can achieve this it offers the potential for an exciting and less hidebound future, in which risks can be taken as we have come to understand that, without certainty, everything is a risk and a leap of faith. This has positive implications for living richer personal lives.

In the business world adaptability and the removal of assumptions about certainties can stimulate creativity and innovation. The pandemic has given us an opportunity to rid ourselves of false 'certainties' and to look at what previously we may have deemed to be impossible.

Resilience

To address the existential givens in a holistic way, as stated earlier, several writers have focused on the need to build resilience. A fundamental assumption of most existential approaches is that encountering harsh existential realities can lead to considerable anxiety, and so it is suggested that there should be 'a move towards a perspective more strongly informed by positive psychology, aimed at developing *existential resilience*, in which existential concerns are regarded as "truths" and not threats, facts and not fears' (van Tongeren and van Tongeren, 2021).

Ratcliffe (2012, 2015) sees *existential feelings* with all their shifts and disturbances as a door to understanding the existential structure of experience. He focuses on loss and the diminution of possibilities, leading to the loss of existential hope, encompassing a loss of a sense of the future domain, and of possible meaningful change for the better, and so empties the world of its significance.

The pandemic has forced all of us to engage with our existential feelings as even ignoring them is a form of engagement. Our personal Covid-19 legacy can leave us with a greater fear of our existential truths or open us up to the possibility of living more vividly within all our existential dimensions. The temporality of our existence as individuals, collectives and as a world, has moved to the foreground and we have the freedom to choose what we do with our new existential understanding.

Although we must try to learn from our pandemic experience it is worth remembering that, as Zizek (2020:3) warned us, when drawing on Hegel:

> the only thing we learn from history is that we learn nothing from history ... there is no return to normal, the new 'normal will have to be constructed on the ruins of our old lives, or we will find ourselves in a new barbarism whose signs are clearly discernible.

We are called upon to build a new legacy of learning from our 'lived experience' with the potentiality to engage with existential possibilities more fully.

I started this book with a poem, and it seems right to end with one by the same four-year-old.

I don't want to write

I don't want to write a poem about coronavirus:
I want to write a poem about playing

> But the coronavirus is everywhere
> It's in my playground and at my nursery
> It's in the streets by my house.
>
> I can't go near Maddie
> I can't go in Adam's house.
> I can't see Momo and Granddad.
> I can't see my Grandma.
>
> I don't want to write a poem about coronavirus;
> I want to write a poem about tv and toys.
>
> But the coronavirus is still here.
> It's like the headless horseman in Scooby Doo.
> It's like a scary invisible shark.
>
> I can still play with toys.
> I can still play dressing up.
> I can still cuddle my doggy.
> I can still cuddle mummy

Just as the author declares she is tired of writing about coronavirus, and would much prefer to be focused on playing, fun, sociability, and creativity, I hope that we can now all find ways to move on and engage our fun and creative sides.

We tend to learn most through the challenges and crises which provide the baseline to our existence. They call for us to self-reflect and perhaps consider seeing ourselves differently, doing things differently and experiencing the world differently. There are many lessons to be learnt from our pandemic experience – a key one being that our lives are full of uncertainty and we are temporal beings. We have a short time available to us in which to use our learning to make life more vibrant, fun, caring and creative, no matter how short or long that life may be, and to work towards making our world a more meaningful and empathic place in which to exist. Let us not pass this opportunity by.

References

Adam, D. (2002) *The Salmon of Doubt: Hitchhiking the Galaxy One Last Time*. London: Macmillan.

Canada, A.L., Murphy, P.E., Fitchett, G. and Stein, K. (2016) Re-examining the Contributions of Faith, Meaning, and Peace to Quality of Life: a Report from the American Cancer Society's Study of Cancer Survivors-II (SCS-II). *Ann. Behav. Med.*, 50, 79–86. doi: 10.1007/s12160-015-9735-y.

Coleman P.T. (2021) Coronavirus Will Change the World Permanently. Here's How. *Politico* www.politico.com/news/magazine/2020/03/19/coronavirus-effect-economy-life-society-analysis-covid-135579.

Deurzen, E. van (2021) *Rising from Existential Crisis: Life Beyond Calamity.* Monmouth: PCCS Book.

Existential Academy (2020) Being With Uncertainty. *Existential Academy* www. existentialacademy.com/blog/existential-wisdom-for-extraordinary-times/being-with-uncertainty/ [link no longer live; accessed 12 February 2020].

Harkness, C. (2018) *The Nature of Existence, Health, Wellbeing and the Natural World.* London: Red Globe Press.

Honigsbaum, M. (2019) *The Pandemic Century: One Hundred Years of Panic, Hysteria and Hubris.* London: Hurst & Company.

Hooker, S.A., Masters, K.S., Vagnini, K.M. and Rush, C.L. (2020) Engaging in Personally Meaningful Activities Is Associated with Meaning Salience and Psychological Well-Being. *J. Posit. Psychol.*, 15, 821–831. doi: 10.1080/17439760.2019.1651895.

Johal, S. (2021) *Steady: A Guide to better Mental health Trough and Beyond the Coronavirus Pandemic.* London: Equanimity Ltd.

Lief, J.L. (2001) *A Buddhist Guide to Encountering Mortality.* Boston, MA: Shambhala Publications.

McAdams, D.P. and Janis, L. (2004) 'Narrative Identity and Narrative Therapy', in L. E. Angus and J. McLeod (eds), *The Handbook of Narrative and Psychotherapy: Practice, Theory, and Research.* Newbury Park, CA: Sage Publications, Inc. (pp. 159–173). doi: 10.4135/9781412973496.d13.

Moustakis C. (1996) *Existential Psychotherapy and the Interpretation of Dreams,* Maryland: Jason Aronson Inc. Publishers.

Price-Robertson, R., Bloch-Atelfi, A., Snell, T., Day, E. and O'Neill, G. (2020) Reflections on Psychotherapy and Counselling from COVID-19 Lockdown. *Psychotherapy and Counselling Journal of Australia* pacja.org.au/2020/06/editorial-reflections-on-psychotherapy-and-counselling-from-covid-19-lockdown/.

Peterson, C. (2006). A Primer in Positive Psychology. Oxford: Oxford University Press.

Ratcliffe, M. (2015) *Experiences of Depression: A Study in Phenomenology.* Oxford: Oxford University Press.

Roepke, A.M., Jayawickreme, E. and Riffle, O.M. (2014) Meaning and Health: A Systematic Review. *Appl. Res. Qual. Life*, 9, 1055–1079. doi: 10.1007/s11482-013-9288-9.

Rosen, M (2021) Sticky Mc Stickstick: The Friend Who helped Me Walk Again. London: Walker Books.

Tanaka, T. and Okamoto, S. (2021) Increase in Suicide Following an Initial Decline During the Covid-19 Pandemic in Japan. *Nat Hum Behav.*, 5, 229–238. doi:10.1038/s41562-020-01042-z pmid:33452498.

Tongeren, D.R. van and Showalter Tongeren, S.A. van (2021) Finding Meaning Amidst COVID-19: An Existential Positive Psychology Model of Suffering. *Front. Psychol.* 12:641747. doi: 10.3389/fpsyg.2021.641747.

Trzebiński, J., Cabaski, M. and Czarnecka, J.C. (2020) Reaction to the COVID-19 Pandemic: The Influence of Meaning in Life, Life Satisfaction, Assumptions on World Orderliness and Positivity. *J. Loss Trauma*, 25, 544–557. doi: 10.1080/15325024.2020.1765098.

Vail, K.E., Reed, D.E., Goncy, E.A., Cornelius, T., and Edmondson, D. (2020). Anxiety Buffer Disruption: Self-Evaluation, Death Anxiety, and Stressor Appraisals Among

Low and High Posttraumatic Stress Symptom Samples. J. *Soc. Clin. Psychol.* 39, 353–382. doi: 10.1521/jscp.2020.39.5.353.

VanderWeele, T.J., Fulks, J., Plake, J.F. and Lee, M.T. (2021) National Well-Being Measures Before and During the COVID-19 Pandemic in Online Samples. *J Gen Intern Med.*, 36.1, 248–250. doi:10.1007/s11606-020-06274-3.

Vos, J. (2016) 'Working with Meaning in Life in Mental Health Care: a Systematic Literature Review of the Practices and Effectiveness of Meaning-Centered Therapies', in P. Russo-Netzer (ed.), *Clinical Perspectives on Meaning.* Switzerland: Springer International Publishing (pp. 59–87). doi: 10.1007/978-3-319-41397-6_4.

Vos, J. (2021) *The Psychology of Covid-19: Building Resilience for Future Pandemics.* London: Sage Swifts.

Wong, P.T.P. (2009) 'Positive Existential Psychology', in S. Lopez (ed.), Encyclopedia of Positive Psychology. Oxford: Blackwell (pp. 361–368).

Yalom, I. (1980) Existential Psychotherapy. New York: Basic Books.

Zizek (2020) *Pandemic: Covid-19 Shakes The World.* New York: Polity Press.

Index

absurdity 14, 118–19, 143–4
acceptance 32
Adams, Douglas 160
Adams, Martin 47
adversity 114
ageing 17, 33
Agyapong, Mary Agyeiwaa 56
alienation 146
aloneness 11
anxiety 4–5, 6–7, 11, 36, 150–2, 162
arts and culture 41
Attali, J. 43
authenticity 7–8, 36, 155–6, 162–4
avoidance 116

bad faith 120, 161
Bailenson, Jeremy 31
Baptie, G. 94
Beauvoir, Simone de 47, 54, 89
Beckett, Samuel Barclay 52–3, 58, 60
beliefs 15–16, 18, 84, 157
Bence, Charlotte 41
Berlin, Isaiah 8
Binswanger, L. 16
birthdays 2, 13
Bonhoeffer, Dietrich 141
Boss, Medard 32–3
'boundary situation' 112, 113, 124
Boyatzis, B. 159
Brexit 29, 167
'bubbles' 41
Bugental, J.F.T. 11
business world 137–8, 148–9; anxiety 150–2; authenticity 155–6; existential dimensions 157–9; existential themes 149–57; freedom and responsibility 156–7; meaning 154; relatedness 154–5; temporality/time 153–4; uncertainty 152–3; values and beliefs 157

Cafferkey, Pauline 25
Cameron, Julia 37
Camus, Albert 9, 11, 12, 14, 118, 146, 147
Carter, I. 18
charismatic leaders 3–4
childbirth 91–2
children's experiences 1–2, 169–70
China 25, 26, 35
choice 68
coaching 84–6, 133–5; existential coaching 122–3
Cohn, Hans W. 51
Colbert, Laurence 166
Coleman, P.T. 167
Collins, N.L. 94
communities 137
confidentiality 81–2
coping strategies 116
couple relationships 108–10
Covey, Steven 45
Covid-19 pandemic: big questions 112–13; 'boundary situation' 112, 113, 124; early reactions 25–7; existential legacy 160–70; existential threat 2–5; lockdown see lockdown; long-term impact 78; return to normality 77; rules and restrictions 7, 9, 12, 16, 17, 18–19
creativity 37, 144–6

daimonic 71
Davis, E. 10
death 12–13, 48, 88, 131, 132, 140, 168
defence mechanisms 8, 68, 116

denial 116
dizziness 132–3
Domin, Hilde 145–6
dread 27
dreams 2, 27, 31, 32–3, 130

Eigenwelt 18, 141, 143, 157, 158
Eliot, T.S. 68
embodiment 11–12, 16–17, 30–1, 33
emotions 6
emptiness 143
endings 118
Existential Academy 165
existential coaching 122–3
existential crisis 5, 148
existential leadership 3–4
existential positive psychology model of suffering (EPPMS) 160
existential resilience 114–22, 124, 169–70; coaching 122–3; post-traumatic growth (PTG) 117–18
existential threat: Covid-19 pandemic 2–5; early uses of the term 3
existentialism: absurdity 14, 118–19, 143–4; anxiety 4–5, 6–7, 11, 36, 150–2, 162; authenticity 7–8, 36, 155–6, 162–4; bad faith 120, 161; big questions 112–13; dimensions 16–19, 157–9; *Eigenwelt* 18, 141, 143, 157, 158; emptiness 143; freedom and responsibility 8–9, 18, 27, 37, 42, 47–8, 83–4, 119–20, 141, 156–7, 165–6; human givens 5–16, 115–17, 139; isolation 119, 141–3; 'leap of faith' 14, 42–3, 133; meaning 5, 9–11, 18, 49, 84, 143–4, 154, 164–5; *Mitwelt* 17, 27, 141, 142, 157, 158; mortality/death 12–13, 48, 88, 131, 132, 140, 168; paradox 116, 120, 143; relatedness 11–12, 40–2, 69, 72, 92–6, 101–11, 154–5, 166–8; revolt 14; time and temporality 12–13, 29, 40, 84, 153–4, 168; *trotzdem* 121–2; *Überwelt* 18–19, 141, 143, 157, 158; *Umwelt* 16–17, 27, 29, 141, 142, 157, 158; uncertainty 13–15, 26, 51, 71, 152–3, 168–9; values and beliefs 15–16, 18, 84, 157

Facebook 46
Frankl, Viktor E. 8, 9, 10, 144, 145, 166
free will 144
freedom 8–9, 18, 27, 37, 42, 47–8, 83–4, 119–20, 141, 156–7, 165–6

Freud, Sigmund 32
Fromm, Erich 47
frustration 71

Galileo Commission 21
Gleeson, Sinead 59
growth 47–8
growth mindset 116

Hall, Emylia 87, 91, 92, 94, 95, 96
Hanaway, Monica 122, 141
Hanaway-Oakley, Cleo 166
Hegel, Georg Wilhelm Friedrich 169
Heidegger, Martin 5, 7, 10–11, 12, 14, 17, 38, 68, 88, 93
'horror vacuum' 143
human givens 5–7, 115–17, 139; anxiety 4–5, 6–7, 11, 36, 150–2, 162; authenticity 7–8, 36, 155–6, 162–4; freedom and responsibility 8–9, 18, 27, 37, 42, 47–8, 83–4, 119–20, 141, 156–7, 165–6; meaning 5, 9–11, 18, 49, 84, 143–4, 154, 164–5; mortality/death 12–13, 48, 88, 131, 132, 140, 168; relatedness 11–12, 40–2, 69, 72, 92–6, 101–11, 154–5, 166–8; time and temporality 12–13, 29, 40, 84, 153–4, 168; uncertainty 13–15, 26, 71, 152–3, 168–9; values and beliefs 15–16, 18, 84, 157
humour 119
Husserl, Edmund 10

identity problems 142–3
isolation 92–6, 102–3, 119, 141–3
Italy 35

Jackson, P.Z. 114
Japan 161
Jaspers, Karl 104, 112, 145, 146
Johal, S. 14, 162, 167
Joyce, James 54
Jung, Carl Gustav 21, 32

Kabat-Zinn, Jon 22–3
Kahlo, Frida 33
Kant, Immanuel 21
Kennedy, Errol 37
Kierkegaard, Søren 4, 8, 14, 42, 55

leadership 3–4
'leap of faith' 14, 42–3, 133

Leder, D. 30
live streaming 37–40
lived experiences 22
lockdown 1, 9, 11, 12, 13, 17, 23,
    28, 29; authenticity 36; 'bubbles'
    41; emerging from 49–51, 70–1;
    emotions 36; fears 36; freedom and
    responsibility 37; growth and freedom
    47–8; implications for therapy 73–7;
    initial reactions 35, 36, 45, 52, 66,
    67–70, 101–2; isolation 102–3;
    meaningful moments 48–9; new terms
    35, 40; paradox of freedom 45–51;
    personal impact 72–3; pregnancy
    52, 54–63; procrastination 46, 48–9;
    relatedness 40–2; space 45–7; time and
    temporality 40
Lyon Neuroscience Research Centre 32

Malraux, André 143
martial arts 104
May, Rollo 71, 166
McKee, K. 159
McNamara, Patrick 32
meaning 5, 9–11, 18, 49, 84, 143–4, 154,
    164–5
meditation 120
mental health advice 71
Merleau-Ponty, Maurice 30, 38, 48, 52,
    54, 57, 60
Miller, D. 10
Mitwelt 17, 27, 141, 142, 157, 158
mortality 12–13, 48, 88, 131, 132, 140,
    168
Moustakis, C. 5, 164
Murphy, Cillian 161
musicians 35–40, 41, 42–3
Musser, S.J. 4
myth 33

'new normal' 32, 35
Nietzsche, Friedrich 144
'normality' 3, 77, 103; 'new normal' 32, 35

obsessive compulsive disorder (OCD)
    130–3
online therapy 73–7, 79–82, 106–8,
    126–7; couple therapy 108–10
optimism 70, 78

paradox 116, 120–1, 143
Parker, R. 89

passivity 144–6
Persephone 33
personal narratives 21
phenomenology 5, 19, 52, 54, 57, 66, 80,
    104, 105, 108, 110, 111
physical embodiment 11v12, 16–17,
    30–1, 33
Plath, Sylvia 58
Plato 22
Porter, Max 161
positive psychology 113, 160
post-traumatic growth (PTG) 117–18
pregnancy 87–8; facing the unknown
    96–7; giving birth 91–2; isolation
    and relatedness 92–6; lockdown 52,
    54–63, 96; pandemic effects 89–92,
    97–9; physical dimension 88–9; pure
    obsessive compulsive disorder
    (POCD) 131–2
Price-Robertson, R. 79, 160
procrastination 46, 48–9
psychological health 6
psychotherapy 126–30
pure obsessive compulsive disorder
    (POCD) 130–3

Qigong 104

Rapp Black, Emily 33
Ratcliffe, M. 169
reality 68
Reed, J. 141
relatedness 11–12, 40–2, 69, 72,
    92–6, 101–11, 154–5, 166–8; couple
    relationships 108–10; virtual
    relatedness 106–8
Renner, Rebecca 32
resilience 113–14; existential resilience
    114–22, 124, 169–70
responsibility 8–9, 18, 27, 37, 119–20,
    141, 156–7, 165–6
revolt 14
Revonsuo, A. 32
Rilke, Rainer Maria 25
Rosen, Michael 163
Rubin, Edgar John 53

Sage, Beverly 37
Sartre, Jean-Paul 8, 15, 28, 37, 53, 120,
    141, 145, 161
self-awareness 22
self-deception 8

self-image 143
self-reflection 22, 23
Showalter Tongeren, S.A. 160, 163
Skype 106
Smith, Zadie 61
social change 70, 77–8
social distancing 17, 27, 58
Socrates 22
solidarity 146–7
Solnit, Rebecca 26
Spinelli, Ernesto 49, 155
spiritual dimension 18
Stone, A. 93
streaming 37–40
subjective experience 21
suicidal ideation 104–5, 130, 162

taking stock 49
temporality 12–13, 29, 40, 84, 153–4, 168
therapeutic frame 75–6
therapy: caution, risk and challenge
    82–3; CBT 83; coaching see coaching;
    couple therapy 108–10; online sessions
    73–7, 79–82, 106–8, 126–7; positive
    psychology 113, 160; psychotherapy
    126–30; pure obsessive compulsive
    disorder (POCD) 130–3
time/temporality 12–13, 29, 40, 84,
    153–4, 168
trotzdem 121–2
Trzebiński, J. 164

Überwelt 18–19, 141, 143, 157, 158

Umwelt 16–17, 27, 29, 141, 142, 157, 158
uncertainty 13–15, 26, 51, 71, 152–3,
    168–9
Ungar, M. 114

vaccination 63–4
values 15–16, 18, 84, 157, 84
van Deurzen, E. 3, 10, 16–17, 18, 19, 89,
    122, 164, 167
van Deurzen-Smith, E. 16
van Tongeren, D.R. 160, 163
van Tongeren, S. A. 160, 163
victims 144–6
Villiers de l'Isle-Adam, Auguste de 15
virtual reality therapy (VRT) 77
virtual relatedness 106–7
Vos, J. 115, 168

Waldman, J. 114
Weber, Max 4
Weixel-Dixon, K. 11
What's App groups 137
Winnicott, Donald Woods 126
Wittgenstein, Ludwig 31
Wong, P.T.P. 112
Woolf, Virginia 54
Wuhan 25, 26, 35

Yalom, Irvin 3, 93, 139, 165

Žižek, Slavoj 22, 27, 169
Zoom 30, 31, 45, 46, 50, 74, 79, 80, 105,
    106, 108, 127

Printed in the United States
by Baker & Taylor Publisher Services